How To Buy a Home at a Reasonable Price

How To Buy a Home
at a Reasonable Price

ROBERT IRWIN

McGraw-Hill Book Company
New York   St. Louis   San Francisco   Auckland   Bogotá
Düsseldorf   Johannesburg   London   Madrid   Mexico
Montreal   New Delhi   Panama   Paris   São Paulo
Singapore   Sydney   Tokyo   Toronto

Library of Congress Cataloging in Publication Data

Irwin, Robert, date.
   How to buy a home at a reasonable price.

   Includes index.
   1. House buying—United States. I. Title.
HD1379.I65   643   78-23828
ISBN 0-07-032060-8

1234567890 BPBP 7865432109

The editors for this book were W. Hodson Mogan and
Virginia Fechtmann Blair, the designer was Elliot
Epstein, and the production supervisor was Sally Fliess.
It was set in Garamond by Black Dot, Incorporated.

Printed and bound by The Book Press.

For Jason, David and Marc

Contents

Contents

PREFACE

If you own a home that's big enough for your family, is in a good neighborhood, has low monthly payments and taxes that aren't frightening (and you're not looking to invest), chances are you're not reading this book. You've already got what millions only yearn to own.

On the other hand, if you are reading this book, chances are you're like a lot of other Americans. Your current home is too small, or perhaps the neighborhood has deteriorated, or maybe you're renting and want the income tax advantages of ownership, or property taxes are killing you, or you simply want another house as an investment, or. . . . Whatever your reason, it takes only a few hours of looking to realize that there's a big roadblock to buying a better home. Price.

The price of homes has skyrocketed in recent years, and chances are you find yourself simply unable to afford the home of your dreams. This housing problem is being faced by tens of millions of Americans today, many of whom ask in bewilderment, "What in the world ever happened to the price of real estate?"

We'll see exactly *what* happened and *how* in Chapter One, but first it's important to realize just how serious the housing problem is. To do so, consider for a moment a different sort of difficulty, one that my two young sons, David and Marc, are having.

David, who is two years younger than Marc, is *shorter* than his older brother and has as one of his big ambitions in life to be as *tall* as Marc. Every so often we measure the boys to record their growth. David is always taller than he was before, occasionally even taller than Marc was at the last measuring. But he never quite gets to be as tall as Marc who, of course, also grows. To the boys it seems a futile struggle which Marc always wins.

House hunting today is too often a similar struggle. We want to get a "dream" home, but every time we've saved up enough money for a down payment and increased our earnings to match monthly payments, our dream house goes up in price. Like David, the best we can seem to do is get to where prices used to be.

The boys know, of course, that someday they'll both be fully grown, and there's every chance that David will be as tall as, perhaps even taller than Marc. And in a similar manner, most of us retain the hope that someday soon we'll be able to get the house of our dreams. The trouble is that while boys *have* to grow up, there's nothing written anywhere to say that we'll ever catch up to the latest prices. In fact, the difference between family income and housing costs is widening.

Does this mean, then, that we are being unrealistic in believing we'll someday get our dream house?

Yes, it does.

Unless we heed some of the creative solutions to be discussed shortly, it's as unrealistic for most of us to think of getting our dream house (or for some of us, *any* house) as it is for David to want to be as tall as Marc at the growing stage of life they're both in.

That doesn't mean, of course, that David can't get to be taller by standing on a chair. Or that he can't be perfectly happy remaining shorter. And it doesn't mean that we can't wiggle our way into what we really want in a home by using some sophisticated financing. Or that we can't find a host of other solutions.

Alternatives to the house problem do exist. The purpose of this book is to present them in a clear and easy-to-read manner, always with an eye to saving money. Whatever your motive and financial situation, chances are there is a housing answer available to you. All that's needed is for you to act today and stop believing that sometime in the future you'll outgrow the problem.

ONE

How Did the Price of a Home Get So High? (Will it ever come down?)

If there is any one phrase that is repeated over and over again in real estate it is, "Just ten years ago I could have bought this house (lot, apartment building, etc.) for half what it now costs." It is simply a truism that over the long run, the price of property always goes up. As Will Rogers was so fond of saying, "Better buy some of it now, because they aren't making any more."

Of course, in the short run it doesn't always go up. When a major employer in an area moves away or cuts back the labor force (as happened in Seattle a few years back), it has a depressing effect on local housing and prices drop. During very bad economic times, such as the depression of the 1930s, prices plummet. And when an inner city decays and turns into a slum, prices also can go down. But these instances of falling prices, although severe for the people directly involved, are like a missed step in a horse race as the horses plunge forward. The overall advance of prices in real estate during this century in the United States is staggering. And the rate of increase, as we'll see shortly, has begun to accelerate in the past decade.

Why is property, with housing in particular, increasing in price so fast? There are several reasons.

1. The price of labor and materials has skyrocketed. This has been due in part to actual shortages, and in part to artificially caused shortages such as the drain of men and material caused by the war in Vietnam.

2. Inflation has boosted costs, just as it has driven many investors to buy houses for investment in order to preserve their capital. This reduces the supply of homes available to consumers and forces prices up.

3. High interest rates and tight money also push prices up.

4. In recent years an enormous amount of government regulation of building has resulted in increased costs to the builder, who passes them on to the consumer.

5. People born during the baby boom of the forties and fifties are now entering the housing market in full force, causing increased demand.

6. Finally, there is the incredible rise in the price of land.

While all these are directly responsible for the increase in the cost of housing today (and we'll see how they determine future costs in a few moments), none is nearly as responsible as one seldom recognized culprit. I am speaking of our very concept of what constitutes good housing—our concept of the *ideal* home.

Our idea of the perfect house begins with the land. We all know that there is a limited supply of land and as our population grows, the demand naturally increases. This alone is enough to cause an eventual rise in land prices. But anyone driving or flying across the United States can testify that there are thousands of square miles just sitting there unused. Even today, according to the U.S. Bureau of the Census *Area Measurement Report* (1970), there is only about one American for every 10 acres of land. In a country with so much land available, so much land simply left untouched, we must be decades, perhaps centuries away from the time when we'll use up our supply to the point where there could be a real shortage sufficient to drive prices up significantly.

True.

And not true.

The country has a total of 3,536,855 square miles. Of these, 3,482,752 are rural or farmland. There are only 54,103 square miles we might consider to be urban and incorporated suburban areas. Yet three-fourths of our population lives and works on those 54,103 square miles. That works out to 2,760 people for every square mile of actual residential land in the United States. It's a fact of life, reported in the 1970 *U.S. Census of Population,* that 73.5 percent of our population lives on about 1.5 percent of our land.

It wasn't always that way. Just a short a time as forty years ago, over half our population lived in rural areas. A mass migration to the cities has cut that number to about 25 percent.

Yet even these dramatic statistics don't tell the entire story, for the central cities themselves have lost population just as have the rural areas. Patricia Harris, as Secretary of Housing and Urban Development (HUD), reported that within the last twenty years "44 percent of the population moved from within the central city to another urban location . . . while 15 percent departed the central city for the suburbs." The migration has actually been to a narrow belt around the cities: the suburbs.

Almost everyone wants to live in the suburbs, even though less than 1.5 percent of our land is there.

The most frequently given reason for living in the suburbs is that they are close to the downtown areas yet relatively free of the high crime rates of our central cities. Both reasons are in general true, but are only part of the story. The other part has to do with a great American fantasy called the dream home. This fantasy is ingrained in our culture and goes back to our country's roots. It can be seen in the great plantation houses of the old South and the mansions built by great industrial fortunes in the North. But it is nowhere more dramatically illustrated than by the Gold Rush of the 1850s. Thousands of people streamed across plains and deserts in a desperate attempt to get rich quick. Those that did could be counted in the dozens, but they left behind their mark—in huge mansions in Virginia City and San Francisco, in the ghost towns, and in the big cities of the West. And those who didn't get wealthy pointed to those who did, and indicated that you could always tell the richest person in town, the one with the gold mine, because that person had the biggest house.

In this country (as in many others) wealth and success have always been associated with, among other things, the size and grandioseness of housing. Until fairly recently, however, for the vast majority of our population the problem of getting the biggest house in town was far removed from their daily lives. Simply finding any place at all to live was of paramount importance.

[3]

In 1890 the nationwide average of persons occupying each housing unit was exactly five, according to the Historical Statistics of the U.S. Bureau of the Census (N238–245). That may not seem too uncomfortable until you realize that, based on the size of homes and apartments built in 1890 and still standing today, the typical size of a house or apartment was less than 350 square feet. By comparison, today a two-car garage usually has a minimum size of 360 square feet (18 × 20 feet). Five people occupying such an abode would be cramped indeed by modern standards.

In 1890 average people might dream of the spacious city homes and apartments and large country farms of the wealthy, but that's as close as they came to them.

Creating an even greater split between the well-off and the average person, certain improvements in lifestyle were available before the turn of the century to those who could afford them. Indoor plumbing (which the ancient Romans and the even more ancient Minoans are believed to have enjoyed) was just coming into widespread use. A single bathroom, including a tub, washbasin, and water closet, was considered essential in the home of anyone of financial achievement. And closets were also becoming fashionable. Since colonial times, American homes had traditionally been built without any closet space. Clothes were stored in bureaus, trunks, or wardrobes. The newer, larger homes of the prosperous had a closet in the bedroom and what's more, they had *two* bedrooms in a house.

For the majority of the population, however, housing still had either outdoor plumbing facilities or, in the more modern tenements (prior to the twentieth century the word tenement did not have such an odious connotation, but only meant a large apartment building), one bathroom for each floor.

But we were just entering our modern age at the turn of the century. The economy began a steady climb upward as the emergence of oil as a significant power source created whole new industries, the largest of which was automotive. The automobile, in addition to providing well-paying jobs, also provided the mobility that enabled builders to extend construction to areas which had previously been inaccessible. Prior to the advent of the auto, only real estate in the city proper or located near a railroad line on the outskirts was considered economically developable. Once people had cars, whole new suburbs of "luxury" homes built on what had been cheap farmland could be offered at very reasonable prices, and the public that now had higher-paying jobs could afford them. More homes were built between 1922 and 1930 than had been built in the previous 17 years. Yet, median sales prices dropped from $7,197 in 1922 to $7,146 by 1930.

The building of newer, cheaper homes, based on the average person's idea of luxury in the 1890s, continued through the early part of this century. By 1929 there was hardly a home built anywhere in the country that did not have at least one indoor bathroom and two bedrooms. In addition the houses had plenty of closet space. What had been only a fantasy of hope for the average family in 1890 became a reality for their children. "Good" housing came to mean a rich person's house at an average person's price.

Of course, the rich no longer measured their wealth by the standards of 1890. By 1930 a well-off family in New York, California, or the Midwest had moved into a home that had two or more bathrooms, three or more bedrooms, with perhaps quarters off the kitchen for a servant or two. (In the earlier homes, servants often had small cottages adjacent to the family's home.)

While the average person had caught up to the highest standards of luxury for 1890, the trend-setting wealthy had moved far ahead. This process of catching up might have continued had not the Great Depression of the 1930s arrived. With cheaper, more affordable homes and with higher-paying jobs, more and more people had been buying houses. But the depression kicked the supports out from under the housing industry. According to the U.S. Department of Labor Statistics, unemployment rose to 25 percent and higher in some areas. Many families couldn't keep up mortgage payments and lost their homes. (Before the depression, homes were typically financed with short-term loans. Even though interest rates were low by today's standards, the short-term made payments relatively high.) Those with jobs, seeing what was happening around them, feared going into debt. House sales plummeted. In 1925 a record-setting 573,000 new single-family housing starts were recorded. By 1933, just eight years later, the number had dropped to 76,000, the smallest since records of housing starts were begun back in the nineteenth century.

Government officials faced with the overwhelming problem of getting the country out of hard times opened their doors to suggestions and, among those shouting ideas, some of the loudest came from the construction industry. Its representatives pointed out that during the good times of the 1920s and earlier the economy had been fanned by the great number of individual families buying homes. Now, with so few buying, hundreds of thousands of construction workers were unemployed. If only the government could get people to buy houses again, these idle could be put back to work and the construction industry could literally pull the country out of depression. (It is a fact that between World War II and the recession of 1974 to 1975 the housing industry was the leader in pulling the country out of economic hard times.)

The government's reaction to demands from the housing industry was to analyze the problem in terms of economics and not human values. Government planners reasoned that it was the high down payment and lack of credit that was keeping families from buying housing. If these could be eliminated, the housing industry could be rejuvenated. Out of this reasoning, the Federal Housing Administration was born in 1934. The FHA, as everyone called it, would insure loans for the purchases of homes by qualified buyers, even if purchasers only put 5 percent or less of their own money down on the property. In some cases down payments could be as low as 3 percent. Federal officials thought that with such terms available the public would swarm to new housing, construction would boom, and happy days would be just around the corner.

But the public's reaction to the FHA was only lukewarm. During the teens and twenties of this century the goal of many home buyers was to live like the wealthy. Their home purchases were inspired as much by a desire for what they imagined opulence to be as by a need for shelter. The financial catastrophe of the 1930s was as much a depression of the mind as it was of the economy. Times were once again as bad as they had been for Grandpa and Grandma—worse. People began once again to dream. In the movies Shirley Temple and Busby Berkeley acted out a nation's fantasies in "make-believe" homes that were frequently temples of luxury. While many people could have bought homes during this period, few took advantage of the government program.

The country was torn from its reveries by the urgent demands of survival. At the start of World War II, every able-bodied man up to the age of fifty-five was ordered into military service. (This was soon dropped to the age of forty-five.) Unemployment, which as late as 1940 was still above 9 percent in most areas of the country, suddenly dropped to zero. In fact there was a shortage of workers and for the first time women in large numbers went to work in industry. The country was given a concrete purpose. Where there had been economic stagnation, life suddenly burst forth. The Gross National Product (GNP), probably the best indicator of national economic health, was more than twice as high at the end of the war than at the beginning.

The war effort, however, prevented houses from being built. Shortages of supplies were very common and when construction materials could be found, the necessary labor was not available. As late as 1944, only 118,000 single-family housing units were begun.

Then, almost as suddenly as the war began, it ended. Many economists predicted a return to depression days. But while their precedents were accurate, they did not read the mood of the country. Economic depression was gone and with it went psychological despair. Optimism was the rule. If this country could win a world war with hardly a shot fired on the homeland, then it could beat anything.

The public had become accustomed to working hard and, in war industries, to getting paid well. They assumed they would continue to be well paid and they wanted to spend their money on all those items, including good housing, that had not been available during the war. Only now, partly because of the movie industry, the public had a new idea of what good housing was. It was as the wealthy in the 1930s had lived, not the wealthy of 1890. People in their twenties and thirties wanted to live not as their parents had lived, but as their parents had dreamed of living during the depression. After the war, anything seemed possible.

And it was. In 1946 the FHA was greatly expanded, with a secondary money market created through the Federal National Mortgage Administration (FNMA) to allow many more loans. The Veteran's Administration program offered no down payments to returning vets on GI loans. Labor was no longer needed for war and could be used for construction. Industry could now produce peacetime building materials.

The pent-up demand from the war years, the new optimism, good financing, the availability of workers and materials were all the ingredients necessary for a housing boom. In 1946, the first year after the war, for the first time in history over 1 million new housing units were started. The figure did not drop close to that number again until the recession of 1974 to 1975.

And the type of housing constructed was significant. The first homes were two-bedroom, one-bath affairs reminiscent of the construction of the twenties. But builders soon learned that buyers wanted something more—they wanted to live as they imagined the wealthy lived. So almost immediately the homes grew in size to three bedrooms and two baths (or, as the trade referred to them, $1^1/2$ or $1^3/4$ baths—a second bathroom with a sink and toilet but no tub, or a shower in place of a tub).

The average person couldn't afford servants, but a growing appliance industry filled the need with a vast array of labor-saving devices that we've all come to accept, such as dishwashers, garbage disposals, electric ovens, self-defrosting refrigerators, clothes washers and dryers, and so on.

As the housing industry boomed, so boomed the economy. The pay for workers increased dramatically. According to the *Current Population Report* of the U.S. Bureau of the Census, in 1945 the median family income was $2,189. By 1955, just ten years later, it had more than doubled to $4,418. And in 1955, as we all know, houses were cheap. The median sales price was around $13,000. If we take a rule of thumb frequently used by brokers to determine ability to buy—you can afford to pay $2^1/2$ times your annual income for a home—very nearly half the families in the country could afford new housing. Actually the number was considerably higher, for in many parts of the country, particularly California, developers were offering "cheapies." Basic homes of about 1,100 square feet with three bedrooms, a bath and a half, on a fairly large lot, for as low as $6,000 to $8,000. (Terms were even more fantastic—typically $50 down and payments of under $100 a month including principal, interest, taxes, and insurance!)

In those days anyone would have been a fool not to buy. Almost everyone did. From the Second World War through the early seventies, with a few slowdowns, we've had an almost thirty-year housing boom. Income kept pace with construction costs and people bought and sold regularly. Upon reflection, it was a good time for housing.

All this new construction required a steady supply of cheap land. Builders moved farther and farther out from the cities into the suburbs. Distance from the city no longer was measured in miles, but in minutes. "How many minutes does it take you to drive from your home to work?" was a frequent phrase heard by suburbanites comparing the advantages of each other's homes. As long as there was still plenty of land left reasonably close to the city, there was no problem. Land costs even through the sixties remained fairly low as "urban sprawl" became a familiar term.

The shape of housing, however, began to change. In the effort to emulate the living standards of the wealthy, people sought larger and larger homes. Consequently the average size of new homes began to grow. While a 1,200-square-foot house might have been considered adequate in the 1950s, by 1979 the size considered desirable approached 2,000 square feet.

In addition, what went into homes changed. Twenty-five years ago a basic home had three bedrooms, $1^1/_2$ baths, a living room (with a dining "L" adjacent to it), and a kitchen. Today basic means three to four bedrooms, two to three baths, dining or family room separate from the living room, and a kitchen with a separate eating area. Even this is not the dream home for many of us. We dream of a house with five bedrooms and three baths, and perhaps a den and a sewing room. A three-car garage also would be nice, with a covered patio, double-entrance doors, an arched entrance, beamed ceilings, and so on. Builders have been hard pressed to come up with more and more elaborate luxury houses at affordable prices. In many ways the housing market of the early seventies resembled the auto market of the sixties, which featured ever bigger cars with more and more chrome and horsepower.

(This is not to say that there is anything wrong with desiring a luxury house. It is worth noting that the wealthy no longer share this desire. Many who can afford to, don't live in the "quiet" suburbs any longer. They live in very expensive townhouses in revitalized downtown areas where cultural and economic activities are now booming. And they usually own a second home way out in the country or near a recreational area. One problem with our dreams is that they're usually behind the times.)

While our ideas of a dream home expanded, what it is possible to acquire at a reasonable price has diminished. As late as 1970 the median price of both new and existing homes in the country was about $23,000 ($23,400 for new homes). That was an increase of only $10,000 in fifteen years.

But the 1970s was a time when we all learned about ecology and shortages. One shortage we are just coming to recognize is in residential land. Developers began reaching the extremes of suburban sprawl. Nowhere is this seen more dramatically than in the Los Angeles area. There a drive of half an hour one-way to work is considered short and many breadwinners every workday of the year drive as much as two hours each way just to get to their jobs!

Yet, in what is one of the world's largest cities in terms of land area, there are no more good residential sections available at cheap prices. In order to get cheap land it is necessary to go even farther! Because of the limits of driving, Los Angeles is actually running out of land! (There are still some pockets of inexpensive property available in the extreme east end of the basin, but these are considered undesirable because of the heavy pollution problem.)

The cost to a developer of preparing a tract of land for housing construction also has skyrocketed. Before it was simply a matter of grading and connecting to sewers and utilities. Now environmental impact reports must often be filed to show how a new housing tract will affect an area's ability to handle sewage and garbage, among other needs. (Some concerned economists have predicted that housing construction in California will come to a complete standstill in the 1980s, because by then the state will have reached its capacity to treat existing sewage, and unless new plants are built at what would be prohibitively high costs, new housing would be environmentally unsafe.) In the 1950s a developer could usually get approval to build a tract from all concerned governmental agencies within thirty to sixty days. Now the time required is frequently from eighteen months to two years.

This is not to say that the environment shouldn't be considered. We only have one environment and it is in all our best interests to preserve it. We must, however, understand that we are all bearing the costs in increased prices.

Construction costs have also gone up dramatically during the 1970s. Probably the best indicators of the costs of building are the Boeckh Indexes. Their residential index for 1970 through 1977 is reproduced in Table 1-1.

TABLE 1-1
Boeckh Indexes Reflecting Increases
in Residential Construction Costs
(Courtesy of Boeckh Publications, a Division
of American Appraisal Associates, Inc.)

	Residences* (1972 = 100)
1970	83.8
1971	90.9
1972	100.0
1973	109.1
1974	117.9
1975	125.8
1976	136.2
1977	148.5

*These national average studies reflect construction cost movements based on twenty major locations and are calculated by averaging their index numbers. Construction cost changes in specific locations may vary sharply from the national average. Use the specific city index for accurate calculations.

Note that during this seven-year period the table climbed 64.7 points, which translates to an increase of about 77 percent in the cost of residential construction.

A large part of this increase is due to materials. Lumber, a basic ingredient in home construction, has been increasing in price so rapidly that contractors often can't give bids on jobs because they don't know what the price of wood will be by the time they begin work. The reason for this is not so much a shortage (although increased construction in 1977 into 1979 has put a strain on our existing lumber resources) as it is the increased cost of milling wood, again brought on by environmental factors. Cleaning up lumber mills so they don't pollute is extraordinarily expensive, and ultimately we pay the cost in increased housing prices. This conversion of older plants to environmentally clean ones, and the building of clean new mills, will continue to increase costs through the next decade.

Then there is simply the high rate of inflation the country experienced for much of the seventies. Figure 1-1 shows the inflation rate based on the consumer price index.

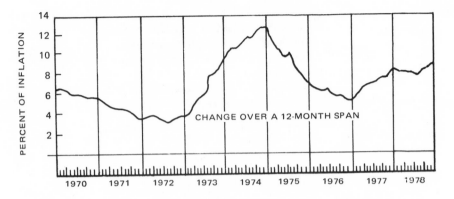

Figure 1–1. Inflation rate in the United States, 1970–1978, *(Based on all items from the Consumer Price Index, 1967-base; computed from unadjusted series, Dept. of Labor, Bureau of Labor Statistics).*

The high inflation—higher in 1974 than in any year in the preceding century—was caused in part by the federal government's attempts to pay for the Vietnam war through manipulation of the economy and finances, in part by the increased costs of imported foreign goods due to the devaluation of the dollar, and in part by the constraints imposed by cartels (such as the oil-exporting countries). The results are higher construction costs for labor and virtually all building materials other than lumber.

The final outcome of environmental controls, increased building costs, shortages of land, and inflation, was predictable—a dramatic increase in the cost of housing. Table 1-2 shows the median prices of existing housing in the United States since 1970 as recorded from actual sales by the Economics and Research Department of the National Association of Realtors.

Note that the price of existing housing has more than doubled in just eight years. Note also that dramatic jumps occurred in 1974 to 1978. There is a fascinating explanation for this which tells us a lot about future costs.

As we've seen, costs of construction and land were rising throughout the seventies, but builders disguised this rise by designing homes with less frills and by building in even more remote areas. In that way they were able to keep prices down. With the recession of 1974 to 1975, the bottom fell out of the housing market. Builders often sold at a loss and went out of business. Those that remained and new ones coming into the field no longer tried to disguise the cost of housing. They built homes they could make money on and passed the costs on to the consumer. So prices of new homes rose. At about this time some very astute people began to notice a very strange thing. New homes, which had always been cheaper than existing homes—an established neighborhood had always been considered a major advantage—suddenly cost more. For example in 1975 the median sales price of a new home was $39,300, as reported by the U.S. Department of Commerce. At the same time the median sales price of an existing home was $35,300, as reported by the National Association of Realtors.

It was more expensive to build a home than to buy an existing one. These astute people began speculating in the used housing market. They would buy existing homes anticipating that once the public found out about the price differential, they would swarm to the existing houses, prices would go up, and they could sell at a profit.

A word should be said about home speculation. The main reason a family buys a home is for shelter. Based on this premise, lenders such as savings and loan associations make very liberal loans on homes compared to other items like automobiles. There have always

TABLE 1-2
Median Sales Price of Existing Single-Family Homes
for the United States
(not seasonally adjusted)

1970	$23,000
1971	24,800
1972	26,700
1973	28,900
1974	32,000
1975	35,300
1976	39,000
1977	42,900
1978 (Aug)	50,300

Percent increase between 1970 and 1978 (9 years)—118%

Source: Department of Economics and Research of the National Association of REALTORS.®

[13]

been a few who bought with an eye toward reselling at a profit, but these were in the minority. When it became apparent that housing was going to go up in price, speculators took advantage of the liberal loans and many bought dozens of houses using financing intended only to allow individual families to buy residences.

One other thing about real estate speculators should be noted. They rarely keep a tight lip. They began boasting about what they were doing and the word got out. More speculators poured into the existing home market, as well as buyers of residences who realized an additional fact: Real estate, as an investment, has greater benefits during inflation than do other types of investment such as stocks or savings accounts. Naturally prices skyrocketed. Nowhere was this more dramatic than on the West Coast. Table 1-3 shows the price of existing homes by region.

The median price means that half the houses in the area at the time were priced above the figure shown and half were priced below. This figure, however, can be deceptive. It is often assumed that there is a spectrum of good houses available both above and below the median price. If the median, for example, were at $50,000, many

TABLE 1-3

Median Sales Price of Existing Single-Family Homes for the United States by Region

(not seasonally adjusted)

	Northeast	North Central	South	West
1970	25,200	20,100	22,200	24,300
1971	27,100	22,100	24,300	26,500
1972	29,800	23,900	26,400	28,400
1973	32,800	25,300	29,000	31,000
1974	35,800	27,700	32,300	34,800
1975	39,300	30,100	34,800	39,600
1976	43,800	34,200	36,400	47,800
1977	44,400	36,700	39,800	57,300
1978 (Aug)	49,600	43,100	46,900	68,300
Percent increase between 1970 and 1978 (9 years)	96%	114%	111%	181%

Source: Department of Economics and Research of the National Association of Realtors.®

buyers would assume that good houses were available for anywhere from $20,000 on the low end to $80,000 or higher on the high end. This is not the case.

It has been my experience that *all* the houses below the median price tend to be considerally less desirable. They include the smaller two-bedroom homes, the older run-down homes, and those in unwanted neighborhoods. Further, if the median price were $50,000, these homes, fully half the market, would tend to be clustered within 40 percent of that median price. That is, they would be within the $30,000 to $50,000 range, with virtually nothing available under $30,000.

On the other hand, desirable homes tend to *start* at the median price and extend upward. This means that the *minimum desirable home* in any given area may cost the median price for all homes and the range (if the median is $50,000) can extend well over $100,000.

What this comes down to is the fact that if the median price of *all* homes is $50,000, the median price of only those homes which are considered desirable or which you yourself would like to own may be considerably higher.

Note that in all areas of the country the cost of housing went up dramatically, but in the West it went far beyond anywhere else. While the median price of an existing house at the end of 1978 nationwide was $50,300, it was over $68,300 in the West. Prices had jumped there over 180 percent in just seven years!

In the summer of 1977 I went across the country to verify for myself the figures on housing costs. I made a point of comparing housing in three cities: Los Angeles, Minneapolis, and Atlanta. Here is what I found: A minimum dream home of 2,000 square feet with three bedrooms, two baths, and family, living, and dining rooms in Los Angeles on the west side of the city (but not Beverly Hills or Encino) would probably cost about $95,000. A similar home (although differences in building designs make comparisons somewhat difficult) in Minneapolis in an area on the west side of the city toward Lake Minnetonka (but not in Edina) might cost around $70,000. A similar home (again comparisions are difficult because of construction differences) on the north side of Atlanta might cost in the $55,000 price range. The typical dream home cost a lot more than the median-priced home indicated on the charts.

Speculation had forced the price of existing homes up. This

caused the price of all residential land to rise and the increased cost of lots was passed on to the consumer in even higher *new* housing costs. This kept the differential between new and used housing costs from closing and forced existing home prices to rise again. This push-pull inflation of housing costs became so dramatic that speculators on the West Coast waited in long lines with regular buyers to buy brand new homes, holding them for six months and then selling at a sizable profit as new housing costs jumped even higher. Along the way the media picked up the story and the high cost of housing suddenly became a national issue.

The housing market peaked in the spring of 1978 on the West Coast and prices leveled off and in some cases dropped slightly. Speculators slowly began to bail out. It would take a year or two two for the West to catch its breath. For the rest of the country, what happened there is a portent of what's to come. By the end of 1978 *new* housing costs were close to a national median of $60,000 and rising rapidly. Yet for most of the country, existing housing still was priced lower. It can only be a matter of time until all of America catches up to what happened on the West Coast.

And there is no end in sight. There is ever less good suburban land to build on. The great American dream house will cost ever more to build and buy. And the gap between income and housing costs continues to widen (see Figure 1-2). Even today the median family income of all families in the United States is still near $17,000.

If you multiply $17,000 by $2\frac{1}{2}$ you get $42,500, which means that the median-income family can't afford the median-priced house (about $50,000) in most areas of the country. On the West Coast, the median-income family probably can't afford any house. Housing prices, in fact, have been going up much faster than family income. Should this trend continue and there is no reason to think it won't, fewer and fewer families will be able to purchase homes in the future.

These statistics can be deceiving. There were nearly 2 million new homes built and sold in 1978, and how could this be if hardly anyone could afford to buy?

Part of the answer lies in the fact that today a good number of families in the United States have two breadwinners. Today the median income for families with two workers is close to $20,000 (the

FAMILY INCOME VS. THE COST OF A HOUSE

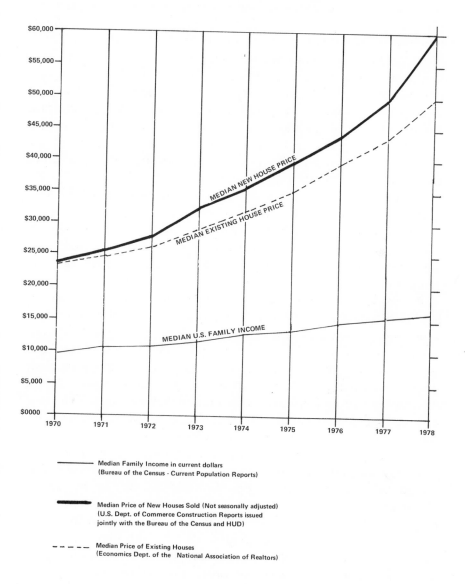

Figure 1–2. Family income versus the cost of a house.

second income is generally about 25 percent that of the first). With two workers, if the entire second salary goes to the house, it is still possible for many families to afford the median-priced home. Other families already owning homes sell them and use their equity to move up to the median-priced home.

Unfortunately the median-priced home tends to lack the luxury features contained in nearly everyone's dream home. In order to get that dream you have to pay a lot more than just the median price. Which means that undoubtedly most of today's buyers are getting second best, third best, or anything at all they can get their hands on. They're just buying in order to get into the market, hoping that they can one day sell and move up to where they really to be.

But by then where they want to be will be much, much higher.

And that's where it's at today.

The housing market is closing down, not opening up. As we mentioned at the beginning of this chapter, the time to have bought was twenty years ago, ten years ago, even just a few years ago. But not any longer.

If this sounds depressing, it's not intended to be. It's merely setting the stage so that you as a home buyer will know where you stand and what you can expect in the future.

There are still many opportunities today and the rest of this book is devoted to explaining them. They may involve throwing aside what is essentially our parents' dream of living as they imagined the wealthy to live and instead reexamining what we want. They may involve finding the courage to be different, to consider how we really want to live and not how we think we ought to live.

Here are your alternatives. They will be discussed in detail in the following chapters, but for the sake of comparison they are presented here in abbreviated form. Consider them, but be careful. Don't make up your mind until you've seen all the evidence. I've heard people say, "I could *never* live in a trailer" or, "A condominium simply doesn't have enough land for me," who later live to eat their words when they moved into these types of housing and *enjoyed* them. The same holds true for other alternatives. Don't let old values keep you from enjoying yourself. Pick a lifestyle and not just a price. You will find what you want.

Single-Family Suburban Homes

Still the most popular housing in the United States, it is also the most expensive. Benefits include a sense of ownership, of fulfilling the American dream. This can sometimes be seen in the friendships that are readily struck up between neighbors who drive about the same distance to work, make about the same income, and have about the same quality house. Living in suburbia can be fun when you feel that you and everyone around you are headed in the same direction in life. Another benefit is financing: the best financing is available for single-family surburban homes. Most houses have at least three bedrooms and two baths and include a large living area. And finally, these homes are frequently located near good schools (although busing has eliminated this benefit in many areas) and shopping.

Disadvantages include: very long distances between home and work and home and cultural activity centers; similarity in architecture within a given tract; a lack of exposure to differing economic and social groups; and, biggest of all, high price.

Condominiums

Condominiums in the minds of many people are a second-best but still acceptable alternative to the suburban single-family home. This is unfortunate, for the condominium offers benefits not found in houses, principally convenience and recreation. In a condominium you should never have to worry about mowing the lawn or painting the outside trim. There will be a gardener and painter to do this work. All the external maintenance needed for a house (and homeowners will agree that there is a lot) is done for the condominium buyer through an owners' association. In addition, while there are exceptionally few homeowners who can afford tennis courts, swimming pools, putting greens, recreational centers, and the like on their own property, these are common in the larger condominium developments.

Finally, there is the additional benefit of companionship. Condominiums are much like apartments in that many families live in the same building. But unlike apartments, your neighbor next door in a condominium owns that unit. This means the neighbor will probably be there for a fairly long period of time, may be in roughly the same financial situation as you, and probably will be using the same recreational facilities. In many condominiums, therefore, you can get to know your neighbors even more quickly than in suburban single-family neighborhoods. A condominium, more than anything else, offers an exciting lifestyle.

The disadvantages of a condominium include: small units (although in recent years many new condos have been built with 2,000 square feet or more of living space); units placed too close together, giving owners a cramped feeling; lack of control over the property (remember, if you don't paint the outside you can't choose the color); inadequate play areas for children; problems with the home-owners' association; and high prices. (See Chapter Four.)

Mobile, Modular, and Manufactured Houses

The mobile home has been around for a long time, but only in the last few years has it come into its own. Today's mobile home park offers many of the advantages of other types of accommodations at a fraction of their price. Which is to say that the most outstanding advantage of mobile, modular and other manufactured homes is their low price. They have other advantages, of course. Frequently these homes are *better* built than other types of housing. Their interior designs offer great variety. Often a buyer can rearrange or choose from a broad selection of interiors as luxurious or as spartan as any home on the market at any price. And, of course, many of the units are mobile, which means that if you don't like the neighborhood, you can pick up your home and move. In addition, most large mobile home parks provide all the recreational amenities we've just discussed as being available in condominiums.

The disadvantages include, at this writing, relatively bland exteriors. Although there are exceptions, you can almost always spot a mobile home by its outside appearance. Architectural diversity, however, is promised for the near future. There remains a certain lack of public acceptance of this form of living. Some single-family suburban homeowners, for example, still look down on owners of mobile homes, and many people still regard mobile home living as a king of second-class lifestyle, although, nothing could be further from the truth. (See Chapter Five.)

Rehabilitating Older Homes

The opportunity to rehabilitate older homes usually comes in central city areas or in neighborhoods which have "burned out." By this I mean areas that years ago were thriving parts of the city and now have become run-down and decayed. These homes offer enormous opportunities to creative buyers.

Their advantages are: bigger homes—three-story houses with over 3,000 square feet are common in many areas; low prices—frequently these are the cheapest houses of all to buy; close proximity to cultural and civic activities; often close proximity to work; a unique house; and a "different" kind of lifestyle.

There are, however, disadvantages. Many such homes are in high crime rate areas; the houses frequently need extensive rehabilitation, which means the buyer must take a chance on an investment of time, money, and hard work; some difficulty in getting financing still exists; local schools may be poor (although busing has significantly helped this problem). (See Chapter Six.)

Additions to Your Present Home

In all the other alternatives we've discussed this far, the presumption is that the buyer will move. When considering adding on to an existing house, there is no buyer. A homeowner, unsatisfied with what he or she has, considers solving the housing problem by remaining in the same place and adding on. This creates a new dimension to the housing dilemma—should I stay where I am or should I move? The answer can only be determined by considering motives for wanting change. (See Chapter Seven for help here.)

Adding on offers great advantages. You don't have to buy land at today's high prices, but can use land connected to your present house which you bought at yesterday's lower prices. You can remain in a neighborhood which you like. You can get more room exactly where you need it. You can do much of the work yourself and save a considerable amount on construction costs.

The disadvantages of adding on to an existing house include: difficulty in getting back all the money you invest in the addition (although as we'll see in Chapter Eight there are ways to solve this problem); remaining in the same neighborhood which you may not like; spending a lot of time, money, and effort and still ending up with a new room attached to the same old house you didn't like in the first place; enormous disruption of your home life while the building goes up. (See Chapters Seven and Eight.)

Building Your Own Home

This is unquestionably the most challenging alternative and it can also be the most rewarding. Advantages include: getting exactly what you want (hopefully), saving money by doing much of the work yourself, building in an area where you couldn't afford to buy a ready-made house, arranging the financing in such a way that you need invest very little of your own money and having an enormously satisfying creative experience.

There are, however, disadvantages. It is not easy to build a home, and someone unfamiliar with the building trades is likely to make costly, time- and effort-consuming errors. You won't know if you'll really like what you're building until it's finished and by then it's too late. There can be headache and worry over getting labor and materials to the right place at the right time, as well as problems arranging and making mortgage payments. Inclement weather can slow the project unexpectedly, thereby increasing costs. Finally, there may be difficulties in finding a place to live if you sell your present house in order to finance the construction of another one. (See Chapter Nine.)

Domes, Log Cabins, Barns, Kits, and Prefabs

Many of the problems of constructing your own home can be avoided by using this alternative. Some kits are made so that you can frame an entire house with no more tools than two wrenches. There is incredible variety; you can have one- to three-story homes, of any imaginable shape and style—truly unique homes.

As always, there are disadvantages. Many of these types of houses are more expensive than other homes, although a few are less. This is because something that is made to be more convenient for the novice builder to assemble, usually costs more. Unusual shapes and designs can cost more because a commercial market big enough to allow mass production savings on them may not yet exist. Also, freighting costs can be a problem—trucking the parts for a home from the factory can be extremely expensive. (See Chapter Ten.)

These are the alternatives to consider when buying a home today. We'll examine the different lifestyles and how money can be saved on each of them in expanded form in the following chapters. But first it might be helpful if the reader had a guide to see just how the alternatives compare with one another.

Quick comparisons can easily be made but accurate comparisons are more difficult. It's like trying to compare a giraffe, an automobile, and an apple. There are similarities, but in truth each is unique. Which all goes to say that Figure 1-3, while certainly helpful, does

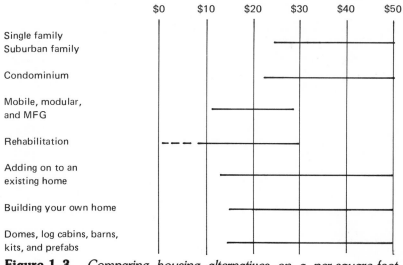

Figure 1–3. *Comparing housing alternatives on a per-square-foot basis (excluding cost of land).*

not tell the entire story and the reader should be wary of jumping to conclusions from it.

Figure 1-3 considers each housing alternative on the basis of square-foot cost in a given year, 1978. This is admittedly a crude method of comparison. Lifestyles and other amenities are not taken into account, nor is the difficulty or ease of obtaining a finished home in one category as opposed to another, nor are other points such as resale potential or availability. Still, the per-square-foot cost is probably the best single method of comparing alternative home costs.

Prices are given for average costs in 1978. They may vary substantially from one section of the country to the other, and will undoubtedly increase with time. The relationship between one alternative and another, however, should be fairly constant from area to area and over a number of years, barring any foreseen technological breakthrough.

TWO

What You Can Really Afford To Buy Today

If you are at all like the rest of us, you'll want that suburban dream house we've talked about. Even if it is a fantasy handed down from generation to generation, it's common knowledge that most of us prefer a good fantasy to a difficult reality. But with the dramatic increase in prices in recent years, will you be able to afford it? For nearly all of us today it's a matter of going from tract to tract, from broker to broker, trying to find a home that will fit both our dreams and our pocketbooks. And in today's market, for far too many of us that means either shattered dreams or burst wallets.

But wouldn't it be ironic if it turned out that you actually could afford your dream house and just didn't know it? Wouldn't it be a shame if you missed out on getting what you really desired just because you didn't know the right way to get it?

Before concluding that you can't get what you want and before considering alternative homes, let's just see how much suburban dream house you can really afford. If you are already quite familiar with financing, you may want to skip this chapter and go on to the next.

To know exactly how expensive a suburban home you can buy, what you really need to know is how much you can borrow. The price of a particular house doesn't matter. What matters is, do you have enough cash to put down and can you make the monthly payments?

There are many myths told and believed about what a family or an individual can borrow on real estate. Some believe that a million dollar piece of property can be purchased for just $500 down if you know the right people. Others believe that unless you put in a lot of cash yourself, a purchase can't, or shouldn't, be made. The truth is in between. It's possible to borrow a great deal on residential real estate, but the limits are quite arbitrary. And in order to understand these limits, a few words must be said about leverage.

The word "leverage" is frequently bandied about when people speak of real estate, but just in case you've forgotten its precise meaning, it all goes back to Archimedes, a Greek scholar who is usually called the father of the lever. Legend has it that Archimedes said, "Give me a point of support and I will move the World." He was referring to the mechanical advantage provided by using a long lever and a pivot point or fulcrum. The principle is clearly seen in the case of a small boy easily moving a rock many times his own weight by placing a long board *under* it and then putting the board *on top* of a small rock near the larger one. Now by pressing down on the extended end of the board, a lever is created which easily moves the large rock (see Figure 2-1).

Real estate borrowing is very similar, as shown in Figure 2-2. A large piece of property can be purchased (moved) by using a lender (fulcrum) and good credit (lever) with a relatively small down payment. How big a house you can purchase depends on how long your credit is and what kind of lender you use.

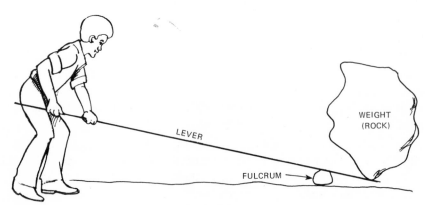

Figure 2-1.

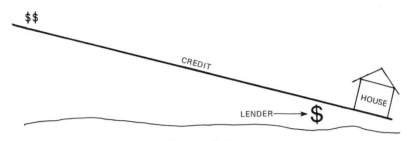

Figure 2–2.

A word of caution needs to be interjected here about a fear that I have heard many people express when thinking of purchasing a house—fear of anything to do with financing. Perhaps it's those big marble bank buildings that give us the idea that there's something arcane about dealing in money. (Perhaps those big institutional structures *are* intended to impress and maybe even intimidate us a little.) Or perhaps it's as simple as a fear of numbers. If so, take heart. The bank's rules are easy to understand. After all, even bankers understand them. And almost no mathematical knowledge is necessary. There are charts and graphs available to give instant answers.

Lenders

Let's start with lenders. Lenders for residential real estate are divided into two groups—banks and savings and loan associations (which together are called lending institutions), and private lenders who are simply individuals like you and me who will loan money on property. By far the single biggest source of real estate loan money in the United States is the savings and loan associations. They are set up primarily to make these kinds of loans. Banks also make loans on real estate, but they derive a majority of their business from commercial accounts. Private lenders are the smallest source of real estate loans, on property which the lending institutions have turned down as too risky. Naturally private lenders tend to charge higher rates of interest.

Appraised Value

If you go to a lending institution—probably a savings and loan association, since they often have funds more readily available and occasionally have slightly lower interest rates (perhaps 0.25 percent lower) than banks—you will quickly find that they are willing to loan a certain percentage of their appraisal of the value of a given piece of property. Their appraisal may not always be as high as the sales price. Typically a savings and loan (S & L) association will lend 80 percent of value. This means that for every $2 you as the buyer put up toward the purchase price, the lender will put up $8. For preferred buyers and preferred properties, these lenders will lend 90 percent. You put up $1 and they'll put up $9 on the purchase price. On rare occasions they will be willing to lend 95 percent. You put up 50 cents and they'll put up $9.50 of every $10 of the purchase.

These percentages are not idly dreamed up by the officers of the lending institutions? They represent the *maximum* amounts they are allowed to lend by state and federal law.

Whether you can get financing for 80 percent of your house purchase or preferred financing of 90 percent is determined by how good your credit standing is. Put another way, how long a lever you can muster depends on how good a risk you are.

It is often the case that buyers could get either an 80 percent or a 90 percent loan, but sometimes real estate agents are afraid to seek the higher loan for fear the lender might turn down the buyer and the whole deal might sour. If you want a bigger loan, you should always try for it. If a lender turns you down, you can always go to another. In almost any area of the country, there is a choice of lenders and being turned down by one does not affect your chances of being accepted by another.

Qualifying

This brings us the matter of *qualifying*. In order to get a mortgage you must meet several criteria and these tend to be the same regardless of which lending institution you go to.

Income

Lending institutions, contrary to what some people believe, are not in the real estate business—they are in the finance business. They want to give mortgages or trust deeds (the types of security instrument used varies from one area of the country to another) on property and then receive interest on their money, with the entire loan plus interest returned at prearranged intervals. Most mortgages today are written for thirty years, but typically they are paid back by the borrower within five to twelve years, usually upon the sale of the house.

In order to qualify for any mortgage you must show that you have the means to pay back the money borrowed plus interest. Since virtually all home mortgages are paid back on a monthly basis, you must show enough income each month to meet the monthly payment.

Lending institutions long ago arrived at a formula for determining how much income is needed to meet a monthly payment. It is interesting to note that there is no scientific basis for their judgment—it is simply that in the 1930s the FHA arbitrarily decided that buyers must be making in income at least four times the total monthly payment on the property they are buying. Ever since, this 4 to 1 ratio has held sway with all lending institutions even though in some families 2 to 1 would be sufficient while in others 6 to 1 is not enough.

The way it works is quite simple, as shown in Table 2-1. If the house you're buying has a mortgage on it in which the monthly

TABLE 2-1
Income Qualifying Example

Principle and interest	$ 200
Taxes	45
Fire insurance	5
Total monthly payment	$ 250
Multiplier	× 4
Income required to qualify	$1,000

payment including both principal and interest is $200, the lender simply adds in the taxes, say $45, and the fire insurance, another $5, coming up with a total monthly payment of $250. Now the lender just multiplies this figure by 4. In order to qualify for the loan in terms of income you must be making $1,000 each month, before taxes.

You might be making $1,000 a month and still not have enough income to qualify *if* the lender determines that either (1) you have other long-term debts like car payments which effectively reduce your income, or (2) you have an insecure job.

How does the lender determine this? You fill out a statement saying what your long-term debts are (lying or making gross exaggerations on the statement is sufficient cause for refusing to give a loan) and, in most cases, you must get your employer to fill out a form indicating how long you have been on your job and what your chances for continued employment are. For self-employed individuals the last two years of federal income tax returns are usually required.

Today, with housing prices and loans so high, many lenders are realizing that the 4 to 1 formula is unreasonable. They are reducing the amount of income required to $3^{1}/_{2}$ to 1 or in some cases lower. Ask your agent about this or if the agent doesn't know, simply start calling all the lenders in town. It may take a few minutes but it could mean the difference between getting your home or not qualifying.

Credit

Once you've qualified by income, you must demonstrate to the lender that you have the willingness to pay back the mortgage. You do this by showing that you've borrowed money from other lenders before and you've always repaid as agreed. The lending institution will have you fill out a credit application and then will secure a credit report from one of many credit-reporting companies across the country. (It is not enough to have never defaulted on a loan—in order to demonstrate good credit you must have borrowed money and repaid it. The person who has never borrowed has as much trouble showing good credit as the one who has borrowed but not repaid.). If you have good credit and sufficient income, you will qualify for the loan. It's that simple. If you have bad credit, or feel you have been discriminated against by being turned down on a loan, you have recourses. To check what you can do to improve your credit or whom to contact in case of discrimination, I suggest you see my earlier book, *Protect Yourself in Real Estate*, McGraw-Hill Book Company, 1977.

Interest Rate

The amount of interest charged by the lender on a loan is arbitrary. The rates are set by the officers of the company and depend on the cost of money from secondary lenders, on the anticipation of future inflation, and on other factors. There is very little the buyer can do to persuade a lender to charge less. Sometimes checking different lending institutions may turn up one that will charge 0.25 percent less than the rest. Don't hesitate to use the lender with the cheapest rate. Money is money.

In the 1950s interest rates of 4 to 6 percent were common. In the period 1957 to 1958 the rates went as high as 7.5 percent. Through the 1960s the rates were generally 6 to 7 percent, and up until the recession and inflation of the mid-1970s rates rarely went higher than 7.5 to 8 percent. Since then they have been as high as 12 percent and rarely lower than 8 percent. Again, check around to be sure you're getting the lowest rate available at the time you're considering buying.

To determine what you can afford to buy, use Table 2-2 (next page). First figure your *monthly income*. You may count both husband and wife's salary, provided each has a job that can be called "steady" work. (Intermittent work such as babysitting probably could not be counted.) Steady work usually means an occupation in which you've been employed for at least six continuous months (although two years may be considered minimum by some lenders) and in which your chances for continued employment are good. If you get paid on a weekly basis, multiply the weekly salary by 4.3 (there are 4.3 weeks in a month). From this monthly salary *deduct* any long-term expenses that will not be paid off within six months, such as car or furniture payments. Do not deduct income taxes.

Once you have determined your monthly income, read down the

TABLE 2-2
Finding the Maximum Price and Loan You Can Get When You Know Monthly Income*

Monthly income	Highest monthly payment (4 to 1)	8% annual interest		9% annual interest		10% annual interest	
		Maximum loan	Maximum price for house	Maximum loan	Maximum price for house	Maximum loan	Maximum price for house
$ 500	$ 125	$ 13,000	$ 16,250	$ 12,000	$ 15,000	$ 11,000	$ 13,750
550	138	14,000	17,500	13,000	16,250	12,000	15,000
600	150	15,000	18,750	14,000	17,500	13,000	16,250
650	163	17,000	21,250	15,000	18,750	14,000	17,500
700	175	18,000	22,500	16,000	20,000	15,000	18,750
750	188	19,000	23,750	18,000	22,500	16,000	20,000
800	200	20,000	25,000	19,000	23,750	17,000	21,250
850	213	22,000	27,500	20,000	25,000	18,000	22,500
900	225	23,000	28,750	21,000	26,250	19,000	23,750
950	238	24,000	30,000	22,000	27,500	20,000	25,000
1,000	250	26,000	32,500	23,000	28,750	21,000	26,250
1,050	263	27,000	33,750	25,000	31,250	22,000	27,500
1,100	275	28,000	35,000	26,000	32,500	23,000	28,750
1,150	288	30,000	37,500	27,000	33,750	25,000	31,250
1,200	300	31,000	38,750	28,000	35,000	26,000	32,500
1,250	313	32,000	40,000	29,000	36,250	27,000	33,750
1,300	325	33,000	41,250	30,000	37,500	28,000	35,000
1,350	338	35,000	43,750	32,000	40,000	29,000	36,250
1,400	350	36,000	45,000	33,000	41,250	30,000	37,500
1,450	363	37,000	46,250	34,000	42,500	31,000	38,750
1,500	375	38,000	47,500	35,000	43,750	32,000	40,000

1,550	388	40,000	50,000	36,000	45,000	33,000	41,250
1,600	400	41,000	51,250	37,000	46,250	34,000	42,500
1,650	413	42,000	52,500	38,000	47,500	35,000	43,750
1,700	425	43,000	53,750	40,000	50,000	36,000	45,000
1,750	438	45,000	56,250	41,000	51,250	37,000	46,250
1,800	450	46,000	57,500	42,000	52,500	39,000	48,750
1,850	463	47,000	58,750	43,000	53,750	40,000	50,000
1,900	475	49,000	61,250	44,000	55,000	41,000	51,250
1,950	488	50,000	62,500	45,000	56,250	42,000	52,500
2,000	500	51,000	63,750	47,000	58,750	43,000	53,750
2,050	513	53,000	66,250	48,000	60,000	44,000	55,000
2,100	525	54,000	67,500	49,000	61,250	45,000	56,250
2,150	538	55,000	68,750	50,000	62,500	46,000	57,500
2,200	550	56,000	70,000	51,000	63,750	47,000	58,750
2,250	563	58,000	72,500	52,000	65,000	48,000	60,000
2,300	575	59,000	73,750	54,000	67,500	49,000	61,250
2,350	588	60,000	75,000	55,000	68,750	50,000	62,500
2,400	600	61,000	76,250	56,000	70,000	51,000	63,750
2,450	613	63,000	78,750	57,000	71,250	52,000	65,000
2,500	625	64,000	80,000	58,000	72,500	53,000	66,250
2,550	638	65,000	81,250	60,000	75,000	55,000	68,750
2,600	650	67,000	83,750	61,000	76,250	56,000	70,000
2,650	663	68,000	85,000	62,000	77,500	57,000	71,250
2,700	675	69,000	86,250	63,000	78,750	58,000	72,500
2,750	688	70,000	87,500	64,000	80,000	59,000	73,750
2,800	700	72,000	90,000	65,000	81,250	60,000	75,000
2,850	713	73,000	91,250	66,000	82,500	61,000	76,250
2,900	725	74,000	92,500	68,000	85,000	62,000	77,500

(Continued)

*For higher interest rates, check the chart on page 168.

TABLE 2-2 continued
Finding the Maximum Price and Loan You Can Get When You Know Monthly Income

Monthly income	Highest monthly payment (4 to 1)	8% annual interest		9% annual interest		10% annual interest	
		Maximum loan	Maximum price for house	Maximum loan	Maximum price for house	Maximum loan	Maximum price for house
2,950	738	76,000	95,000	69,000	86,250	63,000	78,750
3,000	750	77,000	96,250	70,000	87,500	64,000	80,000
3,050	763	78,000	97,500	71,000	88,750	65,000	81,250
3,100	775	79,000	98,750	72,000	90,000	66,000	82,500
3,150	788	80,000	100,000	73,000	91,250	67,000	83,750
3,200	800	82,000	102,500	75,000	93,750	68,000	85,000
3,250	813	83,000	103,750	76,000	95,000	70,000	87,500
3,300	825	84,000	105,000	77,000	96,250	71,000	88,750
3,350	838	86,000	107,500	78,000	97,500	72,000	90,000
3,400	850	87,000	108,750	79,000	98,750	73,000	91,250
3,450	863	88,000	110,000	80,000	100,000	74,000	92,500
3,500	875	89,000	111,250	82,000	102,500	75,000	93,750
3,550	888	91,000	113,750	83,000	103,750	76,000	95,000
3,600	900	92,000	115,000	84,000	105,000	77,000	96,250
3,650	913	93,000	116,250	85,000	106,250	78,000	97,500
3,700	925	95,000	118,750	86,000	107,500	79,000	98,250
3,750	938	96,000	120,000	87,000	108,750	80,000	100,000
3,800	950	97,000	121,250	89,000	111,250	81,000	101,250
3,850	963	98,000	122,500	90,000	112,500	82,000	102,500
3,900	975	100,000	125,000	91,000	113,750	83,000	103,750
3,950	988	101,000	126,250	92,000	115,000	84,000	105,000
4,000	1,000	102,000	127,500	93,000	116,250	86,000	107,500

left-hand side of the table until you find a figure corresponding to your income. If you are between two numbers, take the higher number. Now read across the page. It will show you first the highest total monthly payment, including principal, interest, taxes, and fire insurance, that you can afford on a 4 to 1 ratio. Next it will show you the approximate maximum loan you can afford at three different interest rates: 8, 9, and 10 percent. Then for each of those interest rates it will show you the maximum price you can afford to pay for a house assuming you are getting an 80 percent loan.

NOTE: The total monthly payment figure is arrived at by amortizing (paying off) the loan on a thirty-year basis and adding in 25 percent of the monthly payment for taxes and insurance. This figure will probably be too high for California (after Proposition 13) and for other states with low property taxes. For such areas a closer approximation of what you can get can be found by finding the highest monthly payment, then reading down the chart four to five places before reading across to the maximum loan and price.

If after checking the table you find your income doesn't even come close to buying the dream home you want, don't be discouraged. There are other methods of financing as well as alternatives to the suburban home yet to be considered.

Down Payment

Leverage involves at least three elements: a fulcrum or lender, a lever or credit, and a moving force or down payment. This last is sometimes the largest stumbling block for the potential buyer. To check just how much down payment may be required in a home purchase, see Table 2-3.

To use this table, simply go down the left-hand column to the price of home you are considering and read across to the down payment required. This is the amount of cash you would need, exclusive of closing costs, assuming an 80 percent loan and no other financing.

It is easy to see that as prices go up the amount of cash required to get into a home likewise goes up. For example, the $100,000 home requires $20,000 down, which is a large amount to have in available

TABLE 2-3
Down Payment Required for 80% Loan When You Know the Price

Price	Down payment required to secure an 80% loan	Price	Down payment required to secure an 80% loan
$25,000	$ 5,000	$ 63,000	$12,600
26,000	5,200	64,000	12,800
27,000	5,400	65,000	13,000
28,000	5,600	66,000	13,200
29,000	5,800	67,000	13,400
30,000	6,000	68,000	13,600
31,000	6,200	69,000	13,800
32,000	6,400	70,000	14,000
33,000	6,600	71,000	14,200
34,000	6,800	72,000	14,400
35,000	7,000	73,000	14,600
36,000	7,200	74,000	14,800
37,000	7,400	75,000	15,000
38,000	7,600	76,000	15,200
39,000	7,800	77,000	15,400
40,000	8,000	78,000	15,600
41,000	8,200	79,000	15,800
42,000	8,400	80,000	16,000
43,000	8,600	81,000	16,200
44,000	8,800	82,000	16,400
45,000	9,000	83,000	16,600
46,000	9,200	84,000	16,800
47,000	9,400	85,000	17,000
48,000	9,600	86,000	17,200
49,000	9,800	87,000	17,400
50,000	10,000	88,000	17,600
51,000	10,200	89,000	17,800
52,000	10,400	90,000	18,000
53,000	10,600	91,000	18,200
54,000	10,800	92,000	18,400
55,000	11,000	93,000	18,600
56,000	11,200	94,000	18,800
57,000	11,400	95,000	19,000
58,000	11,600	96,000	19,200
59,000	11,800	97,000	19,400
60,000	12,000	98,000	19,600
61,000	12,200	99,000	19,800
62,000	12,400	100,000	20,000

cash. Many people who have the income do not have sufficient savings or an existing residence to sell from which they can withdraw funds to place as down payment on a new residence.

A great deal of thinking has gone into reducing down payments to bring more buyers into the market. One method is the 90 percent loan, which can be given by some savings and loan associations. In many cases these lenders only issue this type of loan if they purchase an insurance policy from a special insurance company guaranteeing the repayment of the loan in the event you default. While it is unnecessary to go into detail on this Private Mortgage Insurance (PMI), it is important to note that it will cost the borrower (you) an additional 0.25 percent interest a year. This means that the effective rate on an 80 percent loan might be 9 percent while on a 90 percent loan it might be $9^{1}/_{4}$ percent a year. (Once you pay the loan down to 80 percent of the value of the house the PMI insurance can usually be removed by simply issuing a request to the lender, thereby saving you $^{1}/_{4}$ percent in interest.)

In order to get a PMI loan, however, it now becomes necessary to satisfy two parties—the lender and the insurance company, and the insurer usually has stricter rules than the lender (after all, in case you don't pay, the insurer would be out quite a bit of money). PMI loans, therefore, are normally only available to borrowers who have sterling credit and who qualify at a minimum of the 4 to 1 ratio for a piece of property. In addition, the property must also qualify—usually it must be the three-bedroom, two-bath suburban delight we talked about in the last chapter. The insurer wants this type of home because in the event you default and the property must be resold, the insurer knows the largest number of buyers are looking for it. Finally, there is an upper limit or maximum loan amount on PMIs. This has been $55,000.

Another drawback to the 90 percent loan, whether a PMI or uninsured, is that the actual price of a piece of property you can qualify for is less at 90 percent than at 80 percent. Consider Table 2-4. Note that the amount of *loan* you can qualify for remains the same whether it is for 80 percent or 90 percent. Only the total price you can pay varies and it is less for the smaller down payment.

TABLE 2-4
Effect on Price between Putting 20% Down and 10% Down
When You Know Your Maximum Loan Amount

Maximum loan	20% down maximum price	10% down maximum price
$20,000	$25,000	$22,222
25,000	31,250	27,777
30,000	37,500	33,333
35,000	43,750	38,888
40,000	50,000	44,444
45,000	56,250	50,000
50,000	62,500	55,555
55,000	68,750	61,111
60,000	75,000	66,666

Second Mortgage

Another method of lowering the down payment is the second mortgage. In its most common form the seller takes back 10 percent of the sales price in the form of a short-term mortgage—usually two to five years. This means that you, the borrower, can get an 80 percent loan from a lender and then another 10 percent from the seller. You only have to put down 10 percent and yet can still have a high purchase price.

The disadvantage of the second mortgage are higher payments, usually a higher interest rate, and a shorter term. "Seconds," as they are commonly called, rarely go for under 10 percent a year interest. They must be paid off in a few years, which means you'll have to come up with the cash anyway either by refinancing the house or by taking it out of savings.

Some of these disadvantages can be overcome. Often it is possible to pay just the interest (or very close to it) each month, thereby reducing the montly payments on the second. One percent a month of the unpaid balance is a typical payback on a second mortgage. For a $10,000 second that's only $100 a month. Also many sellers prefer cash to seconds and only accept them in order to get a quick sale. After the sale the seller may be planning to sell the second for cash and it may be possible to buy it yourself from the seller at a discount as high as 40 percent. For a $10,000 second, this would mean paying off the note for just $6,000. Check with your agent or financial advisor here.

These are essentially the only conventional methods of reducing the down payment. Most lenders will allow a 10 percent second with 10 percent down on an 80 percent mortgage, but will not grant a first mortgage of 80 percent on anything less than 10 percent down. Some unscrupulous agents and sellers will try illegitimate means of changing this formula, such as faking a sales price much higher than the real sales price so that the buyer gets the home without any down payment, just for the price of the mortgage. Two sales agreements and the consent of buyer, seller, and agent are required in such schemes and with so many participants, the schemes often go awry when one party or the other feels cheated. When word of what's happening reaches the lender, the loan is almost always cancelled and criminal prosecution might follow.

Government Loans

What we've been discussing until now is called in the trade "conventional" financing. In addition, there is government-assisted financing through two branches of the federal government and in some cases through individual state governments. Check with your state's real estate department for further information on state financing. Federal government financing assistance through the Department of Housing and Urban Development (HUD) by means of their Federal Housing Administration (FHA) programs account for only about 10 percent of all residential mortgages. Bureaucratic delays and added expense (1 percent of the loan amount to the buyer and anywhere from 0 to 10 percent in cost of the loan amount for the seller!) have served to cut back on the volume of these loans over the years. Federal assistance through the Veterans Administration is available to veterans.

The FHA Program

The big advantage of the FHA program is lower down payments. The FHA program is in reality an entire series of loan assistance programs under nine titles with many subdivisions. Included are loans for flood assistance and home improvement. What we're concerned with primarily is Title II, Section 203, which insures a lender so that if you take out a mortgage and don't pay it back, the government will make good the amount you borrowed. The government doesn't advance any money, but acts as an insuring agent.

This type of mortgage is available to anyone who can qualify under FHA regulations. These rules are essentially the same as for conventional loans. A 4 to 1 income-to-debt ratio is required as is good credit. They can be arranged through almost any bank or savings and loan association. Table 2-5 indicates the maximum loans allowed and down payments available.

The FHA also sets a maximum interest rate which is frequently lower than the current conventional loan rate There is a statutory maximum interest rate of 6 percent on FHA loans, but each year the federal government has allowed the program to adjust its rates higher in relation to current mortgage levels. No second mortgages are allowed under FHA loans.

Veterans Administration Loans

These loans are available to veterans and are frequently called GI loans. Unlike the FHA loan which insures the lender, the Veterans Administration (VA) loan *guarantees* repayment of the amount borrowed up to a maximum of $17,500. While there is no maximum purchase price, the maximum loan is usually about $70,000. The big advantage is that there is *no down payment requirement* on these loans.

As in the FHA loans, the mortgage must be obtained through a bank or savings and loan association, and a VA appraiser comes out and determines the appraised value, giving a "Certificate of Reasonable Value" (CRV) on the property. The loan is based on this amount. The veteran-buyer can pay more for the property than the CRV, but must make up the difference in cash.

Qualifying for VA loans is similar to FHA and conventional except that the VA often likes the borrower to be making better than four times the monthly payment in income. Eligibility for this program changes almost yearly as it is updated by the government. In general an individual must have served on active duty for 181 days

TABLE 2-5
FHA Loan Program for Single-Family Homes
(FHA Title II, Section 203)
Maximum Loan Amount $60,000
Interest Rate changes—check with lender (8.5% at this writing)
Down Payment Requirements: 3% down of the first $25,000 of appraised value, 5% down of the appraised value over $25,000

Appraised value	Maximum loan	Down required
$20,000	$19,400	$ 600
25,000	24,200	750
30,000	29,000	1,000
35,000	33,750	1,250
40,000	38,500	1,500
45,000	43,250	1,750
50,000	48,000	2,000
55,000	52,750	2,250
60,000	57,500	2,500
62,750	60,000	2,750

Note: Under this program the down payment is considerably less than under conventional financing—always less than 5 percent. The maximum loan, however, is $60,000. For houses above $62,750 in value, this loan is of limited use. The FHA has its own appraisers who give their own estimate of the market value of the home. If their appraised value happens to be less than the selling price, the loan will be computed on their value. This could mean a larger down payment for the buyer. On the plus side, the FHA requires a strict structural inspection before insuring the loan and this helps to ensure that the buyer will receive a home in good condition.

or more within certain time limits. Check with any bank or savings and loan association for the current requirements.

Flexible or Graduated Payment Mortgage Program

Realizing the difficulty many families are experiencing in coming up with the required monthly income to qualify for large loans, some savings and loan associations and the federal government through a HUD-FHA program have found a creative method of reducing the size of the monthly payment in the early years of the mortgage and making up for this reduction by increasing the size in later years. This can substantially reduce the initial monthly payment and mean the difference between getting your dream home or not being able to afford it.

A word of caution about this program. Very few savings and loan associations and almost no banks offer a conventional flexible payment plan at this writing. In order to get a conventional flexible payment plan you'll have to do considerable shopping around. Many major lending institutions do offer the FHA-HUD plan called the "Graduated Payment Mortgage" (GPM) and that plan will be discussed here.

The FHA plan applies to the Section 203 program for reducing down payments that we were just discussing. (By combining the two programs, you can get a small down payment and reduced monthly payments!) It is, unfortunately, limited to the $60,000 maximum for that program.

To see how the FHA-GPM works, consider Table 2-6. This table assumes that you are borrowing $35,000 at $8^{1}/_{2}$ percent interest for thirty years. The GPM offers five different repayment plans which reduce the original monthly payment more or less dramatically. The buyer has the choice of which program to take.

Note that for plan III, a normal $269 level monthly payment is reduced to $203 the first year or a reduction of $66—nearly 25 percent! Each year after the first year on plan III the payment increases until at year five it becomes slightly higher than the original $269 level payment. After year five it jumps up to $291 or $22 higher than the level payment and stays at this amount for the remainder of the loan. This plan offers the greatest initial reduction in payment, but payments increase rapidly for the first five years to a high level. Plan V, on the other hand, also offers a substantial reduction in initial payment, but it does not reach the $291 level until ten years have passed.

Each plan offers advantages and disadvantages. To get a better understanding of each plan, Table 2-7 shows the rate of graduation and the terms for each. The greater the rate of increase or the longer the period of increase, the lower the mortgage payments in early

TABLE 2-6
Comparison of Payment Schedules of
Level Payment Mortgage and GPM
(U.S. Dept. of Housing and Urban Development)
$35,000 Loan—8½ Percent Interest, 30-Year Term

Year	Level payment loan	GPM plans				
		I	II	III	IV	V
1	$269	$245	$223	$203	$243	$223
2	269	251	234	218	248	230
3	269	257	245	234	253	237
4	269	264	258	252	258	244
5	269	270	271	271	263	251
6	269	277	284	291	269	258
7	269	277	284	4291	274	266
8	269	277	284	291	280	274
9	269	277	284	291	285	282
10	269	277	284	291	291	291
11+	269	277	284	291	297	300

Note: Because of the increasing mortgage amount during the early years of the loan, a slightly higher down payment may be required on a GPM loan than with a standard level payment mortgage.

years. If you are a young family that expects to have a quick and substantial growth in income, you could select a Graduated Payment Mortgage with a five-year term and a 7.5 percent rate of graduation. A family with more normal growth in income might choose the 3 percent, ten-year plan.

Under a 3 percent, ten-year plan, the monthly mortgage payment on a $35,000 mortgage would be reduced by $46 in the first year from $269 on a similar, standard-level payment mortgage to $223 on the GPM. For the next ten years, the payment would increase by 3 percent each year. In the third year, the GPM payment would be $32 less each month. By the eighth year, the GPM payment would be $5 more than the level payment. From the eleventh to the thirtieth year, the buyer would be paying a flat $300 a month.

TABLE 2-7
Rates and Terms of Graduation Available on a GPM

Plan	Rate of graduation	Term of graduation
I	2.5%	5 years
II	5	5
III	7.5	5
IV	2	10
V	3	10

Variable Rate Mortgages

Finally a word might be said about the variable rate mortgage (VRM). At the present time these are the only mortgages available from many state-chartered savings and loan associations, particularly on the West Coast. Federally chartered lending institutions still offer fixed rate mortgages.

A VRM simply means that the interest rate will fluctuate up or down according to a set index. This index is usually the cost to the lender of borrowing money from a federal agency such as the Federal Home Loan Bank Board, and that cost is itself tied into many rates, not the least important of which is the rate of inflation. What it all means is that if you have a VRM with an initial rate of 8 percent, several years later the rate could go up to 9 percent or 10 percent or higher. Or conversely it might drop to 7 or 6 percent. These fluctuations in a VRM are not determined according to the whim of the lender. The government controls VRMs. In California, for example, at the present time a change in interest rate is allowed only once every six months and then a maximum change of only 0.25 percent is permitted. In addition, the maximum change in rate up or down during the entire length of the loan is usually limited to 2.5 percent. (An added benefit goes with this. If the rate is raised, the borrower has the option of paying off the mortgage without penalty at the time of the change.)

What's the advantage of such a loan, you might well ask. Almost none in terms of lowering either cash down payment requirements or monthly payments. The real advantage is that it allows lenders to offer loans during times when money is hard to get. This means that a VRM is better than no loan at all. Because of the flexible nature of the interest rate, the closing costs in terms of "points" or percentages of the loan charged for making it can be kept to a minimum.

Closing Costs

Finally we come to a matter that we've skipped over in several places: closing costs. Closing costs for the buyer will usually amount to only 2 to 4 percent of the total purchase price, so by comparison they may seem small. However, since closing costs are normally paid in cash in addition to the down payment, when you consider the money you need in order to buy the house, they can be significant. For example, if you're buying a $50,000 house and putting the normal 20 percent down, you would need to come up with $10,000 in cash. If, in addition, closing costs ran 3 percent or $1,500 your cash requirements are now $11,500 in order to complete the transaction. While the closing costs are only 3 percent of the total price, in this example they are 13 percent of the total *cash* required.

Many buyers lament the high closing costs they have to pay. But they should take comfort from the fact that sellers' closing costs are much higher. The seller has one big item to pay that the buyer doesn't and that is the commission. Generally the seller is responsible for the entire fee to the agent. (It could be argued that the buyer pays part of this fee in a higher purchase price.) This rule, however, is not written in stone. There is nothing to prevent an agent from collecting a commission from a buyer (if you allow it).

The buyer's closing costs are usually about half the total closing costs with the exception of the commission. Local custom determines who pays what fees and customs vary a lot from area to area. In one county within a state, for example, a buyer's costs on a house might be $1,100 while in another county in the same state they could be $1,500. Normally the agent(s) will inform you how closing costs are divided in your area and will expect you to pay your fair share.

This raises an interesting point. While custom dictates the share of closing costs that buyer and seller are to pay, this division also is not written in stone. With certain notable exceptions, such as the choice of a title insurance company, either a buyer or a seller may demand that the other party pay all or a larger portion of the costs. This is usually done by means of a contingency clause included in the sales agreement. Such a clause specifies that the buyer, for example, will only purchase the house if the seller pays *all* the closing costs. If the seller is desperate to sell, he or she may sign.

Before you run off and insist that every purchase agreement you sign include such a clause, a word of caution. More frequently than not, particularly in a fast market, sellers will not accept such clauses. After all, why should they sell their house to you and pay your costs too when they can easily find another buyer who'll pay the buyer's share. Including such a clause in a sales agreement could cause you to lose a deal.

Asking the seller to pay the buyer's closing costs is really asking that party to take less. Let's assume the closing costs for the buyer are $1,500 and the asking price for a house is $40,000. If you as a buyer offer full price but insist that the seller pay your costs, your offer is really $38,500. All of which brings us to the matter of getting your closing costs financed.

Financing the Closing Costs

Closing costs are normally paid in cash by both parties to the transaction. It is sometimes possible for the buyer, in effect, to have the closing costs financed. Consider the following transaction handled from two perspectives.

In the first case, a buyer wants to purchase a $50,000 home on which the closing costs will be $1,500. The buyer figures the home is not worth the full asking price, and wants to offer something less. We'll say that the amount the buyer offers is $48,500 with each party paying normal closing costs. If the seller accepts, the deal for the buyer is shown in Table 2-8. In this instance, the buyer must come up with $11,200 in cash in order to complete the transaction.

In the second case, the price asked is the same. This buyer,

TABLE 2-8

Price	$48,500
Down payment (20%)	$ 9,700
Closing costs	1,500
Cash required	$11,200

however, offers full price insisting that the seller pay the buyer's closing costs. The deal now for the buyer is shown in Table 2-9. Notice that in the second deal the buyer needed to come up with $1,200 less cash than in the first deal.

Does this mean that the buyer is getting away without paying any closing costs? No, it means that the buyer is *financing* them. In the first case the mortgage would be $38,800 (80 percent of the selling price of $48,500). In the second case the mortgage would be $40,000 (80 percent of the selling price of $50,000). Although in the second case the buyer had $1,200 less *cash* to pay, he or she ends up with a $1,200 higher mortgage. The two cases are compared in Table 2-10.

Notice that in both cases the seller is asked to accept the same amount of money for the house: $48,500. To the seller it should make little difference whether the price is actually $48,500 or $50,000 less closing costs. The seller gets the same amount. It could, however, make a big difference to you, if you're short of cash. It could also make a difference to the lender.

You will recall that the lender makes an appraisal on the value of the property. If the house is actually worth $50,000 in the eyes of the lender, it shouldn't make any difference whether you use case 1 or case 2. On the other hand, if the lender appraises the house as having a maximum value of only $48,500, you would not be able to use case 2 since the maximum loan would be 80 percent or $38,800.

Closing Cost Items

Escrow The items that make up the closing costs are generally similar across the country, although there are a few significant differences. In most of the country real estate transactions are handled through an escrow. This is an independent third party, usually a corporation, that acts for both buyer and seller holding and

TABLE 2-9

Price	$50,000	
Down payment (20%)		$10,000
Closing costs to buyer		0
Cash required		$10,000

TABLE 2-10

	Case 1	Case 2
Mortgage	$38,800	$40,000
Down payment	9,700	10,000
Price	$48,500	$50,000
Closing costs to buyer	1,500	0
Total investment	$50,000	$50,000

preparing documents and eventually recording the deed and dispersing the monies. An escrow acts as a kind of protection. It ensures that the seller doesn't let go of the property until the buyer has paid all the necessary money. And that the buyer's money isn't dispersed until the seller has delivered clear title. For this service the escrow company charges a fee.

In parts of the East Coast, particularly in some of the New England states, the function of the escrow is handled by attorneys. The buyer has an attorney, the seller has an attorney, and in many cases even the lender has an attorney. This means that in some areas of the country no attorneys' fees will appear as closing costs, but there will be a hefty escrow charge. In other areas there may be no escrow charge, but there could be hefty attorneys' fees. If an agent is handling your transaction, he or she will tell what the local custom is. If not, you can find out by calling a broker, an attorney, or if available, an escrow office.

The actual dollar costs of escrow or attorney services (as with most other costs listed below) vary considerably between states and even cities. In addition it is adjusted according to the selling price—the higher the price, the higher the fees. The best way to see if the price you are asked to pay is appropriate is to check with another escrow company or another attorney. Many lawyers who handle real estate work have set fees and will gladly discuss them with you. Do this *before* you accept their services.

Points Almost every time you get a new mortgage there are points to pay. A point is equal to 1 percent of the loan amount. One point on a

$10,000 loan is $100. Who must pay the points to get a loan is a matter of agreement, as we've seen earlier (except in the case of an FHA loan where the buyer may not pay more than 1 point).

Points may be either one of two things. They may be a discount on the mortgage (advance interest) as is frequently the case with FHA and VA loans. Or they may be an origination fee as is frequently the case with conventional loans. (The buyer's point on an FHA loan is usually termed an origination fee; a seller's point is usually termed a discount.)

It may be useful to know the difference between an origination fee and a discount. An origination fee is a one-time charge made by the lender for setting up the loan. It usually includes the costs of the appraisal, paper work, and any loss of interest on the loaned money for the time between when you, the borrower, start paying interest on it and the time the lender makes it available for lending (usually just a few days).

A discount is an interest penalty paid to compensate a lender for making a loan at less than the going market interest rate. FHA loans, for example, are typically 0.50 percent or more lower than the current market interest rate. Lenders charge discount points to make up for this loss of interest.

The number of points you have to pay depends on the market conditions. When money is tight, a high premium may be charged to get any loan. This is in addition to high interest rates. When money is easy to obtain, points could be low. I have seen as much as 10 to 12 points charged to obtain government loans. Today, however, typically 1 to 1½ points on conventional loans might be charged.

Title Insurance This ensures that the buyer gets a good title to the property. Normally the buyer pays the full fee, although it may be split between buyer and seller. Like the escrow charge, title insurance fees are tied to the price of the property. There may be two title insurance policies to buy. Many lenders require a standardized American Land Title Association (ALTA) policy. This requires two fees: one for a "standard" policy and another for the ALTA. Again, both are usually paid by the buyer. If you feel that the fee(s) is too high or if you want to know what the fee will be for a given price of a house in your area, call several title companies. Usually they will be happy to discuss their fees and services with you.

[49]

Prorations These are not really fees. They are simply a division of the continuing costs of owning a piece of real estate between buyer and seller so that each pays a fair share. Taxes are normally prorated. So is insurance if the buyer picks up the seller's old policy. Prorations are necessary because taxes, insurance, and some other costs are not paid daily but in one or two installments a year. Depending on when the sale takes place, the seller may owe the buyer for monies due but not yet paid. Or the buyer may owe the seller for money already paid but not yet due.

What is crucial about prorations is the date on which they are made. Normally this is the day the deed is transferred (also called the day escrow closes). This is appropriate since before that point in time the seller owns the property and after it belongs to the buyer. There can be important legal consequences of determining the date of prorations for each transaction and an attorney or other knowledgeable party should be consulted when in doubt on a particular purchase.

Items which may be prorated include:

1. Property taxes (including tax reserves)

2. Insurance (including reserves)

3. Rents (if appropriate)

4. Water, gas, and electric bills

5. Coal or oil on hand

6. Garbage removal

7. Any other continuing item related to the property

Credit Report The fee for this is normally much less than $50 and is usually paid by the buyer, although it can be paid by the seller if both parties agree. There is little opportunity to bargain here as the lender will usually specify which credit-reporting company must be used.

Appraisal Fee If you've hired an independent appraiser, you'll have to pay a fee, which you discuss at the time of the hiring. If you did not hire an appraiser, there should be no appraisal fee. Lenders do not normally charge separate appraisal fees on mortgages.

Mortgage Service Charge   The buyer usually pays this one-time fee. It goes to an independent company that reports to the lender the amount of taxes due on the property so that the lender can pay them out of your impounds. It is usually under $50 and there is little room for bargaining as the lender will specify which service to use.

Impounds   If your monthly payment on your mortgage will include taxes and insurance, you will have to come up with enough money at the close of escrow to cover the first installment on your taxes and at least the first year's payment on your fire insurance. The lender will set these amounts.

The only way you can effectively reduce them is by changing the date escrow closes. If you can manage to close escrow just after a tax payment was made by the previous owner, you probably will have ample time to establish your tax fund in monthly payments before the next tax installment is due; hence your impounds costs at closing should be very low.

Many lenders require an extra month of taxes and insurance as a buffer in case you don't make a payment or in cases taxes rise. If the lender requires more than this amount, you should check to see if you can get a better deal from another lender. In the past, interest has not been paid by lenders on impounded money; new federal laws may soon require that at least a nominal interest rate (around 2 percent) be paid. Impounds are normally required on any loan that is higher than 80 percent of the selling price of the property.

Notary Fee   Notarizing or witnessing documents is usually performed by the escrow officer and in many cases is done as part of the normal escrow charges. Where an extra charge is made, it shouldn't be more than a few dollars for each document notarized.

Recording Fee for Deed and Mortgages   In most areas this fee is under $5 for each document. If you question the amount being charged, call your county or city recorder's office and ask what the regular recording fee is.

Transfer Tax   Until 1967 the federal government charged a revenue stamp tax on the conveyance (transfer of title) of real estate. When this law was repealed the states instituted their own transfer tax.

Other Items Land survey, soil engineer's report, structural engineer's report, termite report, or clearance, etc., are special items which the buyer, the seller, or the lender may insist upon. The costs and who will pay them should be arranged beforehand.

What To Do Now?

What we've seen is that what we can buy is determined not so much by price as by how much cash we can put down and how big a monthly payment we can handle, that is, by how much leverage we can swing. If after going through this chapter you decide that your suburban dream home is out of the question, what do you do now? Do you buy something you don't like and hope to trade up in a few years? Do you rent, waiting for your income to go up? Or do you wring your hands in despair?

The nature of this book is to present alternatives, and those we'll come to shortly. Before we do, there is one last course of action to pursue—getting the seller to reduce the price to a level you can afford. Just how realistic is this approach?

THREE

How To Get a Seller To Lower the Price

Price in real estate is not like price on a jar of mayonnaise or a pair of pants. It's more like the price on an automobile and a whole lot more like prices at an old-fashioned bartering stand. The seller asks, the buyer offers, and a deal is made only when the two get together. Frequently, depending on market conditions and the seller's need to get out, you can get the home of your dreams for considerably less than the asking price.

How Do You Offer Less?

Typically you will work through a real estate agent. Many buyers erroneously feel that they can get a better deal by buying direct from a seller. Having done it both ways, my observation is that sellers who try to sell "by owner" offer two big disadvantages to buyers. First, such sellers tend to have an exaggerated view of their home's worth. Often they will say they are only trying to save themselves the commission. (But even so, what advantage does that offer the buyer?) And second, offering less requires bargaining and in real estate it's better if you have someone else do your bargaining for you. It's a lot easier for a seller to take if an agent says there's a buyer who's offering $5,000 less than if you make the offer directly yourself. When the seller gets mad and says the buyer is a cheapskate and no-good jerk who's trying to steal the house, what do you as a direct buyer say? An agent can easily agree with the seller, calm him or her down, and perhaps get a deal for you.

So if you want to get a home for less than the asking price, the first rule is to *find a good agent, one who will work with you.*

This is extremely important because some agents work against their buyers. Typically this type of agent will show a house and if a prospective buyer appears to like it, quickly will draw up a purchase agreement simply writing in the asking price. If the buyer, on the other hand, is only moderately enthusiastic, the agent may suggest a price a few hundred dollars lower to get the buyer more interested. If the buyer is only slightly enthusiastic, the agent may suggest offering a price thousands lower hoping to get any kind of an offer.

From this one could conclude that you get a better deal the less you like the house. Many times this is true. Agents often want you to offer the highest price for reasons we'll see in a moment. To get around this you have two options. First, you can become an actor or actress and disguise your real feelings. Praise the house you can't stand to the heavens. And complain bitterly about the one you like. This has certain drawbacks. Many agents have learned from bitter experience that the house the client complains the most about is really the one he or she wants. In fact there is a rule in selling real estate that goes, "The sale doesn't begin until the customer says *no.*"

The second option is to find an agent who will work with you. This type of person is not the pushy sort, but will instead be willing to let you take the time to find what you want and then will be agreeable about submitting any offer you make. Frequently this agent is a salesperson, working under a broker. He or she is new to the business and is learning along with you. This can be terrific for you when looking for a house, but can be to your disadvantage when your offer is finally submitted. You don't want the agent who is trying to get the price down for you to be a timid lamb. He or she should be a lion. The experienced broker usually fills this bill. Ideally then, you'll work with a salesperson but have the broker submit the offer.

Now, why does the agent often want you to submit the *highest* price?

In almost all cases the broker is the agent of the seller and gets paid when and *only* when a buyer is found who is ready, willing, and able to meet the seller's terms. And one of the seller's terms is price. If the agent can get you to offer full price (and the other terms the seller is asking) the agent is almost guaranteed of making a commission, in many cases even if the seller decides not to sell!

If you make an offer for *less* than the asking price (or for different terms), the agent must now convince the seller to agree to your offer in order to get a commission. It's easy to see why it can be to the agent's advantage to get you to offer the highest price.

But what is to the agent's advantage may not be to yours. That's why it is important to find an agent who will work with you, that is, will gladly present your offer even though it may be for much less than the asking price. How do you find such an agent? Only trial and error will lead you to one.

Many people believe that there is an additional reason why an agent may want you to make the highest offer—in order to get a bigger commission. The sales commission is almost always tied directly to the sale price. Commonly it is from 4 to 7 percent of whatever the sales price may be. It stands to reason, therefore, that the higher the price the higher the commission.

It's been my experience that most agents do not try to get the buyer to pay more in order to get a higher commission, at least not on residential property. The belief that agents do fails to take into account the biggest motivation an agent has—to make any deal at all. Remember the agent gets *no* commission unless there is a sale.

But let's consider just what money is involved. Let's say an agent is selling a house at a 5 percent commission. The sales price is $50,000. You want to offer $47,000 and the agent wants you to offer full price. Is the agent simply hoping to complete the deal or trying for a bigger commission? Let's see just how much more commission the agent will get if you go along with the higher price.

Five percent of $47,000 is $2,350. Five percent of $50,000 is $2,500. The difference is $150. Would an agent jeopardize a chance at a commission of $2,350 just to make an additional $150? Would you?

We're assuming the agent in question is a broker and listed the property. If another agent listed the property, as is most often the case, then the commission will be split. On a typical 50-50 split at $47,000 the agent dealing with you would get $1,175. At $50,000 the amount would be $1,250. The difference is now only $75. If the agent working with you is a salesperson and not a broker, the commission would be split further making the increase to be achieved by getting a higher price even less. (At a 60-40 split the agent now stands to get only $45 more.) With higher-priced houses, of course, these differences increase.

My experience with agents is that they are more concerned to get the deal at all than to get a few more bucks in the commission. The time they'd spend trying to get you, the buyer, to come up with more money *for this reason* could be better spent selling another buyer another house. Agents know that their most valuable asset is the time they have to offer and they try not to waste it.

How Do You Find the Ideal Agent?

An honest answer is that the only way is trial and error. There are some clues along the way. Check to be sure your agent is a Realtor. This is a registered trademark of the National Association of Realtors and can only be used by its members. The national association makes an effort to see that its members maintain high ethical standards.

Avoid any agents that try to high pressure you into buying something you don't want. When dealing with such agents you can always hold the upper hand by simply walking away from them (or threatening to do so). Many people feel the agent is doing them a favor by showing them around different houses. They begin to feel guilty they haven't bought and may buy something they're not entirely happy with because the agent has "put such a lot of time and effort into helping us."

Their attitude is wrong. They're the one's doing the agent a favor. If the agent can't find them the right house, the agent has wasted their time, not the other way around, and owes the potential buyers an apology.

How Much Lower than the Asking Price Should You Offer?

Each case is different, but there are several things that can guide you. Find out why the seller is moving. A seller who's been transferred, who's bought another house and must leave the area, or who's in the middle of a divorce may be willing to take much less than the asking price. Finding out the reason for sale, however, is not as simple as it looks. Don't rely entirely on your agent. After all, it's to the agent's advantage to get you to offer high. Don't rely on the seller's agent, if different from yours, for the same reason. The second rule for getting a house for less is to *talk directly to the seller.* Get to know your ''adversary'' and find out his or her strong and weak points.

The third rule is: *Know the market.* This you will learn very quickly if you spend some time looking at houses. If they're selling rapidly and prices are advancing, it's most unlikely you'll be able to get away with more than a minor reduction in price. If things are slow and homes aren't selling, you have a much better chance. You'll get to know what a house in a given tract is going for (market value) after you check out a few (see Chapter Seven for tips on comparative shopping) and you'll know if the house you're looking at is overpriced, at market, or is undervalued. And you can act according-ly. In general, real estate has the hottest market in the late spring and summer and the slowest around Christmas. So buy in the winter and sell in the summer.

Once you know the market, the seller, and have a willing agent, the rest is up to you. Common sense pays off here. But be careful. Don't fall in love with the place. Don't decide that you absolutely must have it. If you can't afford to pay full price and if the seller refuses your low offer, you'll be heartbroken. Try to keep your emotions a distance from the dealings. Remember that making an offer is business.

How much you should actually offer will differ in each case, but here are some guidelines. Should you find a house that is going for $50,000, the seller has no immediate need to move and the market is not up or down, you can figure the following: Any seller is likely to accept an offer of just a few hundred dollars less than the asking price. A seller will think twice about accepting an offer a few thousand dollars less, but might go along to make the sale. A seller is likely to think hard about an offer of $2,500 (5 percent) less and is likely to turn it down unless there is some shrewd persuading by your agent. A seller is likely not even to think about an offer of $5,000 (10 percent) less, but simply reject it out of hand regardless of the agent's efforts.

This means that you are unlikely to be successful with a low offer the first time out. You may in fact have to try many offers on many houses before you're able to buy one at your price. If, as in our example, you're only able to pay $45,000 or less and you're looking in an area of $50,000 or higher homes, you should look to buy when the market is slow and you should look for a seller who must get out immediately. The fourth and final rule is: *Don't expect to be successful on very low offers very often.*

If you can only afford to offer $30,000 on a $50,000 house, forget it. Chances are the owner owes more than you're offering and couldn't sell even if he or she wanted to. If you are in this situation, then it is definitely time for you to consider the alternatives to your dream home.

FOUR

Condominiums—The Popular Alternative

Let's consider two types of people who might buy a condominium.

Sharon is in her early fifties. She is divorced. Her three children have all grown up and left her big three-bedroom, two-bath suburban house. Now Sharon lives in the house alone. She does all the upkeep and maintenance work. At least twice a month there are lawns to be mowed, flowered areas to be weeded, and general yard upkeep to be done. In addition, several times a year there are storm windows to put up or take down, painting, plumbing repairs, and so on. The list seems endless.

When her children were living at home, it all seemed worthwhile. But now that they've left and she's divorced, she feels like a stranger in the neighborhood. Old friends who lived next door and whose children are also grown have sold their house and moved. And the family that moved in is much younger with young children.

Sharon made up her mind to move. She wanted to buy and her choice was a condominium.

Using the equity she had in the house, she purchased a high-rise condominium in an urban area. It's near where she works and has cut her commuting time. It is also close to shopping and a college, where Sharon has begun taking courses to get the degree she never finished before she was married.

Her condo doesn't have a swimming pool, but it does have a sauna and a recreation room. She's met several other owners and they have formed a bridge group. Most important to Sharon, she never needs to do any outside maintenance work. For Sharon, the move couldn't have been more ideal.

A similar result, but for different reasons, happened for Marlene and Jim.

Marlene and Jim have been married a little over a year and they've lived in an apartment the entire time. They are both in their late twenties, both have good jobs, and they don't plan to have children for at least three or four years. And they want to own a home.

Their reasons for wanting a home are multiple. They want the tax break (deductions for property taxes and mortgage interest) that homeowners get. They also want to start building an equity in a piece of property that they can eventually use when they might have a family and want to purchase a big house. But they don't want to give up the freedom offered by apartment living. Their current building offers a swimming pool, a sauna, and no maintenance responsibilities for them.

After spending considerable time looking, they also purchased a condominium.

The condo they purchased is in a suburban area. It is one of nearly fifty units; there are three large buildings placed side by side. The entire development does have a swimming pool and a sauna and in addition it has three tennis courts, which appealed strongly to Marlene and Jim. It also has a recreation hall where get-togethers for the condominium owners are held on a regular basis.

For Marlene and Jim, the purchase also couldn't have been more ideal. It provided them home ownership as well as a style of life that they wanted.

All of which serves to illustrate that a condominium purchase is as much a matter of lifestyle as of money. Of course, the type of lifestyle depends to a large degree on the type of condominium you purchase. Sharon elected to get a high-rise downtown condominium; Marlene and Jim, a suburban one.

There are at least three distinct varieties of condominium, differentiated by location.

Suburban Condominium

Suburban condominiums come in all shapes and sizes. They may be small buildings of no more than four units. Or they could be large projects of several hundred units. They have in common that they share roughly the same area of the community as single-family suburban houses. In many areas, in fact, suburban condominiums and suburban single-family houses are built side by side.

Besides the convenience of maintenance-free living and the recreational opportunities, suburban condos offer the chance to live in very desirable areas, as we have discussed, for a fraction of the cost of single-family houses. (Although condominiums do cost less, generally, than their single-family counterparts, the reduced cost is in absolute price, not in relative price. You don't necessarily get more for your money, as we'll see shortly.)

Suburban condominiums also frequently cater to families with children. They may have indoor-outdoor play areas, and even baby-sitting services. In this respect they are unusual, since according to a study conducted by the Department of Housing and Urban Development in 1975, most condominium owners do not have children living at home.

Frequently large suburban condominiums are separated into those that will accept children and those that won't. Those that won't sometimes have a provision in their by-laws that the condo will not be sold to a buyer with children. It is not clear whether or not this is enforceable or even if it makes sense. There is little a homeowners' association can do if a family buys a condominium and subsequently has children. Buyers who are looking for adult condominiums, however, should be very careful to check out who lives in the building they anticipate purchasing. In terms of the noise level alone, the difference between a condominium with families with children and one with only adults can be enormous.

Most of the small condominiums are suburban. These buildings frequently have four or fewer units. They often do not have the recreational amenities of large developments, and sometimes owners must provide some of the external maintenance since there is not a large enough base of ownership to afford to hire regular gardeners, plumbers, etc. These small units, however, frequently offer larger interiors or more yard area. Some people prefer them because they are more like houses.

High-Rise Condominiums

These condominiums are usually located in central city areas. They may or may not have all the recreational amenities, but they offer one enormous advantage—they are usually close to downtown shopping and work.

They are frequently very expensive. Over $100,000 for such a condominium in Manhattan or Chicago or Los Angeles is not unusual. However, they are often considered to be the only alternative to renting. In such central city areas modern single-family housing may not be available at any price. (Rehabilitation does offer a sound alternative today, as we will see in Chapter Six.)

Modern high-rise condominiums also offer some security for owners who live in high crime areas. Frequently the buildings have security personnel, television cameras, and other guard systems.

Recreational Condominiums

Recreational condominiums are built near recreational areas such as the seashore, the mountains, skiing facilities, lakes, and so on. Usually they are large buildings or a large group of smaller buildings. Most have all the recreational amenities including swimming pools.

As in the high-rise condominiums, the recreational ones tend to be expensive. Their cost, in an absolute sense, is almost always lower than buying a single-family home in the same area. Developers often sell them as the only way a buyer can *afford* to live near a recreational center.

Many recreational condominium owners buy their units intending to rent them out for part of the year and use them for part. The condominium becomes a second, vacation home. Such use has both advantages and disadvantages for owners.

For those who live permanently in the condominium, it can be disruptive to have short-term tenants moving in and out on a hotellike basis next door. To overcome this problem, many condominium bylaws require that a unit be rented for a minimum of one month. This helps to maintain the stability of the lifestyle, although it makes it more difficult for those owning the unit as a vacation home to rent it out. Nevertheless, in good resort areas, monthly tenants who are willing to pay high rents can be found in large numbers.

In addition, those considering buying a condominium for use as a vacation home and also as a tax shelter should carefully reconsider their purchase. The 1976 tax reform act severely restricted the use of "paper losses" on all vacation property used both for business (rental) and pleasure. Check with your accountant on this first.

Recreational condominium units tend to be clustered much closer together than other condominiums. As we'll see shortly, increased density frequently can be a problem. Because of the proximity to recreational activities, however, studies have shown that owners are usually more than willing to put up with cramped buildings.

In all three types of condominiums, the two biggest advantages of ownership remain recreation and convenience. If you are gregarious and if you hate to mow the lawn and paint the house, chances are you'll love condominium life. In a well-run condo you are freed from much of what many consider the drudgery involved in owning a single-family house. And because you don't have to spend time on upkeep, you have the time to take advantage of the readily available recreational opportunities. On top of all this you can have the benefits of owning your own home—tax breaks and increased equity as the property appreciates. It is no wonder that condominiums are increasing in popularity all the time.

We'll go into just how affordable condominiums really are and some of the disadvantages of this type of ownership in just a moment, but first let's consider what a condominium really is.

What Exactly Is a Condominium?

The word "condominium" comes from Latin and combines two elements: "dominium" meaning "control," and "con" meaning "with" (other people). The concept can best be understood in terms of Figures 4-1 and 4-2.

In a traditional "single estate," or ownership of real property where an individual owns a single home on a lot, the ownership covers more than just the surface of the land. Imagine visible lines

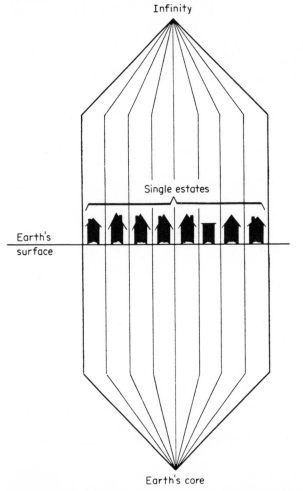

Figure 4–1. Traditional real estate, where ownership extends both above the property to infinity and below to the center of the earth's core. *(Based on a chart taken from "Questions About Condominiums," Department of Housing and Urban Development, U.S. Government Printing Office, 1974, 0–557–488.)*

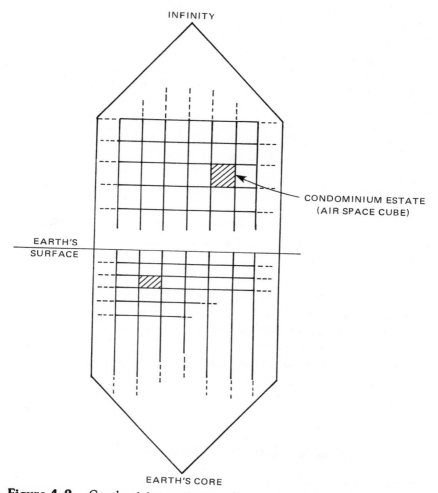

Figure 4–2. Condominium estates, where ownership is limited in the vertical as well as the traditional horizontal planes. *(Based on a chart from "Questions About Condominiums," Department of Housing and Urban Development, U.S. Government Printing Office, 1974, 0–557–488.)*

extending from the edges of the lot all the way down to the earth's core and in the other direction all the way out to infinity—this is the area owned in a single estate. Often owners who have retained mineral rights deep below the surface can sell these to a mining, oil, or gas company. Similarly, owners are protected from anyone building anything directly over their property (although not neces-

[65]

sarily from someone erecting a tall building next door that cuts out the sunshine).

To understand a "condominium estate," imagine horizontal lines now intersecting the vertical lines of Figure 4-1. These horizontal lines bisect the vertical planes and prevent them from continuing upward or downward. They form cubes of air space often called "space estates." In real life the horizontal and vertical lines will appear as the ceiling, floor, and walls of the condominium. Individual ownership applies only within the air-space cube. Ownership in common with the other dwellers of the building applies to the supporting structure, the land (down to the earth's core), and the air space above the building.

When you purchase a condominium, you in reality purchase two estates (or ownerships). You buy a single, undivided estate within your own air-space cube. If, however, that were all you bought, your ownership would hang suspended in space. So you also buy an undivided or common interest in the building and other property. This undivided interest extends right up to the boundaries of the land the condominium building rests on.

The kind of condominium ownership we've been discussing is essentially what most people think of—a large building several stories tall with many units, each individually owned. There is another kind of condominium ownership: the PUD.

Planned Unit Developments (PUDS)

A planned unit development (PUD) is closer in ownership to a house than a condominium. In a PUD, unlike a condominium, there are no air-space cubes. Like a single estate, the ownership runs down to the earth's core and up to infinity. However, the ownership is only for ground directly below and the space directly above the individual unit. Once you go out the front or back door and enter the hallway, it becomes shared ownership property. A diagram of a typical PUD is shown in Figure 4-3.

Of necessity, a PUD only has units spaced horizontally. There are no units vertically, one on top of the other, as this would mean that the owner's air-space rights would be violated. Typically PUDS have common side walls, walkways, etc. The property around the unit, including parking areas, common greens, recreational areas, and so

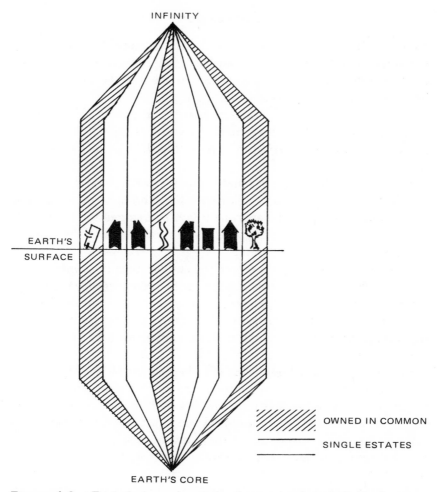

INFINITY

EARTH'S
SURFACE

OWNED IN COMMON

SINGLE ESTATES

EARTH'S CORE

Figure 4-3. Typical planned unit development, where individual ownership exists within individual unit extending both upward and downward, but
where community ownership exists for recreational facilities, walkways, open
areas, and everything outside the unit. *(Based on a chart from "Questions
About Condominiums," Department of Housing and Urban Development,
U.S. Government Printing Office, 1974, 0-557-488.)*

on is owned by a homeowners association. The owner must pay dues
to the association for the upkeep of the common area.

The biggest advantage of the PUD over the condominium is the
decreased density. Usually there is more common area and less
building, that is, fewer units per acre.

Conversion

And then there are the conversions. A conversion is usually a conventional apartment building that has been converted into a space estate condominium. The advantages as well as the problems can best be explained by taking an example.

Let's suppose you're living in an apartment (paying $300 a month rent) and one day the owner comes to you and says, "I've sold my apartment building to Mrs. Jones, here. She'll be collecting the rent from now on."

Mrs. Jones shakes your hand, smiles sweetly, and says, "I've decided to convert my new apartment building to a condominium. I'm willing to sell you the apartment you're living in for $35,000. If you don't want to buy it, you'll have to move. You have three months to make up your mind."

Once you get over the shock of the sudden turn of events (which are happening in much this manner with increasing frequency all across the country), you realize you have an important decision to make, a decision that is of great importance to others who are also thinking of purchasing a condominium conversion. As a tenant you have a great advantage over outside buyers. Since you're living in the building, you already know what it's like before you buy. You know how convenient (or inconvenient) it is to get to the washroom in the basement and you know whether or not there's good heating in the winter and good air conditioning in the summer. And nobody can tell you any fancy stories about there always being hot water when you know if you don't take a shower by 7 A.M. it's going to be lukewarm.

All of which raises an obvious but most important point to consider when buying a condominium conversion. It's like buying an old apartment.

Of course, new owners usually promise new amenities. They'll put in a new swimming pool and recreational hall. And they'll station a guard at the entranceway and make sure the door is always locked so it will be a "secure" building. And they'll completely repaint each unit and all the hallways and the main entrance room downstairs. And they'll fix that old elevator that's never worked right.

A conversion can be an excellent development for all concerned, if it's done properly—if all the needed repairs and deferred maintenance on the old building are taken care of and if the building is modernized. On the other hand, if only cosmetic changes are made, as is the case in some conversions, the new buyer simply gets an old headache. It's been my experience that where more than mere cosmetic changes are made and where all the facts are explained, I've seen more than half of former tenants buy. In some cases that figure has gone as high as 90 percent. Usually tenants (and others) find conversions to be a good deal.

These are the different types of condominium you are likely to run into. There is one additional kind of group ownership that is frequently confused with the condominium—the cooperative.

Cooperatives

Prior to 1970 most group-owned projects were cooperatives, particularly in New York State and other areas of the East Coast. A good portion of these cooperatives came into existence as the result of a quirk in the income tax laws. Investors through the 1960s built moderate-income rental housing and operated such buildings at a loss, at least on paper. They were simply tax shelters. Through tax breaks these projects made a profit for their owners. However, when it came time to dispose of the property, because of the way in which the tax laws are written, a substantial penalty could have been levied on the investors in a straightforward sale. One way to reduce this penalty was to sell the project to the tenants as a cooperative.

Of course, not all cooperatives started this way. Some were existing apartment buildings where the tenants on their own initiated a drive to purchase the property. And in other cases new properties were built and sold as cooperatives.

There is little physical difference between a cooperative and a condominium. Both are usually large buildings with individual units that are owned rather than rented. It's the ownership that's different.

In a cooperative, rather than having title to the space estate we saw for a condominium, the owner usually has stock in a corporation. The corporation owns the entire building, and ownership of stock in the corporation allows the owner to occupy and pay the costs of an individual unit. Taxes are assessed on the entire building, and then the corporation levies the appropriate tax amount on individual owners. The same holds true for other costs. Owning a cooperative unit is in many ways similar to tenancy in an apartment building.

Until about 1970 most new group housing was of the cooperative type. Since then condominium laws have been adopted by most states and nearly all subsequent development has been of the condominium type. (As of this writing there is no federal, nation-wide law defining condominium ownership, although there is some federal protection against fraud in the purchase of a condominium.) The reason for the switch is probably the advantage in ownership that a condominium offers. A condo owner, like a house owner, can sell the unit with or without the approval of the other homeowners (although some condominium bylaws provide that the homeowners association has the right of first refusal to purchase any unit offered for sale).

In a cooperative the "owner" is in effect a tenant of the corporation, albeit a stock-owning tenant. When it comes time to sell, the corporation has a certain voice in who will occupy the unit. In addition, in some cooperatives the stock may only be sold back to the corporation. These limitations may prevent an owner from receiving the full appreciation in equity that may have occurred to the unit during the term of ownership.

This kind of "overcontrol" of the cooperative by the corporation sometimes has its good points. In a condominium it is almost impossible to remove an obnoxious neighbor/owner. In a coop the corporation can often handle such a problem with great dispatch.

Townhouses

One should be careful of the term "townhouse." This is a most misused word. It can be and frequently is used to describe an individual housing unit, a condominium, a PUD, and on some occasions, even a cooperative. The word townhouse usually just means a house which has a common wall with another house.

Is a Condominium Really Cheaper than a Single-Family House?

It is a fact of construction that it does not cost less to build a condominium than a house. Although there is some savings acquired through the use of common walls (two separate units share a single wall between them), this often tends to be lost due to the additional costs for a pool, recreation room, or elevator.

The common denominator is the "per square foot" cost, and it is not appreciably cheaper to build a condominium, per square foot, than a house. If the rate in your area happens to be $30 a square foot for a house, it's probably very close to that for a condominium.

How then, can suburban and recreational condominium units be priced anywhere from 20 to 40 percent less than single-family homes in the same area? There are two reasons. The first is that the condo units tend to be smaller than comparable homes. While it is possible to find a three-bedroom condominium with 3,000 or more square feet, most of these are the high-rise, costly variety. Typically, a recreational or suburban condo may have closer to 1,100 square feet and two bedrooms. A home in the same area may have 1,700 square feet and three bedrooms. Most condominiums are less expensive simply because they are smaller.

The second reason the condominium is cheaper is because less land is used in building it. It is frequently possible to put four condominium units on land that would only hold two single-family homes. As additional floors are added, this savings on land increases dramatically. One development with which I am familiar has 104 units on land that would only accommodate ten or fewer houses! This savings in the amount of land used is offset somewhat, but not entirely, by the additional cost of land zoned for condominiums. By per square of building to lot, condominium land tends to sell for less than single-family housing land.

A condominium may be cheaper than a house, but not nearly as much cheaper as many developers would like buyers to believe. Nonetheless, this lower absolute cost can be important.

It's very difficult to find a new house built with all the modern conveniences that has just 900 square feet. On the other hand, a condominium of this size is not unusual at all. If all you need is a small unit (perhaps your children have grown and moved away, or perhaps you don't have any), a condo can be the answer. It's the same reasoning that goes, why should you buy a station wagon when you only need a compact? Why spend twice as much on a big house when you'd only end up wasting half the living area?

Condominium Disadvantages

As with all alternatives, there are tradeoffs. While you get maintenance-free living, a recreation-oriented lifestyle, and lower absolute cost, you have to give up other things. Here are a few of the problems.

Control When you purchase a condominium you are actually buying a hybrid, a cross between a house and an apartment. While developers are quick to point out that you will have the benefits of house and apartment, the best of both worlds so to speak, you may also end up with the drawbacks of both.

If you buy a condominium, don't expect to be master of all you survey. As a homeowner you are in charge of all your property— front, side, and back yards, and the house—but as owner of a condominium you control only the inside of your unit. Once past the front door you are just one of many owners, a member of a team. And as is the case in team sports, in a condominium there will be times when you will have to forego your personal preference for the good of the whole project.

When you buy a condominium, in addition to getting a new mortgage and the keys to your unit, you will join a homeowners association (HOA). Membership in this organization is not optional—it is required as part of your ownership. Failure to join and, more important, failure to pay monthly membership dues can sometimes result in the loss of your unit.

The HOA has enormous responsibilities for the condominium project as a whole. It is responsible for the maintenance and repair of all areas outside of the individual units. That includes external walls, hallways, plumbing (except within the unit), most electrical and sewer equipment, swimming pool pumps and filters, landscaping, external painting, etc. The list is long . . . and costly.

In order to maintain the condominium building and make repairs, the HOA must raise money and it can do this in only one way: by assessing its members. Depending on the bylaws, the individual owners will be required to pay a monthly fee to cover all HOA costs. This fee is usually flexible, that is, it can go up.

Underestimated Homeowners Dues One of the biggest problems in buying a new condominium is that the HOA fee may be underestimated by the builder-developer. Frequently when the condominium is brand new, repairs and maintenance are at a minimum. Sometimes builder-developers will base HOA dues on these initially low costs and the dues, consequently, will be low.

But as the building gets older, costs of maintaining and repairing the facilities increase sharply. If no funds have been set aside to take care of these costs, they will come upon the HOA as a crisis. In order to pay for the repair work the HOA may have to borrow money and sharply increase dues to cover loan payments. In an improperly run HOA with unrealistically low initial dues, there will eventually be a series of crises. Monthly dues will fluctuate widely as things break down and, without adequate reserves to fix them, heavy assessments are made on the owners to fund repairs.

Why would some builder-developers initially underestimate dues? The reason is that a builder-developer may want low dues to induce people to buy remaining unsold units. After the units are all sold, however, the real costs of operation may become painfully apparent.

Reserves for future maintenance and repairs need to be set aside today to meet tomorrow's costs. Any delay in establishing these funds means less time to accumulate the money before the need arises. I have seen dues rise 100 to 200 percent in badly run HOAs. These dues can be as much as 30 percent or more of the mortgage and tax cost of each unit.

To keep costs at a minimum and to see that things are run properly (and to have some voice in, for example, what color paint will be used on the outside of the building), you as a condominium owner will eventually want or feel forced to run for office in the HOA organization. This requires time and effort and there is usually no financial compensation. The board which runs the HOA will usually meet once a month, but individual committees such as finance, recreation, or maintenance may wind up meeting weekly or more often as problems arise. As a director of the HOA, you have to answer to the other owners—their complaints, needs, and wants.

It can be a time-consuming and thankless job. In projects I have seen, the burn-out rate for the best managers is just a year or so.

In well-planned condo projects builder-developers set the dues high enough initially to meet both current and future needs. In addition, they stick around long enough to train the owners to run things efficiently and then leave. In less ideal setups, maintenance costs are seriously underestimated and builder-developers provide little guidance. They may suddenly disappear, dropping the operation in the lap of the unprepared HOA and creating a financial nightmare. Occasionally the builder-developer does not leave at all, but instead seeks to retain control for the life of the condominium and this can be the worst problem of all.

Long-term Leases   Another problem related to builder-developers has to do with long-term leases. Although this problem has been largely controlled in many states by laws enacted to prevent abuse, it still does occur and is worth mentioning just in case the reader should run into it.

In some condominium projects the HOA would not gain title to the recreational facilities, such as the swimming pool, tennis courts, and saunas. Instead title would remain with the builder-developer, who would then lease these facilities to the homeowners. The developer would often point out advantages to the purchasers of this arrangement. For example, the owners might not know how to properly maintain such facilities while the builder-developer, presumably, is a pro in business and can handle it easily. In many cases this is a valid argument.

The abuse of the long-term lease, however, comes from its payment schedule. In many cases such leases were written with high payments and escalator clauses tied to a national cost-of-living index. As the cost of living increased, so did the monthly payments on the lease. In the last few years the cost of living has skyrocketed, and payments on some of these leases have gone up similarly. In one condominium project in Florida the developer reportedly made $200,000 profit on the recreational lease over the first 2½ years of its existence!

When the owners objected, they found that the homeowners

association was tied to the long-term lease. It couldn't be broken. If they refused to make their monthly dues payments to the association for the lease payment, their property could be tied up to enforce payment.

The best solution to the problems created by a bad builder-developer is not to buy into such a condominium, since changing the contract can be extremely hard once it is set. The way to do this is to carefully check the documents involved *before* a purchase is made. Unfortunately, these documents can be very complex.

Complex Documents The documents used to create a condominium are often beyond the grasp of the individual buyer or even many attorneys unfamiliar with condominium law. This contrasts with the fairly standard documents used in nearly all other types of residential real estate purchases.

This problem occurs not only at the time of purchase. It can have lasting effects if the documents are written in such a manner as to bind the owner to conditions that later prove to be undesirable.

The problem is complicated by the fact, as we've noted, that condominium estates are created by the laws of each state and no standard form is used nationwide. This unfortunately means that there is no established norm which prospective buyers can use to compare their documents.

The situation is not hopeless, however. One aid to the consumer comes from the Department of Housing and Urban Development through the Federal Housing Administration (HUD-FHA). If a condominium is built using financing insured by HUD-FHA, the government under the National Housing Act attempts to oversee that the builder conforms to minimum building specifications, which are often set quite high. Further, when a consumer purchases a condominium and government-insured FHA financing is used (under Section 234, Condominium Program), the sales agreements, homeowners association bylaws, and other documents are standardized. In short, if you buy a *new* condominium and the builder is able to offer you a FHA-insured loan, many of the items you need to watch out for have already been checked out by the federal government. To a lesser degree this is true with VA loans also.

Unfortunately a great many condos are not built using government-insured financing. Then it is up to the purchaser to investigate the role of the HOA and other potential problems from the documents. I suggest that any buyer, before making a purchase, take the documents to an attorney who specializes in or at least is familiar with condominium work for an opinion. The documents include the enabling declaration and the bylaws of the homeowners association.

Enabling Declaration

One of the most important documents in a condominium sale and the one that probably causes the most problems is the "enabling declaration." It is also sometimes referred to as the master deed; the declaration of conditions, covenants, and restrictions; or the plan of condominium ownershp These are some of the areas in the enabling declaration to watch out for:

Legal Descriptions There must be a section which describes the units and the common elements of the condominiums. It is important that all such descriptions be accurate. If title insurance is purchased, normally the title company will insist on the accuracy of this part of the document. The lender will also be watching out for its accuracy. Of more immediate concern to the purchaser are the provisions which specify how the common property, such as streets, parking lots, and recreational facilities, are held. They are usually owned by a nonprofit homeowners association or are leased to the condominium owners by the original developer. If they are leased, the buyer should be very careful to be sure the conditions of the lease are not unreasonable.

Percentage Interest Another section of the declaration will usually specify an owner's percentage interest in the undivided portion of the project. It is often expressed in terms of a ratio of a unit to the total number of units. This ratio is of great importance for it will determine among other things the voting power the owner has in the homeowners association, the amount the owner will have to pay for maintenance operation assessments, the amount of real estate tax to be assessed against that owner, and the amount of money a lender will lend.

There are at least four different ways the ratio can be determined: by market price, by builder's value, by the amount of living area, and by equal shares (each owner has equal interest regardless of the size or value of the unit).

Since the ratios are often initially determined by state law, there is usually little an individual buyer can do to change them. However, the buyer should watch out for clauses which allow the ratio to be changed once the condominium is established. This could affect your responsibilities and payments.

Changes Any changes to the declaration normally require the consent of 100 percent of the owners. This is an important clause and any deviation from the 100 percent figure should make the buyer take special notice. What this means is that no changes can be made unless the buyer of each unit agrees. This is tremendous protection for each unit owner. Unfortunately, it also severely limits the ability of a homeowners association to respond to unexpected problems.

A related problem has to do with delegating the policymaking powers of the association's board of directors. Sometimes duties are delegated in the declaration to a professional management company at a high and escalating fee. Since it takes 100 percent of the owners to change the declaration, the developer or the management company could buy just one unit and prevent the board from changing its policy. One way to avoid this is to give no authority to the board in the enabling declaration other than to hire a manager who will be under its control. Authority for all other operations can be in the bylaws, which can be changed by a majority of owners.

Bylaws of the Homeowners Association

The bylaws establish rules for any future owners, tenants, or employees. They also establish many conditions which determine how pleasant living in the condominium will be. A prospective purchaser should check them out carefully with an attorney. Here are some of the things to watch out for:

Enactment of the Bylaws Bylaws are a secondary agreement and require assent by all the unit owners. To avoid problems, sometimes it's a good idea for the bylaws to provide that merely occupying or renting any unit indicates that the owner ratifies and accepts the bylaws and agrees to comply with them.

[77]

Administration of the Condominium The bylaws usually provide that someone, often the developer, will administer the condominium until the first annual meeting of the owners. They also usually specify that at that meeting the administration will be turned over to an association board of directors elected by the owners.

Voting Rights The bylaws usually specify what constitutes a quorum for doing business at a meeting, the method of voting, the use of proxies, and the manner in which board members can be removed for objectional action. They also specify which bylaws can be amended and how (usually only a majority vote is needed).

Qualifications and Responsibilities of the Members of the Board of Directors These should be spelled out in the bylaws.

Items Relating to Individual Owners and Their Rights and Responsibilities As Co-Owners The bylaws also usually specify the collection of monthly charges and special assessments, including the method of enforcing payment from those who refuse (including the developer); the use of the common areas; the establishment of a budget and reserve funds; provision for professional management where needed; the right of entry to the project and rules governing conduct by owners, visitors, and tenants; the rules for the use of recreational facilities; provision for fire insurance for the common area; provision for liability insurance; restrictions on changes in the exterior of the individual units; and restrictions governing the use of the property for residential purposes provided by local and state zoning ordinances.

Selling or Renting

When purchasing a condominium, most people anticipate that the value will go up. In recent years in most areas this has certainly been the case (although in places where major industry has died or other local adverse conditions have occurred, prices have reversed). Condominiums in general have done about as well as other real estate. My own personal observation has been that while high-rise and recreational condominiums have appreciated right along with single-family homes, suburban condos have not risen in value as quickly as nearby single-family homes. I suspect the reason is that most people do not yet consider them to be equivalent to houses.

The important thing to remember about the appreciation of value in a condominium is that the *entire* project must appreciate in order for your individual unit to go up in price. While it is possible for a unit's owner to improve the inside—upgrading the carpeting, hanging decorative wallpaper, repainting, and the like—all units are maintained by the homeowners association on the outside, including painting, mowing of lawns, and landscaping. Usually there is nothing individual owners can do to make the outside of their unit outstanding; in fact, most bylaws prohibit unit owners from making their units externally distinguishable in any way from other units. Consequently, with minor differences caused by interior upgrading, any one condominium unit will be worth no more than any similar unit in the project. For any unit to appreciate in value, they all must. In a large condominium with, for example, 200 similar units, it is easy to see that before prices can rise, the demand must be very large to compensate for the large supply. Individual condominium units suffer from the same handicap that often keeps homes in a tract with identical houses from rising dramatically in price—lack of uniqueness.

When buying a condominium, therefore, as with most real estate purchases, it is crucial that you consider the resale potential. Very often those very factors that led you to buy will be the same ones that will lead someone else to buy. Proximity to the seashore, for example, can outweigh a lot of other disadvantages like high price or small units. On the other hand, if the reason you're buying is because the present owner is forced to sell at a low price because perhaps the condo is poorly located, or the units are small, or it is run-down, when the time comes to sell you also may have to take a low price for the same reason. A good rule of thumb is to buy quality—quality location first, then quality in size and construction.

Problems can also occur when renting a unit out. As we've already mentioned, the bylaws may prohibit an owner from renting out for a period of less than a month. The bylaws may also prohibit advertising a unit for rent by placing signs on the property. It can be extremely difficult directing prospective tenants to your unit if you can't post a "for rent" sign. This problem is alleviated in many recreational condominiums where the HOA operates a rental office for the benefit of the owners.

Density

Density has been called the single biggest problem for condominiums, but density is a two-edged sword. Before we consider the disadvantages, let's recall the advantages. As we've already pointed out, many units close together can provide companionship and recreational opportunities. Children can have friends to play with, adults can easily meet and associate with other adults. Bridge, poker, and bingo groups frequently form. Weekend parties are common. On the other hand, density can mean trouble.

Density doesn't necessarily mean how physically close together units are, but rather how many units are placed on an acre of ground. The number of units per acre varies enormously from one project to another. If the project is several stories tall, it is possible to have many units per acre and still have a lot of open space. In one- or two-level condominiums there might be very little area left for grass and open space. Many studies have been made to determine the optimum units per acre. The results show that much depends on the type of condominiums. For the suburban kind, in general the fewer units per acre, the more satisfied and happy the owners. The optimum level is about *six to eight* units per acre. An acre is 43,560 square feet. Assuming each unit is about 1,500 square feet, horizontally, six units would be 9,000 square feet, leaving over 30,000 square feet for recreational facilities, parking, pathways, and lawns.

The big advantage of having so few units per acre is increased privacy. One unit's windows do not face the windows or doors of another unit, a big complaint among cramped owners. Children have play areas away from the living areas so they can play without disturbing the adults. Cars can be parked far enough away from the units to reduce noise and smells.

There are exceptions to the density rule. If the neighborhood surrounding the condominium is a park, there is less objection to high-density living. If the surrounding neighborhood is composed of other condos or of apartments, even low density can be objectionable.

With recreational and high-rise condominiums, increased density is often offset by the desirability of the location. As many as thirty units or more per acre can be located without objection near such facilities. In such cases, some owners may use their units as second or vacation homes and leave them unoccupied much of the time.

Developers are well aware of the density problem. They have two ways of handling it. One is to build fewer units per acre, arrange them in small clusters rather than large buildings, and provide pleasant views and a lot of recreational facilities. This, however, usually results in very high-priced units and restricts the number that the builder can sell. The alternative is to disguise a high-density project and try to trick buyers into thinking it really is a low-density one. Many techniques are used here. One of the most common is staggering the buildings. The average person can easily judge the size of a building if it has straight walls, but if the walls are staggered and walkways meander and trees are placed at unusual spots, it can be very difficult. Another technique is to have a large grassy open area in front of the project. The average person is then less likely to notice tiny, cramped garden areas inside. This illusion is simply a matter of first impression. If the first impression is of roominess, subsequent cramped impressions will be less strong than they otherwise would be.

In a disguised high-density condo the parking may butt right up against the back of the building or perhaps be underneath it. If no windows face the parking, from the inside the impression may be that cars are not around. When a car starts, however, noise and smells often enter the units.

An open patio is also a common feature of a disguised high-density condo. Closing in a patio for each unit not only takes up a considerable amount of space, but requires a lot of additional open space to keep that closed-in patio from looking cramped. A developer therefore will often build a patio without walls. This appears to give the individual unit some private territory, but really just adds additional space to the common area, making the project appear roomier than it is.

The big advantage of the disguised high-density condo is that because the builder can put more units on an acre, they can be sold for less.

Lifestyle

Thus far we've considered condominium lifestyle only as a plus. It can, however, be a disadvantage if you get a condominium with the *wrong* lifestyle.

A childless young couple might reasonably hope to have other units in the project similarly occupied by younger people. A retired person, on the other hand, might buy expecting few children in the project. Both these expectations can be dashed, however, if proper care is not taken before purchase to see what sort of lifestyle the project as a whole will offer.

In existing condominiums, the solution to this problem is simple: just walk around and see who lives there. In a new development, the answer is not so simple. Perhaps less than half the units have been sold at the time you buy. How will you know who will occupy the remainder? You could try asking the developer, who is also the seller. Most developers are honest and will reply that their project was built for young marrieds or for people with children or for elderly couples. They will honestly try to dissuade someone from buying if that person would not enjoy the lifestyle. However, with the recession in the mid-1970s and with overbuilding in many areas, some builders were faced with the choice of selling to anyone or going into foreclosure. It's not difficult to imagine which choice they made. There are also some unscrupulous developers who would lie to make a sale regardless of economic conditions.

My suggestion is that if you are interested in a condominium and the lifestyle is a major concern, you should wait until it is 75 to 80 percent sold before buying your unit. If you're afraid you might miss out, you can ask to put a deposit down to hold the place for a month or more while you decide, but make sure it will be returned if you don't buy. During this time you can observe who's moving in and decide whether they will coincide with your desired lifestyle.

For a full or nearly full condominium, I next suggest you try an experiment—rent a unit first.

Experimenting with Condominium Life

If you're considering making a purchase, why not rent a unit in the building for a month first? Almost any larger condo will have a few units for rent. You'll have the opportunity to meet the other people who live there. You'll be able to determine whether the units and the open areas are big enough for you or are too cramped. Chances are you'll find out any problems with renting or selling that the owners are having. You'll also learn a lot about how the HOA is operating (if it's operating) and you'll learn firsthand, from other owners, if the builder-developer has become a real problem.

In addition, you'll have the opportunity to try out the recreational facilities. You'll use the swimming pool and the sauna. You'll see if you enjoy meeting with other owners in the recreation hall. And you'll find out whether the elevator works and if there's hot water after 7 A.M. in the morning. This trial period is not meant to take the place of having a competent attorney check over the documents for you.

You might love it. And you might not. In either event, you'll only be out one month's rent.

Is It for You?

Do the advantages outweigh the disadvantages? Do lower initial cost (in comparison to nearby single-family houses), low maintenance, and the recreation-oriented lifestyle offset perhaps small quarters, potentially high homeowners association dues, loss of control, and the need to take a hand in the direction of the project? What about problems with renting and resale? What about the opportunity a condominium offers to own a good home near the beach or right downtown?

Many people have pronounced the condominium to be the housing of the future. "We'll all be living in condos one day," is a phrase I've often heard. Perhaps. And again, perhaps not. There are other alternatives.

[83]

FIVE

Tomorrow's Answer Today—
Mobile, Modular, Manufactured Houses

Suppose you decide to purchase a new Ford and you've been given a delivery date. On the appointed day a large truck pulls up to where you live and drops a new transmission on your driveway. While you stand there looking in amazement at the transmission, another truck pulls up and tips two front fenders onto your lawn. As you stand there scratching your head the second truck driver shouts that they're temporarily out of stock in rear fenders, but he'll have them to you within three weeks.

Later that day the parts for your car's engine arrive. The next day the suspension system and a completely dismantled rear end. On and on go the deliveries until the end of the week. Then the parts simply sit in a large mound on your driveway and lawn over the weekend.

The following Monday a crew arrives and begins assembling your car, piece by piece. When you ask how long it will take, they estimate six weeks, depending of course on the weather and availability of parts.

Would you call Ford and complain?

You bet you would. You bought a car and you expect a complete car delivered to you. But if instead of a car you bought a house and the same thing happened (the parts being housing materials delivered to a lot), would you complain? Not if you're like everybody else. You'd accept it as the conventional way of building and not think twice about it.

Why is it that the advances in construction that Henry Ford

[84]

introduced more than half a century ago are so taken for granted when it comes to cars and so alien when it comes to houses? If you can build a car on an assembly line in a few hours, why not a house?

There is no reason why not. Houses can be and are built on assembly lines—it takes about two to three days to construct one over 1,800 square feet in size, from nothing to finished product.

And the savings that can be realized by assembly line production of cars can also be applied to housing. Across the country from New York to California it is possible to buy a manufactured home delivered from a dealer at about $14 to $20 a square foot. Of course, you must also pay for installing the unit on a lot, anywhere from $1,500 to $5,000 ($1 to $3 a square foot for an 1,800-square-foot unit). This compares with prices of $30 a square foot for traditionally built homes.

Manufactured housing, known as MFG (the term includes a whole group of subheadings but in this chapter we'll just concentrate on mobile homes and modular houses), is roughly at the same stage today that Henry Ford was just a few years after he introduced his assembly line automobiles. He was still in competition with the original hand-built car builders, but his lower-priced products were in great demand and he was turning them out as fast as he could.

There is an important difference, however, between the development of the automobile and that of the manufactured home—public acceptance. Modern manufactured housing has been in existence for over half a century and yet today there is still only one such house constructed for about every three traditional housing units. The public has failed to accept the manufactured home concept. But if they're cheaper to make and presumably just as good, one would expect they would have taken over the entire market. After all, how much of the market do handmade cars represent today?

The public has failed to fully accept the manufactured home concept.

Why?

The answer has a lot to do with attitudes. Manufactured homes originally went by another name, a name that today brings shudders and dread to their sales representatives: "trailers." At one time, and still today for many people, the word trailer conjured up images of ghastly wooden and tin contraptions hauled around by battered automobiles mostly during the 1930s and 1940s. These early trailers did not have bathrooms and only the most primitive kitchens. They were often used by transients whom the general public considered to be a subculture. In fact a term was even devised to describe them, "gypsy wagons."

Although the gypsy wagons of the past were in fact the ancestors of today's manufactured homes, they are as far removed from them as civilized man is from the cave dwellers. To understand today's product, it is necessary to get a historical perspective on manufactured homes.

Most people believe that the first house trailers were introduced shortly after the turn of the century about the same time the automobile came into vogue. They were not. They were actually introduced in America in the late 1700s by travelers moving from the East Coast to what was then the frontier, which we now call the Midwest. They received their biggest impetus during the 1800s when tens of thousands pulled up stakes and moved to the gold fields of California and its neighboring states. These immigrants used giant Conestoga wagons which were really nothing more than houses on wooden and metal wheels pulled by mules, horses, or oxen.

It was only natural that when the automobile finally replaced the horse and other animals as the primary source of family locomotion, the Conestoga gave way to the house trailer, which in its earliest stages was nothing more than a wagon to which had been affixed a metal axle and rubber tires. It is no coincidence that when Arthur G. Sherman established the first large-scale production of trailer coaches in 1929, he called his operation the Covered Wagon Company.

But while the public accepted the Conestoga wagon, its acceptance of the house trailer was limited. Through the thirties both General Motors and Ford did not enter the field largely because they felt the market potential was too small. Even as late as 1940 with dozens of companies manufacturing them, there were only about 10,000 trailers introduced. They were used primarily by families on vacation, by workers located in remote areas, and by vagabonds— hence the term gypsy wagon.

It is indeed ironic that what may very well turn out to be an excellent answer to America's housing needs might have been overlooked entirely because of bad publicity had it not been for World War II. Faced with an acute housing shortage near defense plants (which were occasionally located in out-of-the-way places), the government bought large numbers of manufactured homes. This captive market kept manufacturers in business and even allowed them to expand. Unfortunately the products they turned out were not much different from the earlier versions.

It wasn't until after World War II that the public began to see manufactured housing in a new light. Traveling across the country as a form of leisure activity came into vogue and giant new trailers which boasted if not the size then at least the convenience of regular homes came into existence. In the early fifties the most popular television show was "I Love Lucy" and the stars decided to cash in on their success by making a popular movie. It was called *The Long Long Trailer* and featured them traveling in a car hauling a brand new house trailer.

By 1955 there were over 200 manufacturers of house trailers, although still only about 125,000 units a year were being built. Then in the 1960s the industry underwent a metamorphosis. Manufacturers discovered that increasingly purchasers were no longer hauling their house trailers from place to place, but rather were living in them as permanent residences. This was particularly the case with the elderly and the poor. The manufacturers, sniffing a new market, began promoting a new breed of trailer, one that shunned the word *trailer* itself and its connotation of being hauled behind something. They substituted the term "mobile home," meaning a house that could be transported from the place of manufacture to a semipermanent site. The new mobile homes were 10 to 14 feet wide and often 40 or more feet long. A special truck was used to move them.

Within a decade industry giants were producing double-wide homes (two units placed side by side) 60 feet long and even triple-wide units. And these units were no longer placed in "trailer courts" but instead were located in "Mobile Home Parks." While the distinction between these two terms may at first seem superficial, it is not. The older trailer courts typically gave the impression of impermanence. A kind of rustic atmosphere might be given by trees and shrubs while asphalt or cement lanes might wander between closely placed "pads" or parking areas onto which a wide assortment of trailers were in essence "camped." Frequently these early trailer courts, while providing sewer and utility connections by means of hoses and pipes, offered public toilets and showers as their only other amenity. And because the court's revenue came from renting out space, the pads were frequently jammed close together to increase the park owner's profit. The closest thing one sees today to those early trailer courts is a campground near a recreational area in the height of the season.

A modern mobile home park is something totally different. A very suburban atmosphere permeates the area. Roads and sidewalks are of similar quality to those in traditional neighborhoods. There is strict architectural control of the mobile home units, which must usually be designed to look like traditional homes. In addition, the units are not simply "parked" on pads. Rather their wheels have been removed and they are semipermanently attached to either peripheral or pier foundations. Their sewer and utility connections are not visible and usually conform to local building codes. And finally, around each unit the owner must normally build and maintain walls, gardens, and a separate driveway and carport for an automobile. For all practical purposes, when you drive into a mobile home park today you might very well be driving into a traditional suburban neighborhood. Only the similarity of construction and the relative smallness of the lots reveal the true identity.

Amenities in modern parks frequently include a swimming pool, whirlpool baths, a recreational room often with attached billiard and music rooms and kitchen, a sauna, tennis courts, a putting green, and other items normally associated with high-level leisure living. If you're unfamiliar with a modern mobile home park, drive through one—you'll be astounded.

Then Came "Modular" Homes

Mobile homes are not real estate. They were always considered vehicular in nature. But in the 1950s enterprising manufacturers asked why the assembly line techniques used to produce trailers couldn't also be used to produce houses. They began building what is essentially a mobile home without the steel trailer understructure. These new modular homes were delivered to their building sites b means of large trailers or dollies. The interior walls might be made of drywall (plaster) while the mobile homes had almost exclusively wood paneling. The modular homes also had steeper roofs than their mobile cousins did, more like traditional homes.

The development of the modular home industry remained small through the 1960s. An important reason was that in order to gain approval for use on a building site, a modular home had to conform to the building code of the particular area in which it was installed. This meant that manufacturers were limited, regionally, in the development of their product. Also public acceptance was not quickly forthcoming, a problem similar to the one we've seen with mobile homes.

In 1970 when George Romney was Secretary of the Department of Housing and Urban Development an energetic attempt was made to greatly expand the use of the modular home. It was seen by many government officials as a solution to the housing problem: It offered plentiful, cheap housing for everyone.

The program was called Operation Breakthrough and many of the country's largest home builders began constructing modular homes. The result was a business disaster. The public did not throng to the modular homes and many companies were forced out of business. Operation Breakthrough went broke.

The reasons for the failure of the program were many, but those involved frequently pointed to the inability of the manufacturers to develop a good dealer-distribution network and the fact that large companies could not easily adjust to the seasonal nature of home building (great demand for several months, then months of slack before the demand picks up again). Perhaps it was simply that at the beginning of the 1970s people were not yet really considering alternatives to the traditional home.

This is not to say that the modular home industry is dead. Far from it. Thousands of modular units are produced each year across the United States by dozens of companies. These include homes that are one, two, and in some cases three stories high and sell for prices in a few instances in excess of $200,000! The diversity of homes available from the modular manufacturing industry truly staggers the mind as shown in Figures 5-1, 5-2, and 5-3. (see the appendix for a list of

Figure 5–1 Modular home. *(Courtesy of Fuqua Homes, Inc., Arlington, Texas.)*

Figure 5–2. Modular home. *(Courtesy of Nationwide Homes, Martinsville, Virginia.)*

manufacturers). Nonetheless, the modular home industry has never achieved the growth and production rate of the mobile home industry.

The Building Code Challenge

Mobile home builders did not ignore the idea aborted in the modular Operation Breakthrough. They reasoned that if properly presented, a manufactured home would be accepted by a growing number of home buyers and therein lay the potential for a big new market. There was the problem of names: Mobile had come to mean highly movable; modular meant permanently placed on a site. To now call mobile homes "modular" would be to take on any onus associated with the failure of Operation Breakthough. The solution used was to ignore the terminology problem. After 1970 mobile home builders in ever-increasing numbers began to build what under the old definition could only be considered modular homes, but they hardly

Figure 5–3. Modular home. *(Courtesy of Continental Homes, Roanoke, Virginia.)*

[91]

ever refer to them as such. Today, for mobile home builders, the words "mobile" and "modular" have come to mean roughly the same thing. (Of course, the exclusively modular home manufacturers still insist there is a difference.)

Modular, however (as opposed to mobile), means real estate to lenders. If mobile homes could be classified as real estate, they would be eligible for those long-term thirty-year loans commonly found on traditional homes. We were saying earlier that mobile homes had always been considered vehicular in nature, that is, they require that a license fee be paid to the state. To a lender it makes little difference whether the product is a car, recreational vehicle, or house, as long as it's licensed as a vehicle by the state it only qualifies for one type of loan—a "chattel" or personal loan.

But these chattel loans tend to be for relatively short terms and high interest rates. Even today a chattel loan on a mobile home is rarely given for as long as fifteen years and then requires the borrower to pay 2 to 3 percent interest per year more than on a real estate loan. If the borrower-buyer of a manufactured house could get a property loan, then he or she would be looking at a lower interest rate, thirty years to pay back, and what it all comes down to, drastically reduced monthly payments. Lower payments would greatly increase the number of buyers, making expansion of the industry profitable and therefore possible.

But the biggest initial obstacle to getting mobile homes classified as real estate had to do with building codes. To fully understand the importance of building codes to the public, consider what is probably the world's first such code—the Code of Hammurabi written about 4,000 years ago in Babylon. It included the condition that if a builder built a home and it fell in and killed the occupant, then the builder would be slain as punishment. If a child of the occupant were killed, a child of the builder would be put to death. If goods of the occupant were destroyed, then the builder would replace all that was lost and in addition restore the house without cost. And so on.

The building Code of Hammurabi tried to ensure a minimum standard of safe construction by placing heavy penalties on poor work. Similarly, in all parts of the United States there are building codes administered by city, county, or township officials to protect home buyers from shoddy construction. Codes today emphasize good workmanship rather than specify punishment (although the consumer revolution is exacting heavier penalties for bad work). Modern building codes indicate exactly how construction is to be done and what maximum loads materials, joints, trusses, and so on can stand. They also specify how electrical, plumbing, heating, and other work is to be performed. But the one thing that the Code of Hammurabi had over modern codes was its uniformity. There was only one Code of Hammurabi for all Babylon. There are a great many building codes for the United States.

These codes include: the Uniform Building Code (UBC) used by many local governments as a model building code; the Building Officials and Code Administrators International, Inc., code (BOCA) used largely in the central and northeastern states; the Southern Building Code Congress International code (SBCC) used in the southeastern states; the International Conference of Building Officials (ICBO) used in the eleven western states; and the Minimum Property Standards (MPS) of the FHA used to qualify for government insured loans!

Before getting mobile homes classified as real estate, their manufacturers would have to satisfy many different codes. This would mean many different models and some of the savings of assembly line production would be lost. It's as if General Motors had to build a different car for each state, or at least each geographical area of the country. Some cities have their own codes independent of their state, compounding the problem even more.

To make matters even worse, mobile homes come out of a vehicular background, not a housing background. Until recently, the industry had almost no building code standards. It was only a little over ten years ago that the first industry-wide standard called ANSI A119.1 of the American National Standards Institute was established. Prior to that, construction quality of mobile homes was left to the conscience of each manufacturer. But ANSI A119.1 was lacking for it was not mandatory in all areas and enforcement in many cases was nonexistent. It was not until 1974 that the federal government passed a code for the building of such units. The Mobile Home Standards code administered by HUD is nationwide and strictly enforced. It was updated and put into widespread use in 1976 and incorporates much of the earlier ANSI code. Today manufacturers of mobile homes who want to have their units classified as real estate must not only be sure that each one passes the Mobile Home Standards code, but also passes the code in force in the particular area in which the until will be placed. If there is to be government financing, as there often is, it must also satisfy the code then in use by the particular agency (HUD or the Veterans Administration) that will insure or guarantee the loan!

As incredible as these hurdles are, the mobile home industry is today moving ever closer to having its products classified as real estate. In fact in many areas they are already commonly considered real property. The last big remaining obstacle has to do with taxation.

Mobile Homes versus Real Estate

Consider the plight of the poor tax assessor (who is given very little sympathy these days). A manufactured home is mobile: It is hauled to the site by a truck so it could easily be considered a vehicle and given a vehicle tax by the state.

But once at the property site it is put on a permanent foundation, hooked up to city sewer lines and public utilities. By these standards, the mobile home should be considered real estate and should be taxed by the local government.

But to further confuse the situation, the MFG is technically still mobile. In theory, if the owner should decide to move it someday, the owner can knock out the foundation, unhook the sewer and utility connections, put the wheels back on, and drive it away. It's a vehicle again!

How can a tax assessor tax such a strange item? This is a problem that has tax assessors staying up nights! While the answer to this problem is obviously difficult, it is made even more so by the stakes riding on the decision, stakes which run into billions of dollars.

From local government's point of view, anytime anyone puts a mobile home on a permanent site, whether it be a lot in the middle of a traditional neighborhood or in a mobile home park, that person draws on the services of the local community. These include sewer hookups (sewer treatment facilities required today by environmental considerations are unbelievably expensive and are paid for in large part by local revenues), schools, fire and police protection, recreational facilities including parks, and a host of other more subtle amenities provided by cities and counties. If, however, the mobile home is considered a vehicle and pays tax accordingly, all such money goes to state coffers and none (or very little) is returned to local government to pay for these services. The surrounding traditional neighborhoods and homes must make up the cost of services used by the mobile home families and this is truly an unfair burden.

From the buyer's viewpoint, however, one of the big selling features of mobile homes is that you don't have to pay high property taxes. Although the initial vehicle tax may be high, even approaching a comparable property tax levy, it *decreases* each year as the mobile home gets older. After a relatively short time, often as short as five years, the vehicle taxes are only a few hundred dollars, much less than they would be if the MFG were taxed as real estate.

This feature is especially appealing to older people, particularly retirees on fixed incomes, as well as couples whose children have grown up and left home. It is this very feature of small or declining taxes that might enable a family to own a home that it otherwise could not afford.

To add weight to this argument, this is not a new problem. Hundreds of thousands of families already have bought mobile homes on the basis of not having to pay real estate taxes. To suddenly change the laws might force a great many of them to lose their property. An unfortunate, not to say inhumane, act.

At this writing, most of the country considers the mobile home to be a vehicle. In some states such as Oregon and Washington it is considered real estate when placed on a lot. This is generally true throughout most of the rural United States. In suburban areas, whether in New York, Atlanta, or Los Angeles, the product is taxed as a vehicle and frequently permitted only in specially designated parks.

But times are changing. In California and in particular southern California the treatment of such units as vehicles is very strict. No long-term real estate financing is available. Yet bills are before city

Figure 5–4. Like automobile manufacturing, the first step in producing a manufactured home is the construction of a frame. In this photo, the frame has just been built and is upside down resting on supports with its wheels in the air. The trailer hitch which will eventually be used to transport it to its lot is off the photo at right. The frame is made of heavy steel with numerous I-beams connecting the two main outside supports.

and county governments to change the rules and within the next few years we may see manufactured home communities spring up not only in Los Angeles, but everywhere.

Can You Stand to Live in a "Trailer" (Pros and Cons)

There's an old saying that manufactured home builders like to use when anyone asks about the quality of their product. It goes something like this: "If you don't think our house is as good as a stick-built [the trade term for traditional homes, built one board or "stick" at a time], try driving one of theirs down the road at 55 miles an hour and go over a railroad crossing."

The MFG builder knows these products will hold together

Figure 5–5. After the substructure is completed, it is turned over and supported by its own wheels. It is then moved to a new position where the floor is added. The floor consists of wooden joists similar to the sort used in stick-built construction. Unlike traditional construction, the boards use special metal joiners and run the entire length of the unit—typically 60 feet. Special batting is added between the wood joists and the metal frame, then insulation is placed between the joists and finally a floorboard, often of pressed wood, is added on top. *(Mobile home construction photos courtesy of Fleetwood Enterprises.)*

because units are delivered via road every day. Nonetheless, many people aware of the strict building codes (you can check with the dealer to find which codes a particular unit is built under) and of the rugged construction still think of them as being "tinny." They think they sag and sway underfoot like a trailer when you walk in them. Nothing could be further from the truth.

The "sagging" or "swaying" idea probably is a throwback to the old image of a trailer which, because it was on wheels, did sag or tilt as you walked across the floor. Today's MFGs use wheels only as transportation to the residence site. There the wheels are usually removed and either a peripheral or pier foundation of cement is used. This means you have cement on top of the natural grade, dirt, then steel beams, then heavy wooden beams, and then floorboard. Such floors are as sturdy as in traditionally built wooden homes. (The only exception would be those houses which are built on a cement slab where the floor has no give at all.)

Manufacturing a House

All the construction techniques and materials used in the building of a manufactured home are essentially the same as those used for stick-built homes. The difference is that the manufactured home is built on an assembly line in a plant.

One well-operated plant will be similar to another. The photographs in Figures 5-4 through 5-12 were taken at Fleetwood Enterprises' "Barrington Homes" plant in Riverside, California. Fleetwood is the world's largest manufacturer of residential-type manufactured housing. In 1978 their total sales were nearly $700 million with almost 40% derived from the MFG field.

Like automobile manufacturing, the first step in producing a manufactured home is the construction of a frame. In the photos on the previous page, the frame has just been built and is upside down resting on supports with its wheels in the air. The trailer hitch which will eventually be used to transport it to its lot is off the photo at right. The frame is made of heavy steel with numerous I-beams connecting the two main outside supports.

After the substructure is completed, it is turned over and supported by its own wheels. It is then moved to a new position where the floor is added. The floor consists of wooden joists similar to the sort used in stick-built construction. Unlike in traditional construction, the boards use special metal joiners and run the entire length of the unit—typically 60 feet! Special batting is added between the wood joists and the metal frame, then insulation is placed between the joists and finally a floorboard, often of pressed wood, is added on top. The final sandwich looks like Figure 5-6.

Once the floor is in place, the unit is moved to the next position where walls are added.

The walls for the entire length of the home are often manufactured in a single unit. Here a 60-foot wall section is lifted up by an overhead crane while a worker finishes installing fiberglass insulation. The wall unit is then moved into place on the home and locked in position. Side walls are then added.

If the home is to be a double-wide, or two units side by side when finished, both sides are built simultaneously to ensure a proper fit. In this case the walls which will meet at the center are made of 2 × 3 inch material on each side. When joined, the center wall will be 6 inches thick. All other walls are made of 2 × 4 wood set 16 inches apart at the center, the same as for traditional houses. All exterior walls on the MFG are heavily insulated.

In this factory all of the cabinets used in the homes are made at the same time the houses are constructed. A section of the plant is set aside for this purpose.

Once the walls are in place, the interior paneling, wiring, and cabinets are installed. Note in Figure 5-10 that the two units have been temporarily placed right next to each other to ensure a perfect match.

The roof with its many manufactured planes looks much like an airplane wing in its early stages of construction. After being built separately, it is lifted up and placed on top of the new home. Roof materials are weight-tested to meet federal load requirements. The final roofing material can be either metal or shingle as the buyer prefers (shingle usually costs several hundred dollars more than metal).

The final homes, once they have been inspected and completed, are moved to a storage area to await delivery to their building sites. In Figure 5-12 all the homes shown are already sold. Note the designation of "A" and "B" on the trailer bodies to indicate matching pairs of double-wides. The exterior is typically high-grade waterproof material. The exterior design will vary dramatically (as will the interior) from manufacturer to manufacturer.

The finished house is hauled to the building site by a heavy truck. Once there, two methods of moving it into place are used, depending on the foundation. The unit can be backed onto its site and then a pier foundation built up to support it. Or, as shown on page 104, a peripheral foundation can be built and the home lifted on top of it by crane. The difference between a pier and peripheral foundation is illustrated in Figures 5-17 and 5-18.

Once the house is in place, the cement, brick, or stone facing

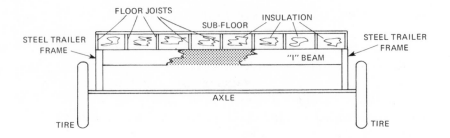

FLOOR JOISTS

SUB-FLOOR   INSULATION

STEEL TRAILER FRAME

STEEL TRAILER FRAME

"I" BEAM

AXLE

TIRE   TIRE

[100]

Figure 5–6.   Understructure of a mobile home.

Figure 5–7.   The walls for the entire length of the home are often manufactured in a single unit. Here a 60-foot wall section is lifted up by an overhead crane while a worker finishes installing fiberglass insulation. This wall unit is then moved into place on the home and locked in position. Side walls are then added.

Figure 5–8.   If the home is to be a double-wide, or two units side by side when finished, both sides are built simultaneously to ensure a proper fit. In this case the walls which will meet at the center are made of 2×3 inch material on each side. When joined, the center wall will be 6 inches thick. All other walls are made of 2×4 wood set 16 inches apart at the centers, the same as for traditional houses. All exterior walls on the MFG are heavily insulated.

Figure 5–9. In this factory all of the cabinets used in the homes are made at the same time that the houses are constructed. A section of the plant is set aside for this purpose.

Figure 5–11. The roof with its many manufactured planes looks much like an airplane wing in its early stages of construction. After being built separately, it is lifted up and placed on top of the new home. Roof materials are weight-tested to meet federal load requirements. The final roofing material can be either metal or shingle as the buyer prefers (shingle usually costs several hundred dollars more than metal).

[102]

Figure 5–10. Once the walls are in place, the interior paneling, wiring, and cabinets are installed. Note in this photo that the two units have been temporarily placed right next to each other to ensure a perfect match.

Figure 5–12. The final homes, once they have been inspected and completed, are moved to a storage area to await delivery to their building sites. In this photo all the homes shown are already sold. Note the designation of "A" and "B" on the trailer bodies to indicate matching pairs of double-wides. The exterior is typically high-grade waterproof material. The exterior design will vary dramatically (as will the interior) from manufacturer to manufacturer.

[104]

Figure 5–13, 5–14, 5–15, 5–16.

The finished house is hauled to the building site by a heavy truck. Once there, two methods of moving it into place are used, depending on the foundation. The unit can be backed onto its site and then a pier foundation built up to support it. Or, as shown here, a peripheral foundation can be built and the home lifted on top of it by crane. Once the house is in place, the cement, brick, or stone facing material is applied, carpeting and finish work is installed inside, and the house is ready to be lived in. Typically this onsite work can be completed in two working days. The cost of site preparation is often sold separately from the cost of the house.

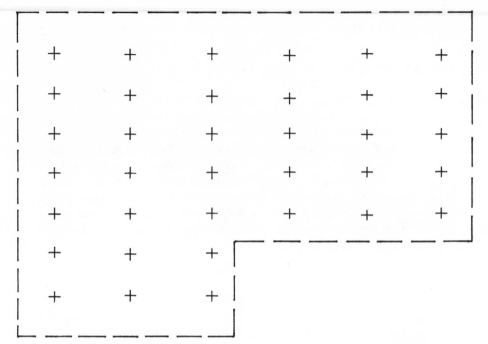

Figure 5–17 Typical pier foundation. Each X denotes a cement support located on the steel trailer frame. A peripheral facade is eventually added for appearance.

Figure 5–18 Typical peripheral foundation. Typically made of cement sunk from a few inches to several feet in the ground for support.

Figure 5-19 Mobile home. *(Courtesy of Skyline Corporation, Elkhart, Indiana.)*

Figure 5-20 Mobile home. *(Courtesy of Fleetwood Enterprises, Inc., Riverside, California.)*

[107]

material is applied, carpeting and finish work is installed inside, and the house is ready to be lived in. Typically this onsite work can be completed in two working days. Site preparation is often sold separately from the cost of the home.

Finished manufactured homes will vary greatly in appearance. Shown in Figures 5-19 and 5-20 are two models, one from Fleetwood and one from Skyline Corporation, the latter the world's largest manufacturer of mobile homes.

It should be noted that the savings in MFG manufacturing arise primarily out of the lower cost of labor that assembly line techniques allow. By concentrating labor at a single place and repeating the same job for the same worker over and again, costs are kept to a minimum. It has been estimated that in constructing a traditional home, the costs are evenly divided between labor and materials—50 percent labor and 50 percent materials. But in MFG construction the costs are roughly 30 percent labor and 70 percent materials.

Almost all traditional homes that are built by developers or builders use union workers, while some of the manufactured home builders use unskilled labor. The savings here are largely passed on to the consumer. (In a larger sense the worker is also the consumer, so it could be argued that this arrangement is counterproductive.) In time it is probably safe to say that most manufactured home plants will become unionized, particularly as the trade unions exert their influence on the industry. This will probably result in an increase in manufacturing costs. Nonetheless, the savings of assembly line production should still make the MFG far less expensive than the traditional home.

"It Doesn't Look like a House"

Assuming that you're convinced the MFG house is at least as well built as a traditional house, the next objection is usually to the appearance. "I don't want to live in any old trailer" is the usual declaration.

I doubt very seriously that anyone who has visited a mobile home of today would make that comment. It refers back to the image of gypsy wagons. Nevertheless mobile homes do not at this time offer the variety nor the structural styles afforded by traditional housing. Beam ceilings, long a feature of traditional housing, are just coming into vogue in mobile homes. Pitched roofs are also just now appearing on mobile homes though the pitch is rarely above 3/12 (3 inches of vertical rise for every 12 inches of horizontal distance), while traditional homes typically have pitches of 4/12 and steeper.

Stucco exteriors, tile roofs, and plaster or gypsum wallboard interiors are hardly ever used in mobile homes for they tend to crack en route to the building site. Brick fronts, however, are often built up once the mobile home is in place. Real wood-burning fireplaces are frequently lacking, although simulated electric heater fireplaces sometimes take their place. And you just don't find a two-story mobile home, at least not yet. Finally, no matter how clever the cosmetics, a mobile home looks like a mobile home and not like a traditional house.

If you really must have any of the features just described, then perhaps the mobile home is not for you. But as one representative of the mobile home industry recently commented, "Anything that can be stick-built, can be built on an assembly line. Just give us time."

Lush wood paneling *is* typically found in mobile homes, as are wet bars, huge open living rooms, and spacious kitchens. Models come in two, three, or four bedrooms and usually with two baths and a washroom. From the inside it is often difficult to tell a mobile home from an expensive custom-built dream home.

The Turtle Problem

Probably the most serious drawback to mobile homes today is finding a place to put it once you buy it. The shortage of suitable sites creates images of a buyer having to carry the home on his or her back like a turtle, forever wandering an endless freeway in search of a permanent place to rest. Usually you don't buy an MFG until you've already got a place to put it. But finding the proper locale can be a serious problem.

How serious a problem depends to a large degree on what area of the country you want or must live in. In California and in particular southern California (where almost 5 percent of the country's population lives) finding a place for your MFG is a real problem. In Oregon and Washington it is almost no problem at all. For the rest of the country the degree of difficulty varies considerably.

There are two parts to the turtle problem. The first goes back to the bad publicity we were speaking of earlier and might be summed up by the statement, "I don't want one of those trailers in my neighborhood." It is a kind of home integration problem that results in restrictive zoning prohibiting the use of manufactured homes in certain neighborhoods.

In one recent incident in southern California, an owner tried to put a manufactured home on a lot in an area where existing houses were selling in the $80,000 price range. The owner paid $30,000 for the lot and was going to put a $25,000 MFG on it. The neighbors complained to the city expressing the fear that the MFG would lower property values. As it turned out, the particular city had no zoning restrictions against MFGs on lots of an acre or larger, which this was. This so incensed the neighbors that they carried around a petition which was eventually signed by enough people in the neighborhood to block location of the MFG on the site.

The owner of the lot, now himself incensed, took out a permit to "stick-build" a home to the same specifications as the MFG would have been. Strangely, there were no protests at all to this. The owner went ahead and stick-built his home at additional cost and was wlecomed into the neighborhood. The home he built was identical to the MFG he had planned to move in!

This story would be humorous if it weren't for the fact that it's absolutely true. Would the property values in the above neighborhood have been lowered if the MFG had been placed there? Since it was an area of custom homes, probably not. Although the MFG itself undoubtedly wouldn't have sold for quite as much as surrounding homes, it probably would have had increased value because of the neighborhood and the owner might have sold it at a healthy profit. Which brings to mind a word of caution. If you're thinking of making a few bucks, or even a lot of bucks by buying a lot in an established neighborhood, putting a quality MFG on it, and then quickly selling, be careful of your neighbors. They may ruin your plans and your pocketbook as well. To be safe you should get prior approval in writing from as many neighbors as possible before putting out any cash or commitment.

The second half of the turtle problem arises when you try to find a mobile home park in which to locate your MFG. In many areas of the country, the supply of new mobile home parks has not kept pace with the demand and consequently there may be a waiting list. If you have children, living in an MFG park can be a serious problem. Many parks are for adults only, and you must be over twenty-one in order to permanently reside there.

There are family parks which take children, but they tend to be in the minority. And even in the family parks there can be restrictions. Some parks, for example, will only take children up to the age of twelve. The reason for the age limit has to do with the confined areas of mobile home parks. Some owners fear that teenage gangs may form and terrorize or vandalize the other tenants. Whether this actually does happen or whether there is only the fear of it happening is not clear. Nonetheless, few mobile home parks will take the entire family. Some parks compromise by organizing separate adult and family sections.

A Relaxed Lifestyle

As we've mentioned, living in a mobile home park (where you are most likely to place your mobile home today) has a great many amenities like recreation halls and swimming pools. It would be incorrect to assume, though, that the lifestyle is the same as it would be if you were living in traditional housing with access to a country club. It's not the same any more than condominium living is the same as living in a house.

In a mobile home park you can usually have the option of whether or not you want gardening. If you want a garden, you'll plant one. If not, you can cement over the areas your unit does not cover. Lots are generally small, only about 50 by 80 feet, so there's not much room for a really large garden.

Your neighbors will be closer together in a mobile home park than if you had a traditional home and, if you use any of the facilities, you'll get to know them quickly. If you're naturally gregarious, a "mixer," this can be great fun and most enjoyable. If you're a loner, this can create a miserable situation for you. It's something to consider seriously before making a purchase.

Typically people buying MFGs to use in mobile home parks are "empty nesters." For them the companionship offered by mobile home living can be ideal. There is usually some activity planned for every evening, like home movies, bingo games, or bridge. The mobile home park lifestyle can make quite enjoyable what could otherwise be a lonely time of life.

Life inside the mobile home is like life in a house. In the bigger units, those that are double-wide with a "tag" or third section added on, the typical size is close to 1,800 square feet. This is large enough to comfortably accommodate a family by today's standards and is spacious if it is only used by a couple. Since so many MFGs are bought by empty nesters many of the units are luxuriously designed and appointed, for this group tends to be affluent. The heartland of empty nester mobile home parks is southern California, with entire communities of hundreds and hundreds of units located on lush grounds.

Typically these luxury units have two bedrooms with a very large living area composed of an open kitchen and bar, living room, and separate dining room. They have rich wood paneling and fine carpeting. And they tend to sell in the $20-to-$24-a-square-foot category. This means that an 1,800-square-foot unit goes for about $40,000, which is still considerably less than a comparably equipped traditional house.

For the rest of the country, the units tend to be more conservative . . . and less expensive.

How to Get the Best Financing on Your Manufactured House

If your mobile home is built to local code and the local government accepts it as real estate, you can get literally the best financing in the world, the same financing as for single-family suburban homes. Thirty years conventional or government-insured or guaranteed loans are available to you at relatively low interest rates. To find out exactly what you can get, check into Chapter Two.

If you pay vehicle tax on your unit, the above financing is probably not available to you. Instead you will have to obtain a chattel or personal loan. The term will be for a maximum of twenty-three years (in most cases fifteen). The interest rate will be higher (at this writing it is 13 percent for these loans, 9 percent for real estate), and your monthly payment will be about one-third more.

But if that's all that is available to you and it means you can get a house at a lower price than anyplace else with payments you can still afford, it remains a good deal. A very famous real estate entrepreneur once was heard to remark, "I'd rather be alive at 18 percent interest, than dead at 10 percent." Harsh, but sound reasoning.

Conventional financing for chattel loans is usually available from banks. Each bank's lending policies will determine its own requirements for qualifying for a loan. Typically they might look something like the figures in Table 5-1.

Many lenders make a distinction between units that are single-wide and those that are double-wide, giving better financing terms to the latter.

As you will quickly notice by comparing Tables 5-1 and 5-2, the financing terms for existing mobile homes are considerably tighter than for new ones. This is because mobile homes which are considered vehicular presumably depreciate each year in the same way an automobile does. Every year you use it, it's worth less. There is even a "Blue Book" that lists the value of used mobile homes. This is exactly the opposite of those MFG homes that are considered to be real estate, where values tend to *increase* annually.

Qualifying for these chattel loans is strict in terms of having good credit, but less stringent when it comes to the amount of income you make. Generally banks want borrowers to maintain a 40 to 50

TABLE 5-1
Lending Policy for a Brand New Mobile Home

Price	Years	Interest rate (%)
Up to $10,000	7	12.16
$10,000 to $15,000	10	11.32
$15,000 to the bank's maximum (usually around $35,000)	15	11.04

TABLE 5-2
Lending Policy for an Existing (Used) Mobile Home

Price	Years	Interest rate (%)
Up to $8,000	5	14.3
$8,000 to $10,000	7	12.93
$10,000 to the bank's maximum	12	12.1

percent debt ratio. A debt ratio is simply your total monthly obligations divided by your *net* monthly income (your take-home pay). If you bring home $800 a month after taxes and your total monthly payments for car, utilities, mobile home loan, space rent, and so on aren't over $400, you would probably qualify for the loan.

$$\frac{\text{Expenses}}{\text{Take-home pay}} \quad \frac{\$400}{\$800} = 50\%$$

In addition, if you've dealt with the bank for a long time and have a good credit history of having borrowed money and repaid promptly, the bank may be quite flexible in both terms and willingness to make a loan. Unlike the strict 4 to 1 ratio on real estate, when it comes to making chattel loans banks consider the person before the property. A cash down payment of 10 to 20 percent may be required.

In addition to this conventional financing, the FHA offers a mobile home loan program under Title I. As with conventional loans, the actual money is borrowed from a lender such as a bank. In the case of an FHA loan, the government insures repayment for a small additional charge which is paid by the lender (but passed on to the borrower). The amount of these loans (see Table 5-3) can cover both the mobile home and the land it is placed on. (We'll discuss ownership of pads in a moment.)

The Veterans Administration also has a program, for qualifying veterans (see Chapter Two for qualification requirements). These terms are outlined in Table 5-4. To purchase a double-wide mobile home and a lot, the maximum loan is $27,500 with a term of twenty years. For the purchase of a mobile home lot *only*, up to $7,500 can be borrowed for a term of up to twelve years. As in the case of FHA

[114]

TABLE 5-3
FHA Loans for Mobile Homes

Maximum loan amount	$16,000 for single-wides
	$24,000 for double-wides or larger (up to 40% higher in Alaska, Guam, and Hawaii)
Maximum term of loan	12 years for single-wides
	23 years for double-wides permanently placed on a building site
Maximum financing charge	12% a year at this writing
Cash down-payment	5% of the first $3,000, 10% for any additional amount (check with lender for recent changes)

loans, the government does not advance any money. For VA loans it guarantees repayment to the lender of a certain percentage of the loan in the event the borrower defaults.

Why Pay Rent?

In many parts of the country, particularly in rural areas, mobile homes are placed on lots owned by the mobile home owner. In most

TABLE 5-4
Veterans Administration Loans for Mobile Homes

Maximum term	12 years for single-wides
	20 years for double-wides
Maximum loan	$12,500 for single-wides
	$20,000 for double-wides
Cash down-payment	none (check with lender for recent changes)

urban areas, however, the mobile home owner rents a lot or pad in a mobile home park. This means that in addition to paying off the mortgage on the mobile home (assuming you didn't buy it for cash), the owner must also pay a monthly rent. In the old trailer courts rents frequently ranged from $35 to $100 a month. In the newer mobile home parks they are rarely under $100 and climb as high as $350 a month or more for the luxurious and well-located parks.

Realizing that many mobile home owners can't afford or don't want high rents, some land owners and developers have built mobile home parks where they sell the individual lots. The prices vary with the location in the park and the size of the lot, but in general they range anywhere from $5,000 to $20,000. The advantage to a mobile home buyer of also purchasing the lot is that the payment for the lot frequently can be *amortized* or paid off each month. That is, it can be included in the same loan as is used to finance the mobile home and over the same period of time. Often this results in a substantially lower monthly payment than paying rent.

It can be a good deal, particularly if the lot is fully improved (graded with all utilities provided) and the park has some excellent recreational facilities. One drawback is that as owner of your lot, you'll have to pay property taxes on it. This means that you could have two tax bills: a licensing or vehicle tax for the mobile home and a property tax for the lot. But these two combined are likely to be lower than the property tax alone on a traditional house. If your mobile home is considered to be a piece of real estate and taxed as real property, then you'll only have one big property tax bill, just like traditional home owners.

One last consideration about financing concerns the cost of mobile homes to you and to the dealer. Many people feel that they pay an unfairly high markup when they buy. In actual fact the markup from manufacturer to dealer is about 30 percent. This means that a home that retails for $20,000 costs the dealer only $14,000. That extra $6,000 is not all profit, however. The dealer must pay for delivering the home to your lot and in many cases the price you pay includes preparing the lot for the home (which costs anywhere from $1,500 to $5,000). In order to sell a manufactured home, the dealer must park a model near a showroom and pay financing charges on it while it sits there. Because of the cost of putting up and tearing down models, dealers rarely change units on display more than once a year. In the end, dealers' profits are more in the 5 to 10 percent range. That (and the fact that demand is so high today) may explain why you're having so much trouble getting a dealer to cut prices for you.

The Final Solution?

Mobile homes are a realistic answer to the skyrocketing cost of housing. Whether they are in fact the best answer for you depends on your housing expectations. They're definitely not that peaceful suburban house you've always dreamed about. In many ways they're better. And in the future they may come closer to the ideal than any of us imagine. In any event, if a manufactured home fits your pocketbook and your lifestyle, don't hesitate to buy one just because it's different.

SIX

Rehabilitation—The Best Deal in Town

Alan and Sheila wanted an unusual house. They felt that the home, more than anything else, determined the quality of the life they would lead. Consequently the shape, the size, the beauty of the house was of utmost importance to them. They agreed that their home must be big, at least 3,000 square feet, hopefully larger. The rooms must also be big; they just couldn't bear tiny, cramped rooms. And they wanted their home to show quality. Real wood paneling should be the rule rather than the exception.

Alan and Sheila, however, were not rich. Alan had a promising job in the electronics division of a space technology laboratory and earned about $16,000 a year. Sheila worked part-time and their total joint income was about $20,000. When they went to an agent and asked to be shown houses, they were disappointed by what they saw. They were shown suburban houses in the $50,000 and under price range and they felt these were small and not built as well as they wanted.

When they carefully explained what they desired, the agent only laughed. She said that a suburban house as big as they wanted and built as well as they wanted would cost perhaps $150,000, if they could find one even at that price. The agent's advice was to be realistic. She suggested they give up their idea of a dream home for the moment. Settle for second or even third best, build up an equity, and eventually move up. When Alan asked how long the agent thought it would take them to build up an equity large enough to get their dream house, the answer he received was not specific. Perhaps five years or ten, the agent replied. A lot depended on how *fast* the property they bought went up in price and how *slow* the type of property they actually wanted appreciated. And, the agent continued, much depended on their income. In ten years, she said, they'd probably be making double their current salary, and then they'd be able to afford more. Sheila asked if property might not also double in cost in ten years. The agent admitted it might. It had done that in the last ten years.

Alan and Sheila were not satisfied with these answers. They decided to look further. They checked out a suburban condominium. They could get a lovely new unit, but it would be smaller than they wanted. They also checked out a high-rise condominium. The location was terrific, but so was the price.

Next they looked at mobile homes. They were most impressed by what they saw. Here they could get a large size (though not nearly as large as they wanted) at a price they could afford. But what they were really committed to was a fine, traditional home.

Being willing to wait, they decided their best alternative was a suburban "fixer-upper," a badly run-down house. Hopefully they could buy such a home cheaply and then, over a period of years, fix it up. They were in for a rude awakening.

The high cost of housing had driven thousands and thousands of other couples to consider the same alternative. For every potential fixer-upper there were hundreds who wanted it. Too often brokers who came across these would simply buy them up themselves before Alan or Sheila could even hear of their existence. After months of looking they decided that, barring a miracle of good fortune, their chances of finding a fixer-upper were slim. (But not impossible. If you want one and are willing to spend a lot of time and energy talking to many brokers, and asking people in run-down houses if they want to sell, you can usually find one.)

Now Sheila and Alan sat down and tried to come to terms with their problem. There were incidental benefits. If they could just buy any house, they could deduct the money they spent on property taxes and interest on the mortgage from their income tax. This would save them a considerable amount of money. In addition, they would be building up an equity so that when they sold they would come away, hopefully, much richer than when they started. But what it really came down to was that they wanted a big, fine place, and couldn't find it. At this point Sheila suggested, "We've looked in all the good areas, how about getting the house we want some place else? Are they cheaper in other parts of the city?"

This got them thinking and they realized that it actually didn't matter so much to them *where* they were living or if they had to fix up the house. What they really wanted was a big house to fall in love with and make their own. Suddenly new possibilities opened up. There must be "undesirable" areas of the city where houses were old and needed repair, where prices were much lower. Immediately they began a search.

What Alan and Sheila found is what buyers all across the country are finding. There are big, sometimes huge houses available at often ridiculously low prices in almost every major city. These are the older homes frequently built between 1890 and 1920 for the wealthy of that period. There is, of course, a problem. The homes are usually located in blighted, decaying neighborhoods where the crime rate is high, the buildings are badly deteriorated and need extensive repairs, and most of the people now living there do so only because they can't afford to live anywhere else.

Alan and Sheila were entering the world of rehabilitating and restoring older buildings. We'll come back to the house they actually found in just a moment, but first let's consider how these big, fine houses happened to get where they are and in the condition they're in.

Before 1850 American cities were much smaller than they are today. The main reason they were smaller has to do with transportation. Walking and riding on horseback were the primary means of getting from one place to another. Since commerce and industry were located in the city, the best residential locations were within easy walking distance. Those who could afford to, the merchants and other wealthy families, lived in the city and walked short distances to work. The poor, on the other hand, lived outside the city and walked far greater distances to work.

Just before the turn of the century, with the expansion of mass transit such as trolley cars and trains, it was possible to conveniently live greater distances from the center of the city. Wealthy families, as we saw in Chapter One, began moving to newer housing farther away from the downtown areas. These areas, with the noise and congestion caused by the businesses and industries, were soon occupied by the laborers who now could live closer to where they worked.

About 1920 the automobile came into its own and the wealthy moved ever farther into what we today call suburbia. The laborers soon followed. After 1920 the city became triple, quadruple the size it had been prior to that time. And the old city, the central area, began a steady decline from which it has never recovered.

Eventually businesses and many industries moved from the center of the city and now these early bedroom communities which had first housed the wealthy and later the workers became of no real use to anyone. Only the very poor, who could not afford to live anywhere else, inhabited these older buildings. And the poor often could not afford to own the property. Instead they rented from landlords who lived far away in suburban homes.

Eventually many of our largest cities like New York, Chicago, and St. Louis, contained dilapidated buildings in areas where social conditions had deteriorated so badly that tenants could not even be found. The owners simply abandoned them rather than pay property taxes. As late as 1975 there were an estimated 50,000 houses a year lost to abandonment in New York City alone.

Realizing what was happening to the central cities, local and federal governments in the 1950s began enthusiastic plans to redevelop these areas. Typically plans called for tearing down existing homes and putting up large low- and moderate-income apartments or cooperative buildings. To say that this has met with limited success is being generous. In the 1970s in St. Louis, one of these apartment projects was dynamited by the city to destroy what had become impossible living conditions within fifteen years of construction. Difficult situations have occurred in other major cities as well. (This is not to say, however, that all urban renewal programs were failures. Some were successfully carried out.)

In the late 1960s some people began to realize that there were real possibilities in central city areas. These individuals began to form save-the-city organizations. Most notable among them were the Citizens Against Slum Housing in Pittsburgh and the Brownstone Revival Committee in New York. Other groups also began forming in most major cities across the country.

Their goals tended to be limited in nature, although the effects of

[121]

their actions have often been broad. In general these people felt that some central city areas (not all) offer benefits to homeowners not found anywhere else in the community, such as large, well-built, and sometimes ornate homes; excellent locations in terms of getting to the business and financial institutions (which have gone back to the central city in the last two decades); and incredibly low cost. You'll recall that in Chapter One we saw that the two greatest reasons for the high price of suburban housing are demand (nearly everyone wants to live there) and the skyrocketing cost of building new houses. These two reasons are reversed in central city areas. Almost no one, until recently, has wanted to live there. And the homes are all old, having been built five to seven decades ago when building costs, compared to today's, were very inexpensive.

Of course there are drawbacks. The kind of central city areas we are talking about are largely slums with decaying houses and social conditions. Groups concerned with saving them must identify those areas which can be saved and those which cannot. The Urban Reinvestment Task Force, which was formed by the Federal Home Loan Bank Board to start Neighborhood Housing Services (on the model of the citizens' group of the same name that had success in Pittsburgh), looks for salvageable neighborhoods to restore. The Brownstone Revival Committee in New York seems to be looking, according to *Back to the City*, published by the Brownstone Revival Committee of New York, Inc., 130 Park Avenue, New York, New York 10017, 1975, for "fine old houses of the nineteenth—and sometimes the eighteenth century . . . waiting to be adopted."

Two types of neighborhood can generally be identified, both of which are usually classified as slum or blighted. The first is the totally decayed neighborhood, with truly dilapidated buildings. Frequently there will be buildings on each block which have been abandoned. The most identifiable trait of this kind of neighborhood is that most of the property owners do not live there, but rent their property out and live elsewhere. In such a neighborhood 60 percent or more of the houses will be rentals.

Houses in this first group, because of the totally decayed nature of the neighborhood, usually cannot be saved on an individual basis. Rehabilitating one house usually does not improve the area at all. The poor social conditions of the neighborhood are likely to drag the house back down and the owners will give up and move.

In the mid-1970s houses in this first group were frequently given away by cities to anyone who would homestead them. The city would offer the house to a buyer for $1 on the condition that the buyer would rehabilitate it. Often the city or the federal government would provide financial assistance to do the work. The owner was said to have purchased the property through "sweat equity." These houses are still available, usually in the worst areas of the big cities. It is often the case, however, that these totally decayed areas cannot be restored without some sort of massive government aid. Improving entire neighborhoods and not just one house at a time is probably the necessary answer.

The second type of neighborhood, that is usually called a slum also has houses which are dilapidated from lack of maintenance. But there are few or no abandoned homes. This neighborhood is poor, old, and declining, but still functioning. Most of the homes have owners living in them. The social fabric of the neighborhood may be wearing thin but it has not yet broken. These neighborhoods are usually on the decline and unless something happens will turn into slums of the first type within a decade or so. These can be saved.

Most private rehabilitation groups are only concerned with this second group. The reasoning is that it is still possible for individuals to buy homes here, rehabilitate, and then live well in them. By doing so they can reverse the downward trend of the neighborhood and create a wholesome community.

Many organizations interested in getting people back to the city sponsor "walking tours" which involve walking prospective buyers through type two neighborhoods so they can see close at hand the homes that are available. In addition many companies will help prospective buyers find homes. In Hartford, Connecticut, for example, the Aetna Life Insurance Company has made a commitment to helping buyers locate housing and figure rehabilitating costs. Brooklyn Union Gas also sponsors some programs. (See the list at the end of this chapter.)

The best way to locate such a group in your city is to check first in the phone book under headings such as Neighborhood Housing Services or urban renewal agencies. City government and homesteading offices may also have information. Another source is to check with some of the larger organizations involved in getting people back to the city. A list of these is given at the end of this chapter. Often these groups may know of an organization that will provide aid in your city if they can't offer it directly themselves. Finally, you can check with lending institutions which have offices near the area you are interested in. These institutions usually work very closely with neighborhood groups and may lead the way to real help.

Alan and Sheila, the couple we met at the beginning of this chapter, spent some time looking for a local group but without success. They were in an area where save-the-neighborhood groups had not yet developed. But although they could not get aid, they did not give up. They decided to proceed on their own using common sense.

Their search led them to neighborhoods that were pretty much type two. The type one neighborhoods simply did not appeal to them. They looked for areas with no abandoned houses, only homes that were old and run-down. And they began specifically looking for a big Victorian-style house.

They contacted brokers until they located the area of the city where just the right big old houses were to be found. Then they went up and down blocks searching for their future home. Eventually they found a good prospect on Horizon Street. It was vacant and for sale by the owner. The house seemed ideal—three stories tall, over 3,500 square feet. The parlor was huge—nearly 30 feet across—and the ceilings were 14 feet tall. There was a narrow wood-paneled hallway, and very large bedrooms on two floors. The kitchen was on the first floor and was tiny, but the dining room was very large. They immediately made plans to knock out a wall between the kitchen and an adjoining pantry and make an eating area. The top floor was a loft, one incredibly large room which they could foresee dividing up into a family room and den. The house only had one bathroom, downstairs, but Alan saw how he might put another one immediately above it on the second floor.

The house was in terrible shape. The old plaster was cracked or falling off in many rooms. Someone years earlier had put composition shingles over the entire front of the house, apparently in an attempt to keep it from deteriorating. The shingles had served their purpose, but made the house look as if the roof had slipped over and down the front. Alan and Sheila immediately realized that this muddled job of rehabilitating would have to be taken off and the original front restored. The wood paneling throughout the house, the heavy wooden doorjambs, and even the wooden floors were scratched and in some places cracked.

But before falling completely in love with the house, they went back and carefully checked the neighborhood. (They had only driven by before.) Its condition was critical.

The street and surrounding neighborhood had obviously been declining for years. But there was a large park nearby, which acted as a kind of anchor, giving the area an inherent quality. This park, in fact, was probably what caused the original builders to put up such an elaborate house. At one time it must have been a home for a very wealthy family.

Although the neighborhood was poor, it was still active. There were no abandoned houses. Alan and Sheila then took a day off and began knocking on the doors of neighboring homes. Some people were reluctant to talk to them, but many did and they quickly learned that most of the homes in the area had owners living in them. They also learned something very interesting: Three other houses nearby had recently been bought by families who were rehabilitating them.

Sheila took the next morning off and went to each of the three houses that had been rehabilitated. In each she found that families like theirs had bought for similar reasons. Only one had been completely rehabilitated—the others were being worked on. But in each case the families who bought were living in the homes.

Sheila and Alan decided it was as good a neighborhood as they were likely to find.

There are several guidelines which Sheila and Alan had learned in their search for a home.

1. *Find a Neighborhood Which Is Not Totally Decayed, but One in Which the Social Fabric Is Still Fairly Intact.*

2. *Find a Neighborhood That Has an Anchor Such As a Park, Shopping Center, or College, or Has a Group Actively Working on Its Preservation.*

3. *Buy Only in an Area Where Someone Else Has Already Pioneered by Rehabilitating Other Homes.*

This last may sound cynical, but it is excellent advice for someone who has never rehabilitated before. It is the novice who is most likely to choose a bad neighborhood. The chances of this happening are greatly reduced by picking an area where others have already made the decision and it seems to be working out.

Sheila remained concerned about the crime rate in the area. Alan went to the local police station and they confirmed that the general area had a high crime rate, but the specific neighborhood their house was located in had a much lower rate of crime. And the rate had been declining ever since the first people began restoring houses there several years earlier. They decided to buy.

The seller was asking only $32,000 for the house. (That's less than $10 a square foot including the cost of the land!) But before they went ahead and made an offer, they wanted to have some idea of what it would cost to do the remodeling work they envisioned.

They called up several contractors who came down and gave them estimates. But these estimates varied so much that they quickly realized that probably they were all inaccurate. The problem was that in rehabilitating, unlike building new, something old first had to be torn down. And no one really knew what would be found after the plaster and other covering materials were removed. If the wiring was ruined or outdated (as probably was the case), its replacement would be expensive. If they found that supporting beams were deteriorated or rotten and would have to be replaced, this also would alter the costs.

Alan and Sheila went to one of the neighbors who was in the process of rehabilitating and asked for advice. The neighbor gave them the name of a contractor who specialized in remodeling work. (They could also have checked with the local National Association of Home Builders affiliate and they would have been given a list of names of remodelers, or they could have checked with the local remodelers association.)

The contractor examined the house and immediately told them that they'd have to rip out about a third of the plaster as it had cracked or otherwise decayed. He indicated that in houses he had done in similar areas, most of the wood beams were in good shape because they were made of either oak or heavy redwood which resisted infestation of termites. But the area was termite plagued, so an extermination was a good idea, preferably once the plaster was off and old boards exposed. He said the old wiring would undoubtedly

[126]

all have to be replaced. Then he went to the wall behind the kitchen sink. He poked around until he found a particular spot where the plaster was cracked and peeled back a piece. He asked Sheila to look and she saw an old pipe there. He took out a rag and wiped it clean. The contractor said it was galvanized iron. Galvanized iron was good plumbing, but not as good as copper or brass used in some early houses. It was, however, far superior to the much older lead plumbing. Undoubtedly some of the plumbing would have to be replaced, but much of it would probably be all right.

Then the contractor tried to get onto the roof to inspect it. When he couldn't, he took out a pair of binoculars and gave it a close look. He said he was looking for missing shingles. (It was a wood shingle roof.) There were a few missing, but it looked okay. A wood shingle roof is probably good for thirty years, he said, so this one obviously wasn't that old. (Metal and some clay roofs last longer.)

The contractor checked the attic for leaks. When none were to be found, it confirmed his feeling that the roof was okay. On the way down from the attic, Alan noticed the contractor bouncing on the stairs. When asked, he replied it was an excellent way to determine if the supports were good. (He had done the same thing with the floors on other levels of the house, but Alan hadn't noticed.) The contractor said the supports seemed to be in good shape.

Next he went to the basement. In old buildings there frequently is no cement foundation. Instead the support beams rest directly on the ground and are called "mud sills." While these may last more than fifty years, they eventually must be replaced at great expense. In this structure, however, there was a foundation of heavy bricks under the support beams. The contractor said this was a good sign, then poked at the bottom beams with a pocket knife. He said he was checking for termites and rot. He found none.

Next he walked over to the furnace. He said it was a natural gas gravity-feed furnace. (Others are coal, oil, or even wood.) He poked at the metal and it broke away. It was rusted. He checked the big heavy ducts leading upward from the furnace. They appeared rusted and rotten also. He said that a gravity-feed furnace operated without a fan. It operated on the principle of hot air rising. It heated air by burning gas or oil and the hot air rose from the basement into the rest of the house, a very efficient heater. Judging by the poor condition of the heater and duct work, however, he judged that a completely new heating system would have to be installed (and air conditioning at the same time if they wanted.) He said that as long as they were doing the work on the house, they should also insulate it. The cost was not that great and it would save them a lot of money on the heating bills.

Then he walked over to the water heater. Alan had trouble identifying it as a water heater because it didn't look like any he had seen before. The contractor whistled and said it was a copper coil heater. Instead of having a tank like modern heaters, this one had a large coil of copper tubing. Gas flames played right on the tubing heating the water inside. He said that it was a very old style, but very efficient when it worked. He pointed to wet dirt around the heater and indicated that it must have many leaks. These heaters were almost impossible to save once they leaked, he noted. A new 50-gallon heater (40 gallons was probably the minimum size they'd want in the house) would have to be purchased.

The cellar had a dirt floor. The contractor went to the center and picked up some of the dirt and felt it with his hand. He noted that it had rained heavily several weeks earlier and that if the cellar flooded, the ground would be damp. This ground, however, was dry as dust, a good sign.

Finally they went back outside and looked at the exterior walls. The contractor sighted along the walls. He said he was checking for bulges that would indicate timbers inside had broken, come loose, or rotted. He found none. Then he pointed to the doorway and asked them to notice how it sagged to the left. Upon closer inspection, Alan and Sheila saw that it did. The contractor explained that since the brick foundation and the lower support boards seemed to be all right, this was probably just due to the warping or slippage of boards near the door. Probably a few extra supports would correct it. (Sagging doorjambs, however, can be the sign of serious problems.)

Then he checked the stucco on the side of the house. It didn't seem to have any major cracks. (Filling cracks and repairing stucco also can be expensive.)

Finally the contractor drew up a list of items to be fixed and their cost. He concluded that the price of rehabilitating the house the way Sheila and Alan wanted would be about $26,000 if it was all hired out, $20,000 if Alan and Sheila did some of the work, and about $12,000 if they did all the work.

Alan and Sheila thanked him and said they'd probably do some of the work themselves and have him do the rest.

The contractor had checked the ten basic elements of every building which need to be looked into:

1. Inside walls

2. Outside walls

3. Structural beams

4. Floors and stairs

5. Roof

6. Attic

7. Electrical, heating, and plumbing systems

8. Termite and other pest infestations

9. Cellar

10. Foundation

(A detailed list of points to check in old homes including many helpful tips on what to look for can be obtained for 50 cents by writing to the Old House Journal, 199 Berkeley Place, Brooklyn, New York 11217.)

Alan and Sheila were satisfied this was the house for them. They offered the seller $30,000 subject to their getting a new first mortgage. They figured about $20,000 to rehabilitate, assuming they did much of the work. Since they had $8,000 in savings, they would need at least $42,000 to do the job.

When the seller accepted the offer, they immediately proceeded to find the financing. Since the house was sold by the owner there was no agent to help. Once again, they were on their own.

Red-lining

Alan and Sheila had read about red-lining. This was a procedure in which lenders allegedly drew a red line around a certain area of a city and refused to make any loans there. Since these were usually run-down areas like the one in which Sheila and Alan were planning to buy, they were concerned that they might not be able to get financing.

Antired-lining advocates (sometimes called green-liners) cite numerous studies which show that institutional lenders have put much more of their money into the suburbs than into central city areas. This, they contend, has kept buyers from being able to purchase central city homes and has kept owners from being able to take out improvement and repair loans.

The problem with most of these studies that I've seen is that they tend to measure only the *supply* of loans, that is, how many mortgages were actually made and where. They don't measure the *demand.* Which raises the question of whether it is possible that fewer loans were made in central city areas primarily because fewer loan requests were made.

More recent studies have attempted to answer this question. Controlled tests in Rochester, New York, and in other areas of the country sponsored by government agencies that regulate lenders indicate that so-called red-lining is more a matter of a family's choice as to where they want to live than it is a policy of quarantine by lenders. It may be simply that in the past fewer people have wanted to buy residences in central city areas. (It is interesting that these studies come after many states and the federal government have passed laws outlining alleged red-lining by lending institutions.)

My own experience has been that I have never seen red-lining discrimination. The lenders I have had experience with have always applied the same risk criteria to all properties without regard to where they are located. Of course, green-liners may point out that this is the very heart of the problem. Central city areas naturally offer greater risk since the areas are run-down and decayed. I would suspect lenders would respond to such an argument by pointing out that they are responsible to their depositors. It only makes sense for them to seek to place loans on the least risky property. To place a loan on a high-risk property when a low-risk property was available might be interpreted by depositors as lacking good business judgment, perhaps even as negligence.

The issue of whether or not red-lining exists is not what primarily interests buyers such as Alan and Sheila who are trying to obtain financing. They simply want to get a loan. Before we go into the type of loan that they actually got, a word more might be said about criteria used by lenders.

In Chapter Two we saw that lenders qualify both buyers and property. Buyers must show that they can repay the mortgage. Property must be of sufficient value to warrant the loan amount on the theory that if foreclosure should occur, the lender can take back the property and resell it for at least the loan amount in a reasonable period of time. See Figure 6-1.

In central city areas in the past, some buyers have been under-qualified. Frequently they made insufficient income to warrant the loan by the old criteria. And because of the location of the property, it made little economic sense to make a loan. If the buyer walked away from the house, the lender would find it difficult or perhaps impossible to resell and recoup the money loaned.

To cope with high-risk borrowers and high-risk property, lenders

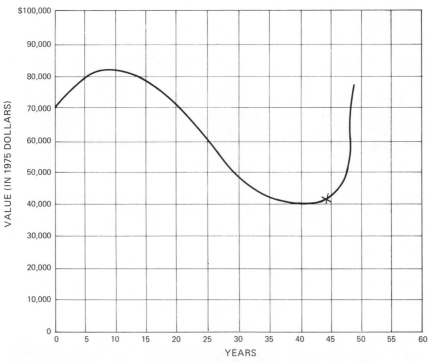

Figure 6–1 Change in value of an older home over a period of fifty years. The "x" indicates where rehabilitation takes place.

[131]

in many cities (often at the urging of the Federal Home Loan Bank Board which regulates savings and loan associations, the largest home lenders) have banded together and formed "mortgage pools." The mortgage pools provide loan money to high-risk borrowers on high-risk property.

Many of these mortgage pools are operated through Neighborhood Housing Services (NHS) started by the Urban Reinvestment Task Force. Currently there are NHS services in operation in dozens of our largest cities across the country with more planned in the near future. (A list of cities with NHS programs is included at the end of this chapter.) When someone with high-risk problems applies to contributing members, they are referred to the service and depending on the degree of risk, loans may be made. In a few cases direct grants have been made. Some lenders in other cities operate such pools independently.

The federal government through HUD has established the Community Development Block Grant Program. Under this program HUD gives cities billions of dollars and the cities then either give loans or grants to individuals and developers concerned with rehabilitating older properties. Since the program is at the local level, it is administered entirely by the cities. The amount of money, eligibility requirements, and method of repayment (if any) vary greatly.

To find out if your city has such a program contact your local urban renewal, housing authority, or homesteading office. They can also tell you if they have any money left in their program or if it's all committed. If you can't get any information there, directly contact HUD, Washington, D.C. 20410, but don't expect to get more than a few helpful hints on where to find money sources. As mentioned, the program is administered entirely on a local level and the Washington office may know very little about what any given city is doing with it.

Searching for a Loan

Alan and Sheila had been renting an apartment in the suburbs. They had been using a local bank and naturally they went there first when applying for a loan. They were immediately turned down.

The loan officer carefully and politely explained that the bank only made loans within a very specific area around each branch (the area is somewhat determined by government rules). Since the bank didn't have a branch near where the new house was, it didn't have any staff prepared to go out and appraise the property. In other words, it wouldn't make the loan. But the loan officer gave them the name of a savings and loan association that was making loans in the area. (Often one lender will be able to refer you to another more likely to make the loan you want.)

Alan and Sheila went to the new lender and found that it would make loans in their neighborhood. But the loan officer pointed out that his institution would only make economically sound loans in that area. In other words, the buyers had to qualify under regular criteria and a fair market appraisal of the house would determine the maximum loan amount.

Sheila said that the asking price had been $32,000 but that they were buying for $30,000. They would also need another $20,000 to cover remodeling work.

The loan officer shook his head. He said that assuming the house appraised for at least $30,000, they wouldn't have any problem getting a conventional 80 percent mortgage for that amount. Getting the other $20,000 would be difficult. But he would see what he could do.

Alan and Sheila took home a loan application and carefully filled it out. They listed all their assets including the $8,000 in the bank. Then they carefully indicated what improvements they intended making. The contractor had told them what items would be best for him to do and what they could easily do. They would do almost all of the tearing out of old plaster, of old plumbing, paneling, and so on. He would handle strengthening any beams, rewiring, replumbing, and putting on a new front. Alan would reduct the house for heating and would install a new furnace. Alan and Sheila would refinish all the wood paneling and floors themselves and do all painting, clean up, and other minor work. The biggest single expense would be the replastering. Alan wanted to do the work, but the contractor had said it was a job strictly for a professional, so Alan agreed to have it hired out. (For additional clues on doing your own remodeling work, check Chapters Seven and Eight.) They included a copy of the contractor's evaluation.

Then they listed those three houses in the neighborhood which had been recently bought and were being renovated. They had found out the purchase prices and put those in as well. Finally they indicated what they felt the house would be worth when it was finished. They took the purchase price and simply added the cost of having the rehabilitation done by a contractor—$30,000 plus $26,000, or $56,000.

They turned in the application, an appraisal was made, and about three weeks later they met again with the loan officer. He said that the property currently did appraise for $30,000. And given his knowledge of the upward trends in the neighborhood (he said he measured this by the fact that people moving in could afford to live elsewhere, if they wanted to. A downward trend would be indicated by people moving in because they couldn't afford to live anywhere else), he felt that their house would be worth at least $56,000 when it was finished. He said his savings and loan association would immediately lend them 80 percent of the purchase price or $24,000 to make the purchase. In addition it would lend them 80 percent of the $56,000 future value (another $20,800), but only as the remodeling work was completed. This seemed perfect and they were elated.

But the bank insisted on two conditions. First, they would have to have all work done by a licensed contractor. Second, they would have to deposit into escrow 20 percent of the $56,000 final value or $11,200. This amount of money, the officer explained, is necessary to show that they are in fact investing $2 for each $8 the lender puts up. $6,000 would be released immediately to make the purchase. The balance would be released as soon as the rehabilitation was completed.

Alan and Sheila pointed out that they only had $8,000 in cash to put up and that would have to take care of all closing costs, which were estimated to be around $1,500. They could only afford to put down about $6,500. They were $3,700 short.

The loan officer sympathized. Alan and Sheila then suggested that what they should do is buy the property and live in it fixing it up a little bit at a time. The loan officer said this was not a good idea for two reasons. The first is that it is almost impossible to live in a house and fix it up at the same time out of money being saved from salary. This process of saving takes a very long period of time, perhaps five years or more. And sitting and looking at work that needs to be done while not being able to afford to do it is distressing and can eventually lead to the remodelers giving up on the entire project.

Second, it is very difficult to go back and arrange for financing a second time. Costs are repeated and lenders are hesitant. They want to know why you didn't borrow enough to complete the job the first time. Did the remodeler miscalculate? If so, that shows a certain inability to handle the project.

Alan and Sheila sought a compromise. Eventually the loan officer agreed that his savings and loan association would release money either to a licensed contractor or to a supplier of materials. In this way Alan and Sheila could buy supplies from the funds to do the work themselves. (See the problems attached to this type of arrangement in Chapter Eight.) The loan officer was adamant about the 20 percent down. He said that it was the lender's policy. He suggested, however, that they contact the city. It had money under the Community Development Block Grant Program.

Sheila and Alan did this. Since it was for home improvement in a distressed area, the city was more than willing to lend them additional money they needed to complete the escrow ($3,700). In addition, the money was at a low interest rate. The city deposited this money with the lender's escrow and Sheila and Alan purchased the house and began rehabilitation.

Not all lenders are as stringent about the 20 percent the buyer must provide. Many will insist on cash down for the purchase price, but will allow the buyers to make up the 20 percent involved in the rehabilitation part of the loan with sweat equity. That is, they can create the equivalent of the money required by improving the property through their own labors.

In other cases it is possible to arrange for the seller to handle the financing. Often the seller will be willing to take back a mortgage at the same or even lower interest rates as a lender and there is less problem (or no problem) qualifying here. A second mortgage would then have to be taken out in order to finance the rehabilitation.

Sheila and Alan quickly learned that the word "rehabilitation" only told half the story. In order to accomplish their goals they had to "restore" the property. This meant returning it to the way it was when new, which turned out to be particularly difficult. Most Victorian-style homes built near the turn of the century were in reality largely prefabricated. The ornate cornices and turned posts, not to mention windows, doors, and some walls were manufactured around the country at different lumber mills. They were sold through catalogues. A builder would pick a cornice from this manufacturer, a window from another and when the material all arrived, would put the house together from often mismatched parts.

Today the materials suppliers no longer exist. Neither does the technology involved in putting together the dissimilar parts. Consequently to restore an old house often means ''stealing'' the missing parts from other houses—a very expensive or even impossible process. Another alternative is to manufacture the parts yourself, but that is even more expensive. Alan and Sheila solved this cost problem by restoring what remained intact in their house and using new material to replace what was gone, always with an eye to keeping the original styling.

It took them eight months but when they finished they were truly pleased. They had two fairly modern bathrooms and a modern kitchen. They also had a Victorian parlor, bedrooms, dining room, hall, and exterior. Their house was enormous by modern standards and exquisite by their own.

While they remodeled they noticed a change in the neighborhood. Other homes were purchased and rehabilitated. There were children playing in the streets where previously people had been concerned to walk for fear of being mugged. And most pleasant of all, they learned that now it cost upwards of $40,000 to buy a run-down house nearby. The changes they had made were helping turn the neighborhood around. More people were choosing that area for the same reasons they had. It was becoming desirable and prices, accordingly, were rising rapidly.

The story of Alan and Sheila's experience is not unique. Today, in fact, it is not even unusual. While actual figures on how many rehabilitations are being done are not available, it must surely run into the tens of thousands. And although this may seem like a drop in the bucket compared to the overall housing needs of the country, it could turn into a tidal wave as more and more families discover the best housing bargain in America today—the rehab.

[136]

Useful Sources of Information

For those interested in rehabilitating older homes the following sources of information may prove useful.

- *The Old House Journal* has been published monthly since October 1973. Individual copy price is $1.50, yearly subscriptions are $12. 199 Berkeley Place, Brooklyn, N.Y. 11217.

  The Old House Journal is filled with information on how to handle the restoration and renovation of old buildings. It frequently gives case histories of what individuals have done and is must reading for anyone involved in rehab work. The journal offers reprints for specific problems such as "Guidelines for Restoring Old Buildings," "Victorian Gardens for Victorian Homes," and "Inspection Checklist for Vintage Houses." These are available for 50 cents each plus postage.

- *The Brownstoner* is published by Back to the City, Inc., 12 East 41 Street, New York, N.Y. 10017. A sample copy will usually be sent if you request it in writing and include postage.

  The Brownstoner gives information on what's happening in the rehabilitation of older brownstone homes in New York and includes some how-to stories. Back to the City sponsors conventions on urban preservation in various cities around the country. Small books on these proceedings may be available in limited quantities for $5 each.

- *The Urban Reinvestment Task Force* helps establish both *Neighborhood Housing Services* (NHS) programs and *Neighborhood Preservation Projects* in cities. The task force has helped set up services in the following cities: NHS of Albuquerque, Inc., Albuquerque, N.Mex.; Grant Park NHS of Atlanta, Inc., Atlanta, Ga.; NHS of Baltimore, Inc., Baltimore, Md.; Boston NHS, Inc., Boston, Mass.; Bridgeport NHS, Inc., Bridgeport, Conn.; NHS of Buffalo, Inc., Buffalo, N.Y.; NHS of Chicago, Inc., Chicago, Ill.; Madisonville Housing Services of NHS, Inc., Cincinnati, Ohio; NHS of Cleveland, Inc., Cleveland, Ohio; NHS of Dallas, Inc., Dallas, Tex.; Hartford NHS, Inc., Hartford, Conn.; Ithaca NHS, Inc., Ithaca, N.Y.; NHS of Jamaica, Inc., Jamaica, N.Y.; NHS of Kansas City, Inc., Kansas City, Mo.; Twin Cities NHS, Inc., Minneapolis/St. Paul, Minn.; Waverly-Bellmont-Hillsboro NHS of Nashville, Nashville, Tenn.; Oakland NHS, Inc., Oakland, Calif.; Philadelphia NHS, Inc., Philadelphia, Pa.; NHS of Phoenix, Inc., Phoenix, Ariz.; NHS of Pittsburgh, Pittsburgh, Pa.; NHS of Racine, Inc., Racine, Wis.; St. Louis Neighborhood Housing Services, Inc., St. Louis, Mo.; San Antonio NHS, Inc., San Antonio, Tex.; Tampa NHS, Inc., Tampa, Fla.; NHS, Inc., Washington, D.C. The Urban Reinvestment Task Force is establishing several dozen more NHS programs in cities across the country. A representative of the task force emphasized that to find out about newly established programs it might be best to contact the head office in Washington, D.C.:

Urban Reinvestment Task Force
1120 19 Street, N.W.
Suite 600
Washington, D.C. 20036

• *The National Association of Home Builders,* 15 and M Streets, N.W., Washington, D.C. 20005

The National Association of Home Builders (NAHB) is primarily a trade group catering to the needs of builders. It has recently initiated a new renovation section that may provide some help to individuals seeking to revitalize older homes. They have issued a booklet entitled

How to Choose a Reputable Remodeler, and can probably steer you toward reputable remodelers in your area. (It might be better to first contact the local NAHB affiliate.)

- *The National Association of Remodelers,* 50 East 42 Street, New York, N.Y. 10017

This is also a trade group serving remodelers. Like the NAHB it may be able to steer you to a reputable remodeler in your area. (Once again, it's probably best to check the phone book for a local affiliate.)

SEVEN

Should You Add On to What You Already Have?

Most American families already own homes. Yet for one reason or another, a family will decide its current housing is inadequate. They will go out looking for something else. An inquisitive family will check out new and used homes as well as alternatives we've already considered. Perhaps when they get through with their investigation, however, their response will be to come back, look lovingly at their old house and say, "It's not that bad."

If the motive for making a move is strong, some sort of change must be made. At this juncture the homeowner commonly investigates the possibility of adding on to the current home. Undoubtedly he or she has heard that as expensive as adding on may be, it is far cheaper than buying something new. And many owners are convinced, often for no good reason, that by putting an addition onto their house they can increase their property's value far and above the cost of the addition.

I have some neighbors who own their house. Recently they went out looking to buy a new or used home. I happened to be in the front yard when they returned. The wife got out of the car, looked lovingly at their house and said, "It's not that bad." The husband replied, "A mighty fine house all right."

I inquired about how their house-hunting went. "Terrible," was the reply. "Everything is much too expensive. We think we'll be better off staying where we are and perhaps just adding on."

This is frequently the process that leads to the decision to add on. Homeowners check out the cost of moving (that is, of substituting their house for another) and are appalled. They return home thankful for what they have. But for one reason or another what they have is inadequate, or else they wouldn't have been looking for something else in the first place. Consequently some change must be accomplished in their housing situation and an addition is considered.

At this point, many owners are convinced, often for no good reason, that an addition can increase their home's value far above the cost of putting it up. "Why move when we can add on and make a profit (on paper) at the same time?" goes the usual argument.

It is true that adding a room can solve some housing problems. Perhaps it can solve yours. It is also true that a room addition can be cheaper than buying something new. After all, when you add on to what you already have you don't need to buy land for the addition. You already own it, purchased with your present house at yesterday's low prices. You will not, however, necessarily make money on the addition or even break even. And an addition will not necessarily solve your basic housing problem. Actually, the cost versus return aspect and the motive aspect for adding on should be kept separate, initially, in order to see if an addition will be right for you. Let's consider motive first.

Will Adding On Solve Your Problem?

Recently I conducted a small survey of twenty-seven families who added on to their homes. Admittedly this is a very small group, yet I was not out to establish statistical proof, but rather to get some idea of the motives people had for enlarging their present homes and to see just how satisfied these families were once they had made the changes. The results are shown in Table 7-1.

In this table the number of families having a particular motive is listed immediately next to the motive. Next whether or not they were satisfied with the addition is noted. And finally, the number of families that moved anyway within one year of completing the addition is given.

The results may be helpful to you if you are contemplating adding on. More than half of those questioned in this small survey indicated

TABLE 7-1
Typical Motives for Adding On to an Existing Home

Motive for adding on	Satisfied	Not satisfied	Moved anyway within one year
Need a bigger house (16)	12	4	5
Don't like the neighborhood (5)		5	5
Need a change (4)	1	3	2
Want a better school for children (3)	—	3	2
Totals	13	15	14

they were *not* satisfied with the addition and more than half moved within one year.

Does this mean that an addition is not a good idea? It depends on your motives. The most common motive given was the desire to have a bigger house. Of those who wanted a bigger house, twelve out of sixteen were satisfied with their decision to add on. Only four were not and, incidentally, those were the families that moved. Of those who didn't like the neighborhood, *none* were satisfied with their addition and all moved! The case is nearly the same for those who said they "wanted my children in a better school district." For those who "needed a change," it's inconclusive.

While drawing conclusions from such a small sample is risky, the results nonetheless seem to indicate that if your motive for change is *external,* that is, you're unhappy with the schools or the neighborhood, you'll probably be best off simply moving. Adding on will mean trying to hide your real reason for wanting change and true motives, like oil in water, eventually tend to rise to the surface.

But if you're satisfied with the external things and simply need more room, by all means consider an addition.

If you have a good motive for adding on, the second question to ask is whether it makes good economic sense. Does a person who adds on to an existing house lose money when it's time to sell? Do they break even? Or is there profit to be made here?

A great deal depends on the house you are adding to, the

neighborhood, and the cost of the addition in comparison to the cost of the house. We'll consider these in a moment. Certain rules of thumb may be used for all types of add-ons in all locations in today's market.

Rules for Getting Your Money Back When Adding On

In general, you will probably not get out the money you put into an addition when it's time to sell if you simply improve the quality of your house without changing its size. If, for example, you put expensive hardwood paneling in the living room, or a connecting door between two bedrooms, or very expensive carpeting throughout—you probably will receive back fewer dollars than you put in. This rule, however, must be qualified. If your house has torn or shabby carpeting or badly worn wood floors or a cracked tile floor, it may be necessary to replace the flooring in order to get the full market value of the house. If this replacement is done with materials suitable to the quality of the house you can usually get your full money's worth back at sale time. The same holds true for modernizing an old-fashioned or decayed bathroom or kitchen. Putting $500 into a badly deteriorated kitchen on a $50,000 house will probably return at least that much on the sales price. Putting $5,000 into the same kitchen probably won't.

(The National Remodeler's Association, a trade organization, has rated the various additions one can add to a house indicating which they feel will bring back the greatest and the smallest return at selling time. Their address is 50 East 42 Street, New York, New York 10017.)

In general you stand the best chance of getting back dollar for dollar if you add to the size of the house. In years past most home buyers were looking for quality—quality kitchens, baths, living rooms, etc. But in today's market with the high cost of building putting space at a premium, buyers tend to look for size. Add an extra bedroom or a family room and it does increase sharply the value of your house. Buyers who have shopped around for a while pretty well know what they can get in both existing and new housing on a per-square-foot basis. When you increase the square

[143]

footage in your home you automatically increase its value in their eyes.

You probably won't get all your money back if you hire someone to do all the work. I've heard the story about a family that hires someone to add a $10,000 room to their $60,000 house. When it's finished and they go to sell, they find the house is worth $75,000. "We've made $5,000 profit on the addition!" they boast.

Probably not. The real question is how much would the house have gone up in value if the addition had not been made? If it would have gone up $7,000 anyway, they actually lost $2,000 by adding on the room. Table 7-2 presents this comparison.

The problem is that the cost of hiring labor is very high. When this is added to the high cost of materials, it is very difficult to get back out the money you stick in. If you do some or all the work yourself, the cost of the addition can frequently be cut substantially from what it would cost to have a contractor do the whole job. Owners who add on in this fashion frequently not only get back dollar for dollar when it's time to sell, but make a profit.

You won't get your money back if you overbuild for your neighborhood. This rule should be cut out and pasted to the set of plans every owner uses for an addition. It is cast in stone. It is immutable. It is one rule not to break.

Neighborhood

Neighborhood influence has everything to do with the *market value* (MV) of your property. Market value is a term used frequently in real estate to simply indicate the price at which a house, given proper exposure to buyers, a willing seller, and stable economic conditions

TABLE 7-2

	With addition	Without
Sales price	$75,000	$67,000
Less cost of addition	10,000	
	$65,000	$67,000

can be expected to sell for in a reasonable amount of time. When adding on, you must be concerned with two market values: the current market value of your home and the projected one after your project is completed. Figuring a break-even point is simple. The projected market value must be as high as all the costs involved in the addition *plus* the current market value. That is to say, once you've found out how much your house is currently worth ($50,000), your estimated value after the addition ($70,000) must be equal to all the costs involved (maximum costs to the break-even point are $20,000).

All this may seem quite simpleminded, but the number of families who plunge into an addition without making this calculation carefully is astonishing.

All right, then how do we determine market value?

In real estate the market value of residential property is almost always determined by the comparison method. This simply means that in order to find out how much one house is worth, find several others like it that have sold recently and their average price is the value of the house in question. This comparison method is used by your tax assessor, by your agent when he or she advises you what price you should list for, and by a lender when determining the value and the amount it will loan on your property. (Note: This method is not used by your fire and hazard insurer. The cost of replacement is used instead.)

You can easily use it yourself, particularly if you live in a tract or other suburban area where homes tend.to be similar (not custom built). Check with an agent to find the recent selling price of homes like yours. Most agents hoping to get a listing will gladly give you this information, particularly since they usually have it handy from their Multiple Listing Service books.

You may or may not be surprised at the market value of your home depending on how aware you are of the real estate market. In a rising market people tend to overestimate their home's worth. In a static market they guess too low. So don't guess at all, but take the time to check it out.

Once you've found your present market value, an easy task, you must now find your future market value: how much your house will be worth with the addition, a much more difficult task. At first glance it may seem that all you have to do is add the cost of the addition to the current market value and there you have it. This, unfortunately, doesn't take into account the importance of the neighborhood.

Put yourself for a moment in the place of a home buyer. If you had $80,000 to spend (an adequate down payment plus the ability to obtain a suitable loan for the balance), would you look in a neighborhood where the homes were generally selling for $50,000? Or would you look in what is probably considered a more exclusive $80,000 neighborhood? If you were a typical buyer, you would search in the more expensive neighborhood. It is a fact of life in real estate that buyers buy neighborhoods before they buy homes.

Consequently, you as a seller would be faced with trying to dispose of an $80,000 investment in an area where buyers are looking for $50,000 homes. The neighborhood will influence the value of your home, in this case, by dragging it down. In order to sell you'll undoubtedly have to lower your price. In an extreme case, particularly in a neighborhood that is blighted or otherwise considered undesirable by home buyers, you could add $30,000 to a $50,000 house and still be able to sell for only $50,000!

A word of caution: Don't dismiss neighborhood influence, thinking that by doing a good job on the addition, by using better materials, a more clever design, or a high-powered sales agent you can overcome it. The difference that all these factors make is minute compared to the difference the neighborhood makes. In some exclusive areas people will literally pay fortunes for shacks, just to be able to say they live there. In other areas huge homes, usually older but still able to give good service as we saw in the last chapter, go begging because of the neighborhood's bad reputation.

How then does one determine the exact neighborhood influence on the future market value? Again we must resort to the comparison method.

Assume you are planning to add a family room to your house. You take the time to go around the neighborhood and see how many other owners have added family rooms or other rooms of any kind, and also, if possible, you find out if any of these homes have sold recently. If they have, your task will come to a quick conclusion. By checking with brokers or if necessary with the current homeowners, try to find out (1) how many square feet were added in the addition, (2) what area of the house was added to (whether bathroom, kitchen, family room, or bedroom), and (3) what the selling price was. You may be able to find out all of these things on a recent sale from a broker who happens to have kept the old listing sheet.

Now compare the addition that was made with what you plan. If the other house added a family room and you plan to add one, your comparison is easy. It may be more difficult to compare your planned living room expansion with an added on bedroom and a bath. In such a case you'll have to make a decision as to whether the situation is similar to yours or so unlike it as to make a comparison impossible.

Assuming that the addition was made in a manner similar to yours, find out the selling price and subtract from it what you know is the current market price for your home. (If your homes are really similar, your market price is what the other home would have sold for without the addition.) Now divide the number of square feet into the difference and you have the per-foot increase in value due to the addition. If the market value is $50,000 and the sales price was $60,000, divide the difference, $10,000, by the square footage, say 300 square feet, and you find out that each foot that was added onto the house increased its value by approximately $33.

In some neighborhoods I have seen, nearly every other house has made a similar addition. Often the original homes only had three bedrooms and nearly everyone added a fourth. In other cases the living area was small and nearly everyone added a family room. Comparisons then are plentiful and a homeowner can quickly acquire three or four comparables.

If it turns out that on the average an addition adds say $30 or more per square foot to the house and you can accurately estimate (see the next section) that your costs will only be $20 a square foot, it's easy to see that there's profit to be made here.

On the other hand, if the addition only adds $15 a square foot and your costs are $20 a foot, you might want to reconsider.

When Comparables Can't Be Found in a Tract Area

In most cases comparisons such as the one just illustrated are difficult to make for there are few comparables nearby. In fact, if you drive around your neighborhood (assuming all the homes are similar) and you see that no additions or almost none have been made, you might consider scrapping the entire idea of adding on. An addition to your property would be unique and in order to get back even the money you put in, you would probably have to have a unique buyer. When it comes time to sell, you don't want to go looking for that one buyer in a thousand who has your exact tastes. You want to appeal to as many potential buyers as possible.

Assuming that there is an occasional addition here and there in your neighborhood, say at least one for every ten houses, I have found Table 7–3 helpful as a rule of thumb. To use this table you simply figure out what percent of the current value the addition will cost, and then read across to how much the addition will actually add to the property's value. If a home costs $50,000 and an addition expected to cost 10 percent or $5,000 is contemplated, it can be expected that on sale the seller will receive back at least an additional $5,000. Table 7-4 shows how Table 7-3 applies at other levels for a $50,000 house.

You will immediately notice that while additions costing a small amount of money add at least dollar for dollar to the value of the house, additions costing a large amount add less and less to the house's value. In fact at a certain point around $60,000 for this house

TABLE 7-3
Calculating How Much of the Cost of the Addition Can Be Returned Upon Sale of the House

Cost of addition in comparison to current market value (MV)	Anticipated return on sale
10%	100%
15	90
20	80
25	75
30	70
35	65
40	60
45	55
50	50

TABLE 7-4
Application of Table 7-3 to a House with a Present Market Value (MV) of $50,000

Cost of addition	Anticipated return of cost of addition upon sale of house	Sales price (future MV)
$ 5,000	100%	$55,000
7,500	90	56,500
10,000	80	58,000
12,500	75	59,120
15,000	70	60,500
17,500	65	61,375
20,000	60	62,000
22,500	55	62,375
25,000	50	62,500

we reach a kind of maximum price that a buyer will pay for a home in the area regardless of almost any kind of addition that is made.

From these two tables, the principle of *overbuilding* should be abundantly clear. Regardless of how much you sink into an addition beyond a certain point, your chances of getting your money out let alone making a profit diminish for each additional dollar you spend. If you're in a tract area of $50,000 homes, you'll get $50,000 buyers. They may be willing to spend a little bit more for a bigger house, but not enough more to make an addition worthwhile.

There is another category (in addition to the tract areas we've been discussing), and that is custom homes. If you live in a suburb where each home is distinct, possibly built by different builders at different times *and* your area is considered highly desirable by buyers (not blighted, relatively crime free, with a good record of increasing values), almost any addition you make up to 50 percent of your house's value will get you back at least dollar for each dollar spent . . . and probably a lot more. The custom home area is where neighborhood influence works to your best advantage.

Neighborhood influence, therefore, works against you the more similar your house is to surrounding homes, provided others haven't already made additions. It works for you the more distinct each house in your area is from its neighbors. If you are in a tract, be careful and investigate thoroughly before adding on. If you've got a custom home in a good area, on the other hand, don't hesitate too much—you're a prime candidate for a profitable addition.

The Bottom Line—Does It Pay To Add On?

As we've seen, if you like the neighborhood but simply want a bigger house, if you can do some or all the work yourself, if you don't overbuild—then you probably can get back dollar for dollar what you put into an addition. If you're careful, make intelligent choices, and have a little bit of luck, you may even make a profit. An addition here would be a good idea for you.

On the other hand, if you like the neighborhood and simply want a bigger house but you hire a contractor to do all the work, you overbuild just a little and you can't get back all the money you stick into an addition when it's time to sell—it may still be a good idea to add on! Although this may sound a bit illogical, it does make perfectly good sense. Consider an addition from another viewpoint—substitution.

The inescapable fact is that you have to live somewhere. Chances are that if you already own a home, particularly if you've owned it for some time, the payments even with the costs of the addition will be less than the payments on a new home. The same may be true of the taxes. And finally, when you go out and compare new homes or other existing homes with the same square footage as your home with the addition, you may find that to buy an acceptable substitute costs as much or more than the amount you can sell your existing home for. It may be less expensive even if you lose a little money on the addition (on paper) to simply keep your added on house than to substitute for another. If the addition was made wisely and fulfills your needs, you, presumably, won't want to move anyway.

Finally, even if you did the work yourself cheaply and you didn't overbuild so that you can get back dollar for dollar invested, *but* you don't like the neighborhood or some other external factor, it probably would be a mistake to add on. If your motive for moving remains just as strong after the addition, as before, chances are you won't be satisfied with your work and you'll move eventually anyway. If that's the case, don't add-on; move, now.

I have heard arguments that even in this last situation, an addition makes good sense. After all, if you do all the work yourself, add on wisely, when it comes time to sell you can get back more than you put in—you can make a profit.

Perhaps, but look at it this way. Most contractors charge roughly half labor and half materials. If your time is at least as valuable as the workpeople who build additions, then (assuming you did all the work yourself) to just break even on labor your addition would have to return $2 on each $1 in materials invested. To make a profit you'd have to do even better. I can tell you from experience that very few additions can return that kind of money.

Should you add on to your existing home? Ask yourself first, why are you really dissatisfied with your home the way it is?

EIGHT

How To Build a Successful Addition

Once you've decided you want to add on but before you go to the bother of plans and getting bids that we'll discuss in a moment, you'd best prepare yourself to face the elements. There will be days when the wind comes whistling through an opening where your dining room wall used to be. When an unexpected rain in June stains some of your bedroom furniture because the roof above has been removed. When a worker pouring cement in the backyard walks across your living room carpet with cement-covered boots on the way to your bathroom.

And there will be emotional strains as well. The roofers have sworn to show up early Saturday to finish the shingles. Saturday dawns bright and clear and quiet. There is not a sound of hammering. Nor on Sunday. For no reason and without explanation workers simply don't appear.

Or you've promised you'll be at the wedding of your sister's daughter but your husband hasn't finished soldering water pipes and he says he can't leave until they're done. Or a thousand other inconveniences that occur when you're living in a half-finished home.

If you can take it all in good spirits, then you're ready to begin a project that can really be fun.

The Ugly Duckling

When creating an addition to a house, you should take into consideration the tastes of at least two parties other than yourself: the potential buyer when you go to sell and the lender who will make the sale possible. If you never intend to sell, then you need only be concerned with pleasing yourself. But even this, as many home adders-on have found out, is more difficult than it first appears.

Pleasing a potential buyer means creating an addition that nearly everyone would find pleasant to look at and enjoyable to live in. It means being conservative in your approach. If you add a bedroom, you don't add unusual angles or forget to put in closets. If it's a new master bedroom, you spend the time and money to also add a master bathroom (people today expect a bath off the master bedroom). If it's to be a new kitchen, you're very careful not to add it onto the back of the garage (where the plumbing happens inconveniently to be located) because a future buyer won't buy with an "outhouse" kitchen. And so forth.

Pleasing the potential lender is much the same. If you add a family room which can only be reached by walking through the garage, even if you find a willing buyer you may find lenders are unwilling to loan as much as you need to make a sale. They may figure, and rightly so, that if they are ever forced to foreclose, they'll have a real problem in finding another buyer crazy enough to like such an arrangement.

Pleasing oneself means making the addition suit your own very personal tastes and your needs (in terms of size, type of room added, and so on). Please all three and you have a successful addition.

Sound simple? It isn't.

To understand the problems involved, let's consider for a moment a profession far removed from home building, but in several important aspects much like it—that of a magazine design or layout artist. It is an unusual profession and most people outside of the business are unaware it exists. This person doesn't usually draw, sketch, or otherwise do what we would normally consider artwork. Yet, he or she is still an artist. The layout artist's major function is to take all the material for a story, such as photos, headlines, captions, and body type and *arrange* them on the page according to a predetermined style. That is laying out or designing a page.

[153]

Easy? Try it sometime. On any given page of almost any magazine there may be from one to ten photos and a lot of typewritten material including the headlines and captions. (There are hundreds, possibly thousands of different styles in which the type itself can be set. This book, for example, is set in Garamond.) The type can be set in bold or italic, in sans serif or serif, large or small. The photos can be blown up or reduced, cropped tight, cropped large, or left uncropped. In a color spread there is the need to decide what colors to use and where, in the background, in the photos, in the type.

And now do it in the dark! You see, the layout artist isn't able to blow up, reduce, or print the type. The job is only to specify what is to be done, and other people—typesetters, paste-up artists, and printers—do the work. The layout artist normally never sees anything more than the original hodgepodge of type and photos handed over by the editors, until the page is finally printed often weeks later and certainly far too late to make any adjustments or changes. But that is the nature of the art. This design or layout artist transforms all the primitive elements into a finished product by using just imagination, and then tells other workers how to get it done. No small accomplishment.

How does the layout artist do this? There is certainly talent involved, but far more important this artist, first as an apprentice and later as an art director has done the job so many hundreds, even thousands of times that he or she knows in advance what doing this, adding that, changing something else will look like when it is finally finished.

But we aren't really concerned with layout artists here; we're concerned with an addition. The similarities may already have become apparent. Like a layout artist, the person responsible for creating an addition must take all the basic elements—the existing house; the desire for a new room or two; the need for windows, doors, closets, plumbing, electrical and heating outlets; the style of construction (should it be the same or different)—and find a pleasant arrangement.

If you're the average person planning to add on and do the original design work yourself, the odds are far and away against your coming up with a successful plan. The reason is that even if you have the necessary talent, you haven't done it enough times to know how something you have in your mind will come out in the finished product. You need a skilled professional to do the arranging or design. If you were putting out a magazine, you'd call upon a layout artist. For a house, you need an architect, and a good one.

I've taken some time to get to this point, but I feel it is sufficiently important to warrant the effort. The final design concept includes where your addition will be located, what it will be, and how it will look. It is the most important aspect of your addition. If you plan to sell, as most people eventually do, this concept will determine how much you'll get, how easy it will be to find a buyer, and whether or not a lender will go along with the resulting price.

Of course, architects don't come cheap. It can easily cost $300 to $500 to have one do a design concept (perhaps not even a set of plans) even if it is done in the architect's spare time on a free-lance basis. But it's worth it, for a good concept will return dollar for dollar and more on the money invested in it. Most people who add on have very limited budgets and plan to skimp here and there and possibly do much of the work themselves. If you have to skimp, skimp on the framing, on the cement work, do the roof yourself, do the electrical work (where permitted) and plumbing yourself (the easiest of all jobs involved in additions!), but don't skimp on the design concept or on the finishing work, drywall taping, texturing, or outside final plastering, for these are the areas where it shows.

One final word should be said here about engaging the services of a general contractor who agrees to come up with a working set of plans as part of the job at no additional cost to you. Beware! If the contractor has done several hundred additions, has a good sense of design, and has someone with architectural talents on staff, the set of plans that you are given may be worth their weight in gold. It's been my experience, however, that too often general contractors have a series of standard plans for additions and that's all they build. You tell them you want a new kitchen or another bathroom and they don't take pains to create special plans to suit your needs and house. They just take out a standard plan, make a few adjustments and . . . instant plans which look to you for all the world as if they were created specially for your job.

Homeowners wanting a successful addition shouldn't want this. If you don't know of a contractor who treats each assignment as unique or if you don't trust the judgment of the contractor you talk to, you should get an architect. Get one who will come to the house, look it

[155]

over, and then talk to you. The architect then has enough information to create a design especially for your house and to draw up a set of plans, hopefully for the same price.

Not too long ago some friends of mine, Jeffrey and Ann, decided to add a family room to their house. Jeff has some basic drafting knowledge and so decided to skip both the architect and the builder with standard plans, preferring to do the design himself.

The set of plans he came up with was of sufficient quality that the city building department passed it and the workers could use it without any major problems. It called for converting his present garage into a family room and then building a new garage in front of his house. (A two-car enclosed garage was required by his city.) He figured on saving a considerable amount of money since the cost of garage construction was cheaper than the cost of house construction.

He didn't take into consideration several things. First, the cost of converting the old garage (cutting windows, putting in additional roof supports as required by the city, converting the old large garage door opening into a more conventional sliding glass door) ate up most of the money he saved in construction. Second, when he was finished his house looked as though it had two garages, one in front of the other. People driving down the street would often slow down and look again, puzzled at why someone would build two garages for one house.

This is not to say that all garage conversions are bad or that you will be unsuccessful doing the design yourself. It is to say that if you're inexperienced, you may not know you've done a poor job until you have finished and it's too late.

One final word of caution while you are still in the design stage. In construction work, everything is done in a standard way. For example, in most areas of the country studs (the tall boards that support the walls) are set 16 inches apart on centers. You can call for them closer together or further apart as local building codes permit, but if you do you raise the cost of construction. Why? Because the insulation that goes between the studs is made to fit at roughly 15 inches wide. You have to get specially cut and usually more costly insulation if you deviate from the standard size. Drywall (Sheetrock) which is commonly nailed onto the studs as the inside wall material usually comes in 8-, 12-, and 16-foot lengths, and in 4-foot widths. These are all multiples of 16 inches (16 × 3 = 48 inches or 4 feet). If you make your studs other than 16 inches apart you will have to make special cuts in the drywall resulting in increased costs in hanging and taping (finishing the wall). Similar problems can occur on the outside wall with lathing materials.

The distance between studs is but one example of the standard way things are done in construction. Other examples are making walls at right angles (90°, not 70° or 35°), having ceilings 8 feet high, doors 82 inches high, and so on endlessly. If you want to keep costs at a minimum, don't design anything out of the ordinary. It won't cost just a little bit more to make your addition different. It will cost a whole lot more.

This applies to adding features as well as just varying sizes and shapes. A freestanding fireplace in the center of a room can cost 2 or 3 times more than a conventional ready-made wall model. A cathedral ceiling (it doesn't really look like a cathedral, it's just in the same "A" shape) will probably cost 2½ times as much as a conventional flat ceiling. It's something to keep in mind when your wife says she wants the whole ceiling to be glass or your husband wants a special workroom built right onto the den.

The High Price of Everything

Once you've got a suitable design, you should find out in advance what it will really cost to transform it into an addition. This can be a very discouraging process. The costs of building materials and labor go up daily and they are already sky-high. Nevertheless, you shouldn't be daunted by the high prices and give up getting estimates. Sometimes people will make a few inquiries and say to themselves, "Oh, I know I can get it done cheaper than that. I'll wait until I reach that stage of the building and worry then." Bad mistake. Plan it all out in advance as though you were getting ready to fight the critical battle of a war.

Show a general contractor your design concept and/or plans, including a description of the kind of materials you want. Are your glass "sliders" going to be standard aluminum or upgraded gold anodized? Will you have inexpensive pine molding painted the color of the room or more expensive hardwood molding stained to your specifications? In a kitchen or bath, exactly what brand of appliances and what quality will you want? You can find the prices and available styles of these items fairly easily by yourself by spending a few hours at building supply stores. Builders can also suggest catalogues through which the materials you want can be ordered by mail and delivered directly to you, although freight charges can be expensive for heavy items. Keep one thing in mind: If *you* buy, the chances are you'll be purchasing at retail. A contractor buys at wholesale. It is possible for you to buy for less by taking advantage of closeout sales, going to auctions advertised in local papers, and checking at discount stores, if you have the time. Get a bid for the total cost of construction from the contractor.

A word about bids is in order here. A bid is merely an estimate, a statement of opinion. If it's in writing and signed by the contractor, then it's a written estimate or opinion. It's still a guess. If the contractor gets two-thirds through with the job and realizes the estimate was grossly underbid, that the opinion was wrong and it's going to cost a lot more to finish, the contractor can do one of two things: go ahead and finish at the original bid taking the loss (a great many contractors who take pride in themselves and their work will do this), or the contractor can tell you the guess was wrong and that it's going to cost more and won't be finished unless you come up with the extra money.

Now the ball is in your court. You can yell and complain, which will most likely do you no good; you can pay the extra amount, which will do your pocketbook no good; or you can try to force the contractor to complete at the original price (which will probably only do wonders for your lawyer's pocketbook). Only if your original bid is in the form of a contract which provides for damages in the event of noncompletion as agreed upon and if the contractor puts up a bond to back up the agreement are you likely to quickly and easily either get the work done as agreed or get enough money back to have it done by someone else. Most contractors, however, won't go along with this or, if they do, will charge so much for the job that you won't want to use them. The point of this discussion is to emphasize that the bid is just a guess. Hopefully it's an educated guess, but don't stack the success of your whole project on it.

It is a good idea to always get bids from at least three different contractors. It's surprising how much they may differ and besides, they may give you valuable clues along the way on how to get this or that done better and cheaper.

If you're going to hire a general contractor, don't be afraid to take the lowest bid but be sure you get references. Find out what the contractor has built recently and who it was built for, then don't hesitate to call up these people and ask their opinion of the work. Most reliable contractors can give you a list pages long to call and are very pleased to have you do it for they take pride in their work.

If you're going to subcontract the work yourself (see the next chapter for clues on doing much of the work yourself), then you'll have to go through the above process with each subcontractor. Here's a list of subcontractors you're likely to need in the order you'll need them.

1. Concrete

2. Framing

3. Electrical*

4. Plumbing

5. Heating (sheet metal)

6. Insulating

7. Plaster (stucco)

8. Drywall (including hanging and taping)

9. Finishing

10. Painting

Your job may also require more specialized subcontractors, such as steel workers or tile masons. It's a good idea to follow the same three bid procedures for *each one.*

For whatever work you plan to do yourself or to hire subcontractors to do, you'll need accurate quotes on the cost of lumber and other materials. This will involve going to lumber and roofing yards,

*If electrical and plumbing work is to be laid inside the concrete, then these subcontractors work before the framing is done. Otherwise they only come afterward.

electrical and plumbing supply houses, and so on. If you happen to have a friend who has a contractor's license who is willing to buy the materials for you, you often can get dramatic reductions from the retail prices (mostly on products other than wood).

The price of materials will fluctuate often from one day to the next. When there's a lot of construction in an area, prices naturally tend to go up. In a slack period they tend to go down. The services of workers will also vary greatly (unless you're working through subcontractors, in which case you will probably be bound into a union wage scale). Workers who free-lance small jobs will usually charge what the market bears. If there is a lot of work, they'll be hard to find and it will cost you a premium to hire them. If it's winter and jobs are few and far between, you may get the work done at a cut-rate price.

Whenever you figure the cost of work and materials, always keep in mind that the figures are generally good only for a few weeks. A month later and they could be significantly higher or lower.

Making the Final Decision

Once you have the cost figures and know what the present and future market values of your house are, you are almost in a position to decide whether to go ahead with your addition or to scrap it. Another bit of information has to be obtained before the answer can be reached, and that has to do with the money you will need to complete the work.

In general, labor and materials must be paid for as the work is completed and as materials are delivered. On occasion it is possible to arrange credit with a lumber yard or other supplier, but normally not for more than thirty days. It is unusual to arrange credit with workers unless they're personal friends.

When paying for labor and materials, you the home builder are not in the driver's seat that you may think you are. If you don't pay for work and materials, nearly every state provides for the use by laborers and suppliers of "mechanic's liens." These are legally binding documents that can effectively tie up the title to your property and prevent you from selling, refinancing, or otherwise disposing of your house. They are to be taken quite seriously and great care should be exercised to avoid them. This means that you normally can't get away with refusing to pay, in some cases, even if you are unsatisfied with the craftsmanship or materials.

When I am having construction done I always write "full and final payment" on my checks and get a "release" or statement from all workers and suppliers indicating that they have been fully paid. If they should then try to put a mechanic's lien on my property I am in a position to have it removed once the matter gets to court.

What this means is that you'll need *all* the money to complete the project either before you start or as soon as any given segment is done. Assuming you don't have a rich uncle or a big bank account there are three ways to get it, all involving mortgaging.

Home Improvement Loan

The first is the home improvement loan which banks and savings and loan associations spend lots of time and money advertising. These loans, according to much of the literature I have seen, purport to be designed to help families add on to their present housing at minimum expense. In my experience most of these loans are for high interest rates and short periods of time, and carry with them restrictions that can make it almost impossible for you to get the work done cheaply. Let's take an example.

The Petersons wanted to add another bedroom and bathroom to their home. As shown in Table 8-1, they figured their present market value at $60,000, their future market value at $75,000, and the cost of the addition at $10,000. They stood to make a profit of $5,000 if their figures were correct.

TABLE 8-1
Determining Profit from Market Value

Present MV	$60,000
Future MV	75,000
Increased value	$15,000
Cost of addition	10,000
Profit	$ 5,000

When they went to their local savings and loan association they were told they could obtain a home improvement loan for the exact amount of their costs ($10,000). The loan would be in the form of a second mortgage on their property for ten years bearing interest at 13 percent a year payable at $150 a month. In addition the money would be given to them only as they supplied bills for completed work from licensed contractors. To be sure the Petersons got the right contractors, the savings and loan association required that they get three bids and submit each so that the lender could make the final choice on who would do the work. When the checks were finally issued, they would be in both the Petersons' and the contractors' names. Both would have to sign to release the money. They were told that this was the way most home improvement loans were handled.

This type of loan has several obvious disadvantages for the Petersons. First, it is only for the $10,000 that the construction is estimated to cost, not for the full $15,000 that the addition will add to the value of the property. Second, if they figured wrong and the addition costs more, they have no money margin for error. They would have to make up the difference from savings or from another loan, which might be very difficult to arrange. Third, besides the high interest rate (13 percent compared to perhaps 9 percent for a first mortgage) and the shorter term (ten years as opposed to thirty years for a first mortgage), the second mortgage offered by the lender has an elaborate payment system that requires the Petersons to use only licensed contractors and then will pay out money only upon submission of bills for work completed or materials supplied. If our couple has the opportunity to save money by paying a worker in cash instead of by check (as is often the case), they can't take advantage of it. If they find they can hire a lather (who prepares the outside of the house for stucco) directly for $100 instead of going through a licensed contractor who will hire the same lather to do the same work but will charge $200, they can't take advantage of this savings either.

The disadvantages are caused by the fact that the lender is in reality giving them a "construction loan" and calling it a "home improvement loan." A construction loan, in the trade, is given for the purpose of allowing a builder to put up new construction on bare land. It allows that construction to serve as collateral for the loan.

For example, when a foundation is poured at a cost of $2,500, the property has been improved and the lender issues a check for $2,500. The foundation serves as the collateral. When the framing has been done at a cost of another $2,500, the property has been improved to the tune of $5,000 and the bank feels confident in releasing an additional amount of money. And so on.

In home improvements, however, in most cases the new construction *need not* stand as collateral for the loan. With the rise in values over recent years, the existing home itself can stand for the full collateral and if it does, two different and far more advantageous loans can be obtained.

Refinancing

Stan and Linda also wanted to add on to their house. They lived in the same tract as the Petersons and their similar addition would also cost $10,000. They also figured their present value at $60,000 and their future value at $75,000.

But Linda and Stan knew they already had considerable equity in their house. They had bought it three years earlier for $42,000 and they had a $32,000 first mortgage. If they were correct in their assessment that their home was worth $60,000, then a lender should be willing to give them 80 percent of its value (see Chapter Two on financing) or up to $48,000.

Without looking for a home improvement loan, they went to a bank and asked about refinancing their home. When the bank examined the property, it agreed with their figures and offered them a new first mortgage. It would refinance the entire property (pay off the old mortgage) for thirty years at 9 percent interest payable at $386 a month. Since the payments on their current first mortgage were $260, the increase in payments was only $126 a month—in return for $16,000 in cash! (The Petersons paid $150 a month for only $10,000 on their home improvement loan.)

In addition, the money would be given to them up front and with no strings attached as soon as the mortgage papers were signed. They could spend it as they wished either on contractors or directly on workers. The bank didn't even care if they didn't spend any of it on the addition at all! Stan and Linda were careful, however, to give the alteration as the reason they wanted the money so the bank couldn't later say it hadn't been informed of their plans.

Stan and Linda went ahead with the addition, which cost them $10,000. When they were done they drew up a value sheet (Table 8-2) to show what they had accomplished.

They now had a new addition, but their equity in the building had gone down $1,000. They also had an extra $6,000 in their pockets, as shown in Table 8-3.

Even deducting the $1,000 in lost equity from the $6,000 in cash, they still came up with a $5,000 profit. They had almost their exact same old equity, a brand new addition, and their profit out of their house in cash! They figured they had done pretty well.

Is this to say that it is always better to refinance and get a new first mortgage than to get a new second mortgage? No, not at all. Thus far we've only considered a second mortgage that had home improvement conditions tied to it.

"No-Strings" Second Mortgages

There are no-strings second mortgages available. You can get these from lenders such as banks, some mortgage companies, credit unions, and occasionally from private individuals who advertise for borrowers in local papers. Just as in refinancing, the lender is only concerned that you have enough equity in the property to justify the mortgage. What you do with the money, as with a new first mortgage, is your own business. Interest rates on these loans, like home-improvement second mortgages, are still much higher than for first mortgages. They are in the 12 to 15 percent range at this writing.

TABLE 8-2
Figuring Values for Addition

Old MV	$60,000
Old first mortgage	32,000
Old equity	$28,000
New MV	$75,000
New mortgage	48,000
New equity	$27,000

TABLE 8-3
Cash Left after Addition

New mortgage	$48,000
Old mortgage	32,000
Cash	$16,000
Less cost of addition	10,000
Cash left	$ 6,000

How do you tell which is better: to get a no-strings second mortgage or to refinance a new first? This question can only be answered by comparing the two types.

Costs of Getting New Loans

When refinancing a new first, the costs are essentially the same as when buying a house. There are mortgage points to pay, title insurance, escrow charges, and so on (see Chapter Two for a more complete list). On a new loan of $25,000, 1½ points is $375. Escrow, title charges, and other costs can quickly swell the figure to $1,000. There is often a penalty for paying off the old loan before it's due. This prepayment penalty can run 2 percent of the loan balance or six months' interest. On a $20,000 existing balance at 7 percent interest, this could be $500 or more. Thus the cost of refinancing a first can run $1,500 or more, regardless of the amount of the loan.

There are also costs of getting a new second mortgage of any kind, but they are usually much lower. There are normally no points to pay (although some lenders require a discount on the mortgage which amounts to the same thing). An abbreviated title insurance policy may be obtained at a reduced cost. The lender, if it's a bank or similar institution, will often run the escrow itself, again at a savings. Because the total amount of the loan is much less and many of the costs are tied to this total, costs will be lower. If refinancing a $20,000 existing mortgage, obtaining a new $25,000 mortgage, and netting $5,000 cash costs $1,500, then a second mortgage for the $5,000 will probably cost closer to $500.

[165]

There are ways to reduce refinancing costs. Very often if you get the new loan from the same lender that made the old one, the lender will waive all prepayment penalties (if the new loan's interest rate is as high or higher than the old, which has been true in recent years). In addition, by going to the same lender you may achieve some of the benefits of getting a second mortgage. The lender may run the escrow and accept a shortened title insurance policy. Costs of $1,500 can be reduced in this manner down to $1,000 or less.

Keeping the Old Low Interest Rate Mortgage

The interest rate on the existing mortgage is another consideration. Many homeowners purchased their houses when interest rates were much lower than they are today. When you refinance you pay off the existing mortgage and lose that old interest rate. If you simply get a new second mortgage, you leave the existing first on the property and continue to receive the benefits of the old interest rate. Whether or not to keep the existing first depends upon the old interest rate, the new interest rate, and the amount of money you need to borrow compared to what you currently owe.

Comparing Refinancing with a New Second Mortgage

Stan and Linda have a cousin who needs to get $3,000 in order to do some minor remodeling. The cousin has an existing first mortgage of $20,000 on her home (the original balance was $25,000) at 5.5 percent interest. Table 8-4 shows what her costs would be both for refinancing and for a no-strings second mortgage.

From this example it should be readily apparent that it would be to the cousin's advantage to get a second mortgage and keep the existing low interest first. The advantages include: lower monthly payments, lower costs in obtaining the loan, and a shorter repayment period for the borrowed money (ten years as opposed to thirty).

If the interest rate on the first mortgage were higher, or if she wanted to borrow more money in relation to the money already owed (in this case $3,000 to $20,000), the figures could swing the

TABLE 8-4
Refinancing versus Getting a New Second Mortgage*
Borrower Needs $3,000

	Years to repay	Amount of loan	Monthly payments	
			Refinancing	New second
New first at 9.5%	30	$24,000	$201	
New second at 13%	10	3,500		$ 52
Existing first at 5.5%	originally			
	30	20,000		142
Totals			$201	$194

* We are assuming that the cost of getting the refinancing will be $1,000 and of getting the second $500. These amounts are added to the loans.

other way. Which all goes to show that each case is different and must be considered on its own merits.

Table 8-5 can help you decide which would be best for you. It shows the monthly payments for loans of different sizes and repayment periods.

Using your present home as collateral instead of taking a construction loan only works if your equity is high enough to cover the mortgage. The way prices have jumped in the last few years, it probably is.

Money for an addition, then, can be arranged in a convenient manner by shopping around for the correct financing. Before you get involved in a home improvement loan be sure you investigate refinancing and no-strings second mortgages.

Now that you've arranged your financing, are you finally ready to begin your addition? You've got the correct cost figures, you've estimated present and future market value, and everything seems all right. But before you begin there's one last consideration. Check out brand new houses. Go see a builder and find out if you can't buy a brand new house for the same total monthly payments that you will be paying after your addition is made. This last bit of research will convince you that you are either making the right move or just being foolish.

The last time I added on to a house, which was within a few months of this writing, I found that the cost of the addition was

TABLE 8-5
Monthly Payments for Each $1,000 You Borrow

To use this table to figure the monthly cost of a mortgage,
find the number corresponding to the years of repayment
and the interest rate for your loan, and multiply that by
the number of thousands of dollars you would borrow.
(The answer will be very close, but not exact.)

Interest rate (%)	Years of Repayment			
	5	10	25	30
5	$18.87	$10.61	$ 5.85	$ 5.37
5.5	19.10	10.86	6.15	5.68
6	19.33	11.11	6.45	6.00
6.5	19.56	11.36	6.76	6.33
7	19.80	11.62	7.07	6.66
7.5	20.04	11.88	7.39	7.00
8	20.28	12.14	7.72	7.34
8.5	20.52	12.40	8.06	7.69
9	20.76	12.67	8.40	8.05
9.5	21.00	12.94	8.74	8.41
10	21.25	13.22	9.09	8.78
10.5	21.49	13.49	9.44	9.15
11	21.74	13.78	9.80	9.52
11.5	21.99	14.06	10.16	9.90
12	22.25	14.35	10.53	10.29
12.5	22.50	14.64	10.90	10.67
13	22.75	14.93	11.28	11.06
13.5	23.01	15.23	11.66	11.45
14	23.27	15.53	12.04	11.85
14.5	23.53	15.83	12.42	12.25
15	23.79	16.13	12.80	12.65

roughly $23 a square foot. This compared to roughly $32 a square foot for new construction. For new construction I also would have paid for land at today's high prices. By adding on I used land I already owned and had paid for at yesterday's low prices.

I began construction confident that I was making the correct move.

Solving an Add-On Problem

Here's a typical addition problem that was solved by a good design. Sarah and John decided after living in their house for a few years that the living area was too small. While the four bedrooms were adequate for their three children, there were no dining or family rooms. A quick glance at the floor plan in Figure 8-1 reveals that the house's living area consisted of only a living room, kitchen, and eating space.

Sarah wanted a formal dining room while John wanted a family room or den where he could romp with the kids. So they went out to look at both new and existing homes. They quickly found that they couldn't afford to move up. They reasoned that their best alternative was to add on the space they needed and to do it as cheaply as possible.

Trying to save money, John decided that he would draw a few

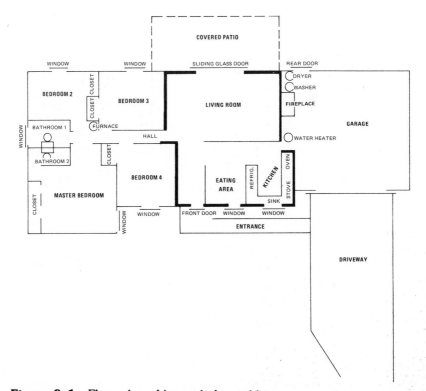

Figure 8–1   Floor plan of house before addition.

[169]

sketches of what they wanted and then have a part-time draftsman friend (who said he would do their plans for free) finish them. He concluded that the cheapest way to construct an addition would be to convert the garage.

Sarah pointed out several drawbacks to this, telling him, "The only entrance is from the kitchen, That's all right for the dining room, but how do you get to the family room?"

John considered this and decided that he would cut a new entrance through the living room wall next to the fireplace. He would cut another opening in the back of the fireplace and it would serve both rooms. It would mean moving the washer and dryer or the water heater, at additional expense, but it couldn't be helped. He gave the sketches to Fred, the draftsman, who drew up plans and estimated the job would cost about $6,000 (see Figure 8-2).

When John took the plans to the city building department he met

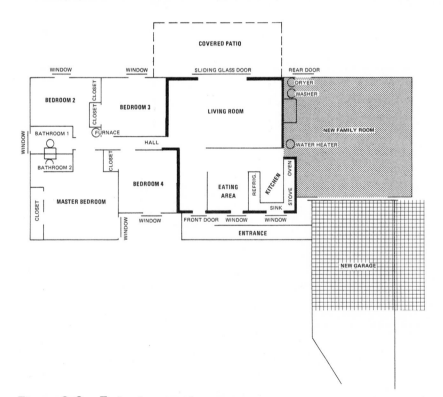

Figure 8–2. Trying to convert garage.

some resistance. He was told that he couldn't cut a new hole in an existing fireplace. The fireplace had to originally have been designed with two openings. He would have to completely tear down the old one and put in a new one. John decided he would leave the fireplace as it was without an opening into the family room. It would look awkward, but it was cheaper. The building department had no further objections.

Only slightly daunted, John moved on to the planning department. Here he was told that while it was perfectly all right to convert the old garage, he would have to build a new one to take its place. John said he planned to add a carport. He was told that wasn't good enough. The city required a two-car *enclosed* garage. John agreed, unhappily.

Then the planning department clerk pulled out a plot map showing the location of John and Sarah's property. John indicated where their house was and the clerk asked, "How far is it from the street?"

John had measured it just that morning to get plans drawn for a carport. "Thirty-seven feet," he answered.

"Can't put a garage there," the clerk replied. "You need 40 feet. There's a 20-foot setback and the code requires garages to be a minimum of 20 feet deep." The clerk explained a setback was the minimum distance allowed between the house and the street.

"Can you put it on the side of the house?" the clerk suggested.

"I only have 5 feet on one side and 15 on the other. The building department said any car area had to be 18 feet wide."

"Then you can't add a garage," the clerk concluded. The clerk said it was possible to get a "variance" allowing them to build with only 37 feet, but they would have to petition the planning commission, a process taking several months. And once their petition was heard, it was unlikely it would be granted since it would make their house stick far out in front of any others on the block—an eyesore. John went home.

Sarah took the plans back to Fred the draftsman and wanted to know how he could have made such a blunder. After all, he was supposed to know city requirements. Fred apologized and said the problem was easily solved. Simply move the new garage 3 feet back into the old one. That would give them the 40 feet they needed and make their new dining and family room only slightly smaller.

[171]

This time Sarah took the plans to the planning commission. They were quickly approved. Smelling victory, she took them back to the building department for final approval. They were turned down. In order to build the new garage 3 feet into the wall, they'd have to sink a new foundation and put a fireproof wall between the two garages. It wasn't shown on the plans. Back she went to see Fred.

This time he didn't have such an easy solution. To do the required work would greatly add to the price. Fred figured the cost now would be above $10,000. Sarah gave up on the garage idea, and on Fred.

Frustrated in their plans to add on, Sarah and John considered instead changing the use of one of their bedrooms. Perhaps they could convert a bedroom to a dining or family room? Perhaps their third or fourth bedroom could have a new doorway put in making it part of the living room or eating area, John suggested (Figure 8-3).

Sarah pointed out the drawbacks to such a plan. They needed all the bedrooms they had for their children, and both the third and fourth bedrooms were too small. John had to agree. He hadn't been too excited about the plan anyway, but he pointed out it would have been cheap.

Next John suggested that perhaps what they should do is convert their existing patio into a new room. It certainly would be quite large enough and shouldn't be too difficult to do (see Figure 8-4). Sarah agreed it would be large, but wouldn't provide a dining area for her. John argued they'd have to compromise—she just wouldn't get the dining area she wanted. Reluctantly Sarah agreed.

John took the idea back to Fred. Sarah wouldn't have anything to do with him. Fred drew up the plans.

When John took them down to the city, the planning commission quickly agreed. But the building department did not. "You can't simply put a room on top of an old patio because the patio doesn't have a proper foundation," John was told. Because his property was on "expansive" soil, which stretched and shrunk with rainfall, he would have to put a footing $2^1/2$ feet deep and 1 foot wide all around the perimeter of the new room. The footing would have to be made out of concrete and steel. To do it he'd have to entirely tear out the existing patio. John immediately saw that it would be very expensive.

He was aghast. He complained, "Why should I have to do so

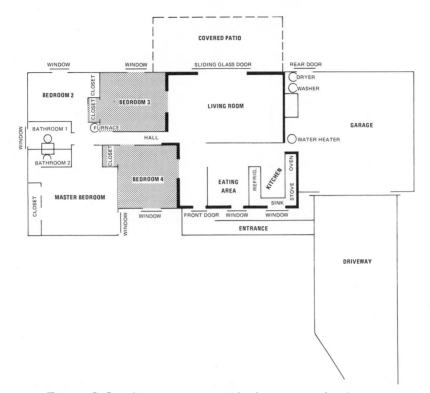

Figure 8–3. Attempt to convert bedrooms to a family area.

much work at the back of my house when I wasn't required to do it when adding a garage to the front?"

"You weren't?" the building department woman asked.

John happened to have his first set of plans with him and took them out and showed them to her.

"Oh," she commented, "you forgot to show your footings here. You'd be required to put these same footings in wherever you added on to your home. The person you originally talked to must have forgotten to point that out, but we would have caught it the first time we inspected the property. You couldn't do it anyway," the woman pointed out, "because the way you have it there the new room completely blocks off any light coming into the existing living room and according to code, every room must have some window area except baths and halls."

[173]

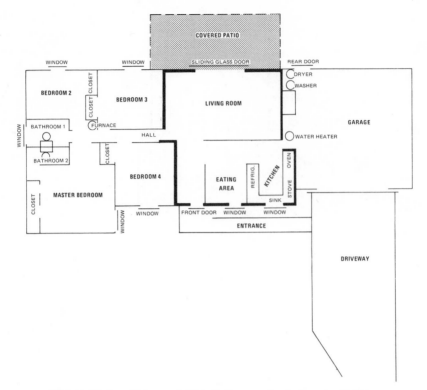

Figure 8–4. Using existing patio as a basis for an addition.

John took his plans back and told Sarah they just couldn't add on. There was no way to do it.

Sarah looked at the plans and said, "We've tried to add on to three sides of the present living area, what about the fourth?" John asked her what she meant and she drew a sketch putting the new family room in front of the house (Figure 8-5).

"You see," Sarah said, "this way we can have a dining room close to the kitchen as well as a family room."

John had to agree it had possibilities so they talked it over further.

There were certain problems. They would need a new entrance to the house and it would be on one side of the family room—admittedly awkward. Also the new room would cut off all light from the existing eating area and make the kitchen very dark. And John wasn't at all sure the planning commission would allow him to put such a structure in front because he still had to maintain a 20-foot

[174]

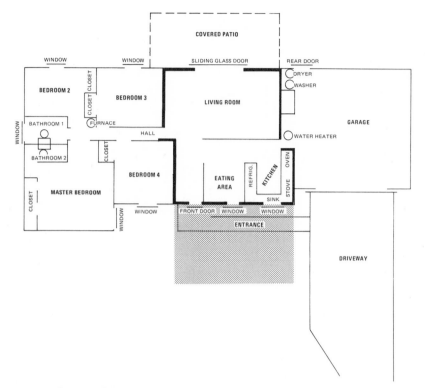

Figure 8–5. Putting the addition in front of the house.

setback. To do that would severely limit the size of the new room. Both Sarah and John decided to drop the idea of putting the addition at the front.

"Why not go up?" John finally suggested. "How do you mean?" Sarah asked.

"Let's put the new room on top of the existing living room." John drew up a detailed sketch himself (by now he too had given up on Fred) and back they both went to the city. The results (Figure 8-6) were discouraging.

The helpful woman at the building department pointed out that indeed it was possible to build up, but it would be costly. She said she wasn't supposed to quote figures, but she guessed it would cost upward of $20,000 by the time they got through reframing and bolstering the bottom room in preparation for the top room.

Sarah and John were about to give up in despair. It seemed

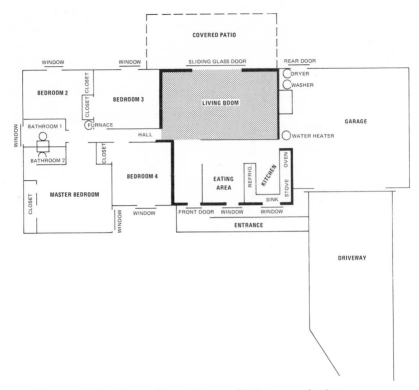

Figure 8–6. Expanding with an addition over the living room.

hopeless. Then Sarah suggested they consult an architect. John pointed out it would be expensive, but Sarah pointed out they didn't have any other choice.

The fee was $350 and the architect, after talking with them and visiting their house, came up with the design shown in Figure 8-7.

"That's crazy," was John's initial reaction and Sarah was puzzled as well. They pointed out that the new design covered up two-thirds of the existing sliding glass door entry from the present living room, more than half the existing patio, and the rear door from the garage. "And what kind of a room would it be?" Sarah demanded. "There's no dining room there."

The architect pointed out the advantage of his design: the new addition would be strictly a family room, but it would be huge—18 × 20 feet, or roughly the size of their garage and far larger than their present living room. A dining alcove would be made at the far end of

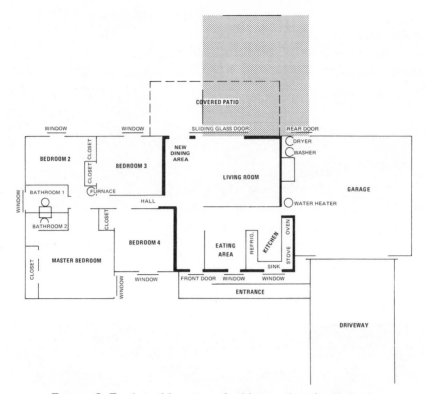

Figure 8–7 Actual location of addition when finally built.

the present living room with a box window added to the wall next to it. This window would be large enough to meet city requirements for lighting and ventilation for the room. In addition, part of the existing patio could be saved and if they wished a new patio could be added at the rear of the addition. The architect's plans called for a cathedral ceiling of exposed spruce and pine and two large sliding glass doors in the room, one leading to the existing patio and one out the back.

"But it looks so awkward," John commented.

"It seems to be just tacked on," Sarah added.

"That's how it looks on the plans. Take my word for it. When it's built, it will be outstanding," the architect replied.

They did. Sarah and John received a set of plans from the architect and took them to the planning and building departments where they were approved without comment. They hired a contractor to pour the cement foundation and a worker to help John construct the

[177]

Figure 8-8 Exterior of home addition nearing completion. Existing portion of home is at right center. Room with patio and cover jutting forward was added on.

Figure 8-9. Interior of home addition after completion with some furniture already in place. Note cathedral ceiling constructed by owners who had no previous building experience.

framing. John did the electrical work (see the discussion in Chapter Nine on licensed work and safety) and a little plumbing and put on the roof himself. They hired other workers to stucco the outside and finish the inside.

Working weekends and evenings, it took them a little less than six weeks to complete the job. The results are shown in Figures 8-8 and 8-9. Total cost of the job? Including the architect's fee, $6,800! The final room was 360 square feet, which worked out to a little under $19 a square foot. Of course the price would have been much higher had John and Sarah not done much of the work themselves.

This addition was actually constructed as recorded here in the city of Thousand Oaks, California, in the summer of 1977.

NINE

How To Build Your Own Home Using 100 Percent Financing

A visit to Gunnar's house is a bit of an adventure. It is a strikingly unusual home with tall beam ceilings, Italian ceramic tile floors, solid wood paneling and even a loft suspended above a huge family room. The home is fairly large and quite comfortable and the owner, an up and coming artist, uses the loft as his studio. A visitor cannot help but comment on the pleasantness of the design and the richness with which it was carried out.

Gunnar enjoys such comments and always points to this wall or that window and describes why it was built a certain way or placed in a certain location. For Gunnar both designed and built the house he and his wife and two sons live in. It is their dream home—exactly what they want in a house. While they don't believe they'll live in it forever, they can foresee no reason why they should move. If you pry a little bit, Gunnar will eventually admit that the best thing about their house is the fact that it was unbelievably cheap.

Gunnar's house, located in northern California, has a market value of about $100,000. Gunnar points out, however, that it only cost him about $30,000 to build and another $30,000 for the lot and finishing done to it.

Gunnar has what he wants in housing, but he didn't use the services of a magician to get it. The $60,000 he paid was a terrific strain on the family income, but the sacrifices were made. It would have been impossible for him, as he points out, to buy an already built home in his neighborhood with a $100,000 price tag. He and his wife have a combined income of around $24,000, making a $60,000 home their maximum. "It was worth the strain," he says. "because I got exactly what I wanted."

We can't all be as fortunate as Gunnar. Or can we? For those of us with the desire and the ability to do the work ourselves it is possible to save an enormous amount of money on home construction. While building your own home may not be the proper answer for you, it is certainly an alternative worth seriously considering.

A great deal of serious inward searching should be done regarding your construction abilities. If your goal, at least in large part, is to save money, then you must do a vast proportion of the work yourself. If you can't (or won't) do this work, then don't build. If you have to hire others to do everything, chances are it will cost more for you to construct a house than to buy one already built by a developer.

How do you know if you're the house builder type? Here's a quick test you can take that will give an indication.

Test

In your present home or apartment:

1. Do you fix the washer in the faucet when it leaks, or do you call someone else?

2. When you were younger (or even today), did you tune your own car?

3. Would you seriously consider building a wooden playhouse for children?

4. If a light switch in the wall of your kitchen breaks, do you know how to fix it?

5. If you had to hammer five nails into a piece of wood, are you confident you could get them all in straight?

6. Are you free of any back problems or other physical

impairments that would keep you from doing hard labor?

7. As a child did you build tree houses or other things with wood?

8. When you buy a bike or toy for a child that needs to be assembled, do you pay little attention to the instructions and immediately know how to put it together?

9. Do you like working with your hands?

10. Do others think of you as handy?

If you can truthfully answer yes to all these questions, you are probably the kind of person who is basically a builder by nature. If you missed a couple of the questions, perhaps you already know you're not the builder type. For you, while you might still be successful at building, chances are it will be a difficult and unenjoyable procedure. And since it involves a great financial and emotional commitment on the part of your whole family, you'd better seriously consider whether saving money on a house is worth risking divorce and an ulcer.

Safety and Licensed Work

Before you pick up a hammer and begin pounding the first nail you should weigh the most important consideration of building anything by yourself—safety. Will what you erect be as safe as what a licensed contractor would build?

It's a tough question. Some city and state governments have answered it for the do-it-yourselfer by requiring that certain work such as electrical, plumbing, and gas be done only by licensed workers. Other local building and safety departments require the do-it-yourselfer to sign a statement that he or she will live in the house for at least one year after doing any such work. I suppose the theory is that you won't build anything unsafe that you're going to live in. Other building departments require the owner to sign a statement that if he or she is going to do any electrical, plumbing, gas, or whatever work, then no licensed mechanic may be hired to do any other part of the job unless special insurance to protect the mechanic is provided. (The safety of the worker seems of more consequence here than the building.)

While these restrictions by various government jurisdictions indicate concern over work done by inexperienced and unlicensed people (be sure and check with your local building and safety department to see what the requirements in your area are), they don't really answer the question of how safe is something which you yourself build?

I can't answer that question either. Only you can.

Building authorities do usually insist on inspection privileges. They will approve plans and then come out at various stages of construction to see that the work is being done in a proper fashion. But most building authorities are overworked and understaffed and my experience has been that very often inspectors give only the most cursory inspections. Bad work (both by do-it-yourselfers and licensed contractors) often goes unnoticed.

The question remains the same, can you build a room or a house in a proper and safe fashion? Again, only you can answer that question.

Many aids are available. Large bookstores carry local building code books. There are also many technical manuals on construction available at bookstores and libraries. Sometimes it is possible to obtain the services of a retired carpenter, plumber, or other worker to help you in your project. Many of these people advertise for part-time work in local papers.

There is no guarantee that a licensed contractor will do any better job than you, even though licensing usually assures you that the person has passed tests on competency in construction techniques and building codes. In my experiences using licensed contractors, skilled helpers, and doing my own work, I've found that licensed contractors are outstanding in one area only. They seem to know exactly the *minimum* in construction materials and labor that is required to pass building and safety inspections.

It still all comes down to whether or not you can do a safe and competent job. If you can't, if you think you can't, if you're worried that you can't, then you shouldn't do any of the work yourself but should hire licensed mechanics to do it all.

Finding a Temporary House

If you are convinced you can do the work, you will have to decide where you will live while you're doing it. Remember, during the construction period, anywhere from six to twenty-four months, you'll need to pay interest on your construction loan plus payments on any mortgage that you have on the lot. This could take up that portion of your income that you normally set aside for shelter. Yet you can't live in your new house until it's finished. This problem is compounded in many cases by the fact that people may need to sell an existing home to get the cash to start construction work. You could be temporarily without a house.

The typical answer to this is to buy a small mobile home and temporarily place it on the building site. The mobile home can be financed and sold when you're done with it, so that all you're out is the money spent on setting it up and taking it down plus depreciation (if any). This means that you and your family could end up living in smaller and less convenient quarters for quite some time, another thing to consider before deciding to build.

Finding the Right Lot

People buy areas before they buy homes. As we pointed out earlier, if you can't afford your dream house, more likely than not the reason is that it is located in a high-priced neighborhood. When you consider building, you don't have the option of buying lots in a wide variety of areas. You are limited to finding a lot in a neighborhood where you want to live. Choice lots, those in the good suburban areas, are quickly disappearing and finding what you want will be no easy task. In many tract areas every piece of land has been built upon and unless a home burns down, no lots are available.

Whether you end up commuting from farther out in the suburbs or you chance upon an empty lot closer in, you will probably find some land suitable for building. Let's assume you've identified the neighborhood you want and you've discovered that there are several lots available. When you ask the prices, you may get a real jolt. As noted earlier, the high cost of suburban homes is due in large part to the skyrocketing cost of land. Lots which five years ago sold for $7,500, today can sell for $50,000 and more.

A typical example of the dramatic increase in prices occurred in northwestern Los Angeles in the mid-1970s. The price of homes in one area, all of which are custom built, went from an average of $55,000 in 1974 to about $95,000 in 1977. That was an increase of $40,000 or about 70 percent in just three years. This same area had a great many lots available, perhaps one lot for every ten houses. As shown in Table 9-1, during the same period the average price of lots went from $15,000 (in 1974) to $40,000 (in 1977), an increase of $25,000 or 166 percent. Of the $40,000 total increase in price during the three years, more than half, $25,000, was a direct increase in the value of the land.

What this table indicates is that while the cost of the buildings increased substantially (about 12 percent a year, close to the inflation rate for building costs), the price of land increased much more, about 50 percent a year. A person buying in this area would save little by constructing a house since the major cause of the high price of homes is the cost of land.

Unfortunately this example tends to be far closer to the rule than the exception. In order to save a significant amount of money by building a home yourself, you must be able to buy the land for the home at a low price. Simply planning to scrimp and save on construction costs will not help enough if you're paying too dearly for the lot.

How does one get land cheaply? In the area we've just been describing, ideally you would have bought the land back in 1974 when it sold for only $15,000 a lot. But assuming you didn't and that you can't find a seller foolish enough to sell for much less than the going rate, you may not be able to buy where you want. In our example, a buyer who can't afford to spend $40,000 for a lot (we'll see in a moment how many of these lot purchases are financed) simply can't build there.

[185]

TABLE 9-1
Comparison of Appreciation Between House and Land

	1974 price	1977 price	Increase	%
House	$40,000	$55,000	$15,000	38
Land	15,000	40,000	25,000	166
Total	$55,000	$95,000	$40,000	70

So what do you do if you're not in the $40,000 a lot category? My suggestion is that you look in other than dream neighborhoods. Perhaps closer in or farther out there are areas that (as Alan and Sheila found in Chapter Six) offer a reasonably priced alternative. If everyone wants to live on the west side of the city, for example, there may be some very beautiful pockets on the east side that are largely overlooked and provide the kind of neighborhood you want at a lot price you can afford. Some economists refer to this as the principle of "contrariness." To get the best buy, go to an area that's currently out of demand. Then if and when it ever becomes in demand, you'll stand to make the most profit.

Calculating What You Can Save by Building Yourself

Going back to our example in northwestern Los Angeles, we find that it cost about $30 a square foot for a builder to erect a house at the time. (Prices for construction vary dramatically from one part of the country to another. Be sure you check with builders in your area for the current price.) For how much cheaper than this can you reasonably expect to build?

It happened that in this area there were quite a number of individuals who were building their own homes. I contacted many of them and picked three who are representative.

Harry worked full-time as a dealer representative for a rug manufacturing company. He was an extremely strong, physical person and felt he could build anything. When it came time to build his own house, he determined he would do the work entirely himself. And he did. He built the frames and poured the concrete (hiring only a finisher to smooth it out). He did all the framing, all the electrical, plumbing, and heating work, and he put on his own roof. The only other job he hired out was stuccoing the outside of his house and texturing the inside walls. He built his home for $16 a square foot! Harry not only saved money on labor, but also on materials. He rented a truck and drove to Oregon where lumber was cheap and hauled back all he needed. He bought everything either on sale or at prices reduced because the goods were "seconds."

Another home builder, Alan, worked for the local telephone company. He too was physical and considered himself a builder by nature. He did much of the work himself, but he hired workers to do the heavy job of pouring concrete. He also hired someone to put up his roof, hang his inside drywall, and put up the outside of his building. Like Harry he made an effort to get his materials cheaply, although he did not go to Oregon for the wood. Alan's price per square foot was about $23.

Jake was a pharmacist and he liked working with his hands. But he was basically no builder. He liked drawing up plans and showing people where things went, but he tended to get bogged down when it came time to do anything. He intended to do the framing himself, but after spending a week of his vacation at it he had only put up three walls. He gave up and hired someone to do the job. In fact he hired contractors to do every job except the painting, which he and his wife did. While he tried to buy his materials cheaply, he usually didn't want to bargain and so ended up paying retail. His home cost him an unbelievable $45 a square foot!

Harry, Alan, and Jake all built homes of about 2,000 square feet. But the cost of building looked like this:

	Cost per square foot	Final cost
Average building cost in the area	$30	$60,000
Harry's house	16	32,000
Alan's house	23	46,000
Jake's house	45	90,000

*From these examples it should be apparent that how much
money you save depends on how much work you do yourself
and how ingenious you are at getting materials at low prices.*

There is one other factor that we have not yet discussed—time. It
took free-spending Jake less than six months to complete his home.
Alan took about thirteen months, while thrifty Harry had just
finished at this writing after more than two years of effort. It costs
money to go fast. If you want to get good buys, you have to wait for
material to be on sale and for labor to be off-season.

Other Costs

We've talked about the cost of the lot and the cost of construction.
There are a few other costs that need to be mentioned. The first is
the cost of preparing the lot for building. This involves clearing,
leveling, and grading a building site; building a road or at least a
driveway to the house; bringing in sewer and utility lines; erecting
support walls on hillside lots, and whatever other problems may be
unique to your lot. Since every piece of property is different, it is
impossible to give a figure for this cost. It could be only $1,000 if a
street is nearby, utilities are available, the lot is level, and so on. Or
it could be tens of thousands for more adverse conditions. We will
arbitrarily assume a figure of $3,000 for lot preparation from here on.

Another cost arises if the city or other local government requires
that you pay to bring sewer lines to the street in front of your house
(this is different from the lot preparation cost of hooking up these
lines). Often this can be in the form of a bond if you don't want to
come up with cash. There is a trend toward requiring builders to pay
a fee to the city ranging from several hundred to a thousand dollars
for the privilege of building. This fee goes into a fund to provide for
new schools, recreational facilities, and so on. There may be
additional incidental fees of this sort.

Finally there will be the cost of permits (which could run into
several hundred dollars), of soil and environmental reports (which
could range from a few hundred to thousands), and of financing. This
last, which we will deal with extensively in a moment, includes the
interest you'll pay on the money borrowed to build your home while
you're not yet living in it.

All these potential costs in buying and preparing a lot should serve to make a purchaser wary. Before you leap in and get entangled in expensive and unexpected expense, it would be wise to get the assistance of a specialist, someone who does this sort of work regularly and can give you instant information about the problems you are likely to run into for your particular lot.

There are several people who will fit the bill. A contractor whom you may use to do some work and who has had experience in such matters can be invaluable. The architect who drew up your plans may be able to help. For a relatively small fee you can acquire the services of a local engineering firm for a few hours. A conversation with a civil or structural engineer can be shockingly enlightening and might save you from making a ghastly mistake.

Financing the Self-Built Home

Thus far we've seen that leverage plays a big role in real estate purchases. While this is true for the purchase of a completed home and for financing an addition, unfortunately it is not true for purchasing a bare lot.

In real estate the property is the collateral for the loan. To be more specific, the major part of the collateral is the *improved* property, that is, the house on it. Unimproved property, such as a lot, is considered very poor collateral. The reason is that a lender, in the event of a foreclosure, is much more likely to be able to dispose of a house than a lot. For every lot buyer there are hundreds of finished home buyers.

Consequently you cannot easily get an 80 percent or higher loan on a lot. In fact many institutional lenders (banks and savings and loan associations) will not loan any money at all on lots. If they do, they'll normally loan only a small percentage of the appraised value—perhaps 50 percent or on rare occasions as high as 70 percent.

This means that when you go shopping for a lot you had best be prepared to come up with a sizable amount of cash yourself. How much? That depends on what other kinds of financing you can obtain.

The owner of a lot may be willing to carry back the mortgage. This means that rather than having to look for a separate lender, the seller

[189]

will be the lender. Sellers will do it because it's often the only way they can sell their lots. They may be in a position to do it (currently own their land free and clear) because they bought years earlier at a much lower price than they are selling it for.

Typically a seller may want 25 percent down and be willing to carry the balance in the form of a mortgage for a short period of time—usually one year and rarely more than five years. Occasionally sellers want 29 percent down with the balance paid over several years. This is so they can take advantage of tax laws which permit them to declare only the profit they actually receive rather than the profit on the whole purchase price, provided they receive no more than 30 percent the first year, the remainder is amortized, and other conditions are met (see your accountant or attorney).

On a $40,000 lot this means that if the seller were willing to carry back 75 percent, you would have to come up with $10,000 immediately (plus closing costs, see Chapter Two) to purchase the land.

If you make such a purchase you could be in deep trouble. Once you start to build, you'll need a construction loan. As discussed in the last chapter, this is a short-term loan in which the lender releases the money as the work is completed, with the building serving as collateral. Almost all lending institutions, however, will only offer a construction mortgage if it is the "first loan" on the property. If you've already given the owner of the land a mortgage to make the lot purchase, that becomes a first loan and you have made it impossible to get a construction loan until you've paid off the existing first $30,000 balance.

It is worthwhile to take a few moments here to discuss the order of loans on property and what is meant by a "first," "second," and "third" mortgage. It all has to do with foreclosure, which is the taking back of the collateral in the event the borrower fails to live up to the terms of the loan, that is, fails to make the monthly payments.

When a lender gives a borrower a mortgage on a piece of property, the documents that give evidence of that loan, often called security instruments (either mortgage papers or trust deed and note depending on the area of the country), are exposed to the public so that at least for legal purposes all people may be aware of their existence. This is accomplished by recording them at a county or township recorder's office. It is called giving *constructive notice.*

Constructive notice serves several important functions, not the smallest of which is to document exactly when the mortgage was placed on the property, the date, and in many cases the time. These are integral parts of the recording procedure. The reason is that the documents recorded *first* have priority over those recorded later. (There are exceptions to this, such as mechanics and tax liens, but we need not concern ourselves with them here.) In the case of mortgages, if a property has three mortgages on it, the one recorded first is called the "first" mortgage, that recorded second is the "second" mortgage, and so on.

Why is this order of recording so critical? As we mentioned, it has to do with foreclosure and collateral. If an individual borrows money on the same property several times and has several mortgages, say a first, second, and third, and then does not keep up the monthly payments, in order to recover the loaned money all three lenders must foreclose (take back the property) and then sell it. At the time of the sale, when the collateral is sold for cash, that cash is paid back to the lenders in the *order* in which the mortgages were recorded. The first mortgage is paid back first. If there is any money left, the second is paid off, and so with the third and any subsequent mortgages. If a piece of property has a first for $10,000, a second for $10,000, and a third for $10,000 and at foreclosure is sold for $15,000, this means that the first mortgage lender takes the first $10,000, the second mortgage lender takes $5,000, and the third mortgage lender gets nothing! (In some cases a deficiency judgment for money not recovered from the sale may be obtained.)

It's easy to see that the most secure instrument is a first mortgage and that's why banks and savings and loans normally insist on these for new construction.

How do you get loans both from the owner of the lot and from a lending institution that insists on a first mortgage? (There can't be two firsts.) There are two basic solutions. The best for you as the builder is probably the *subordinated second mortgage.*

The idea behind this document is really the essence of simplicity. What you are doing is offering the landowner a second mortgage for the $30,000 instead of a first. Admittedly this is not as secure a position for the landowner, but you sweeten the offer by making the second last for only one year (or as long as you expect it will take construction to be completed), and you also agree that the owner has the right to approve any first mortgage you take out and that in the event you don't make payments on the first mortgage construction loan, the landowner has the right to make the payments, foreclose on the second, and take the property back. (This affords the second mortgage holder additional protection.)

There only remains the problem of the order of recording the mortgages. Presumably the mortgage you give the landowner will occur in time before the mortgage you give the bank and we just said the order in which they are recorded makes a loan first or second. The answer is a subordination clause. This is a clause included in the mortgage you give the *landowner* that in effect says that although it was recorded first, as soon as you record a construction loan, the landowner's loan legally will revert to a second mortgage. It will be *subordinate* to the first. To protect the landowner, he or she will usually insist that a clause be inserted that this only be done one time.

In the 1950s and early 1960s this was the usual way that developers bought property from farmers. Developers sometimes abused this method and abandoned half-built tracts, leaving the landowner with the task of taking over dozens of first mortgages (often an overwhelming financial burden). The method is used much less often today. With individual lots and a private party builder it is still possible to use it. To execute the documents properly, you and the landowner should use the services of an attorney. Lawyers who specialize in real estate work may already have such documents prepared and may charge no more than a nominal fee for filling them out.

In areas where demand is high and property is sold very quickly, landowners may refuse to take a subordinated second. Why should they bother with an inferior loan position when they have an excellent chance of selling the property to someone else for cash?

In a case like this your best bet may be to borrow the money to pay off the lot on a personal loan.

If that is impossible, you may still be able to get the property by giving the owner a first with "releases" in it. Releases are simply agreements by the owner that he or she will give up interest in the property under specified conditions. For example, if you are buying a large plot of land, say 5 acres, it might be possible to give the owner $10,000 with a first mortgage for $4\frac{1}{2}$ acres plus a release for the $\frac{1}{2}$ acre that you'll actually build on. This means that when you go to the lending institution, you don't offer them a first on the whole 5 acres but instead only on the ¹/₂-acre construction site. Since the major collateral is the building, many lending institutions will be happy to go along with this. (The landowner retains a $30,000 first on the 4¹/₂ acres.)

It may be possible to get the landowner to change a first to a subordinated second upon the payment of an additional sum of money. Say you come up with $10,000 and give the owner a first. Then when you're ready to build you come up with an additional $10,000 and the owner agrees to change the first to a subordinated second for the remaining $20,000.

The advantage to this is that on occasion it is possible to get a construction loan where the lender advances money *prior* to the construction of each section (sometimes called a land advance). By careful handling of the money and fortuitous timing it may be possible to pay off part of the land and complete the building with the same loan.

100 Percent Financing

Let's assume you've gone ahead and found a $20,000 lot. You put down $10,000 which you either had in the bank or borrowed from a relative, the landowner gave you a $10,000 subordinated second, you've got a set of plans (which we'll discuss in a few moments), and you're ready to get your construction loan. Here's how you might go about getting it.

Let's assume your house will be 2,000 square feet and you're confident that by doing much of the work yourself it can be built for $23 a square foot. You'll need about $46,000 in order to complete the house plus about $3,000 to improve the lot and another $1,000 in financing charges or about $50,000 to complete the job. This is the minimum amount of construction loan you'll apply for.

To get your construction loan, you'll quickly find out that an institutional lender will also want you to have something called a "take-out or permanent loan commitment." A permanent loan commitment is merely a *promise* from a lender that when your house is completed you'll be given a traditional loan. The important thing to remember about the permanent loan is that it is based on the future market value (MV) of your property while the construction loan is based on the cost of building the house.

It is worth noting some other differences between a construction and a permanent loan:

Construction loan	*Take-out (permanent) loan*
Maximum term is usually 18 to 24 months	Maximum term is usually 30 years
Frequently need pay interest only during loan period, paying back entire loan at end of term	Pay back loan and interest (amortize) over 30 years in equal monthly payments
Interest rate is frequently higher than on a take-out loan	Interest rate lower than on a construction loan

It should be easy to see why a lender will not give a construction loan until there is a permanent commitment. The construction loan is short-term and its lender wants to be sure you'll have the money to pay it off when the term is up—hence, the take-out promise. (You often can get both permanent and construction loans from the same lender.)

While in our example we're assuming a $50,000 construction loan, the permanent loan could be for much more. (Remember, it's based on future market value.) Assuming the home (lot plus building costs) will be worth at least $80,000 when finished—we will of course have checked out the area to be sure we're not overbuilding (see Chapter Seven)—a conservative 80 percent permanent loan commitment will be for $64,000. Although it is not usually possible to get loans for above 80 percent, after the building is finished there shouldn't be a problem in declining the original permanent loan from the lender who made the 80 percent commitment—a clause saying that you have this option can be inserted in the commitment—and instead getting another lender to commit 90 percent for a $72,000 loan. Finding a lender who will go 90 percent at this high a price could be difficult but not impossible. Alternatively, an even higher loan can be obtained after the property is finished if it appraises higher than $80,000.

Now that we have the property, the construction loan, and the permanent commitment, let's assume we go ahead and successfully build the house meeting the $23 a square foot price we originally estimated. Further let's say that after construction is finished we exercise our commitment getting that 80 percent permanent loan. Table 9-2 shows what we would do with the $64,000.

We've built our house with only $6,000 of our own money invested. Our permanent loan has paid off everything else.

On the other hand, if we secure a 90 percent loan or get a higher evaluation on our property, the payoffs would look like they do in Table 9-3.

It is possible, therefore, to get financing for 100 percent of your new home when you build it yourself. It's even possible you might get money returned to you in the form of cash profit!

A great deal depends on how cheaply you build. If you were to cut the cost below $23 a square foot in our example, you could either pocket the money saved or reduce the amount of the loan and thereby lower your monthly payments.

This kind of financing may sound a bit strange to a beginner. A reader might reasonably ask, while it looks great on paper, how well does it actually work in the real world. The answer is that it works very well. It is the standard way new buildings are financed, although a developer, while obtaining a permanent commitment, probably wouldn't actually get the permanent loan. The developer would keep the construction loan on the property until the buyer or consumer of the home eventually bought the property.

An 80 percent permanent commitment for the future market value shouldn't be a problem. A 90 percent loan after the house is built shouldn't be a problem unless the price of the property gets

TABLE 9-2
Payoffs from a $64,000 Permanent Loan

Construction loan	$50,000
Subordinated second on lot	10,000
Cash left	4,000
	$64,000

TABLE 9-3
Payoffs from a 90 Percent Loan for $72,000

Construction loan	$50,000
Subordinated second on lot	10,000
Return of original investment in lot	10,000
Cash profit	2,000
	$72,000

high (as it was in our example). Getting a higher evaluation once the home is completed is also not usually difficult. It's quite a difference for a lender to see a house only on a blueprint and to actually be able to walk through it. Lenders are likely to be far more liberal on a completed home than on a paper one.

The House That You Build

As with any project, before you begin work you must have a plan. When building a house, a good plan is not optional, it is essential. It is the plan that your local building department will approve and it is the plan that you and your workers will follow in building the house.

If you are going to need financing, as almost all of us do, you'll have to come up with a set of plans that meet the approval of a lender. If you plan to sell the home you build in the near future, you need to come up with a set of plans that will appeal to a wide variety of buyers. And your plans must meet the local building and safety codes of your municipality.

Designing your house, therefore, becomes an exercise in compromising. You will have to compromise between what you ideally want and what you'll realistically be allowed to build.

Most lending institutions will want a home that has the following standard features: three or more bedrooms, two or more baths, a kitchen (size here is not critical), a living room, a separate dining room or eating area, and a wash area. Anything else, such as a family room, fireplace, or enclosed patio, will serve to enhance the plans.

If you satisfy the lender, chances are you'll satisfy any potential buyer, since the lender is only concerned with reselling the house in the event you default on the payments. One item not usually specified on the plans that you need to be particularly careful of is painting the home unusual colors. Pastels in brown, green, blue, and white are acceptable to most buyers. Vivid tones of red, orange, blue, green, and purple turn most buyers off.

Satisfying the local building department will be your most difficult task. If you're having an architect or competent drafter draw up your plans, this shouldn't be too much of a problem since either of these two people should be familiar with the local building code and will draw the plans up in accordance with it. If you are going to draw the plans yourself or intend to have an unusual feature like a cathedral ceiling, you may need to know what is allowed and what isn't.

The cheapest way to find out is to draw a sketch of what you plan to do and take it down to your local building department. If you can find someone there who has a few moments to give you, he or she can often tell whether or not it will work. If it will, that person can specify exactly the type and size of building materials required.

If your building department doesn't have the personnel to handle your questions, you can purchase a series of books containing the building code adopted by your locale at any large bookstore. The price, however, may be fairly high.

In the last chapter we discussed the need to get an architect to come up with a design when we are adding on to an existing house. An architect's help when we are laying out a house is also helpful, but not as critical. The reason is that there are many sources of good house building plans. Several magazines filled with plans are available, as are a wide variety of books. Or you, the builder, can visit a large number of homes already built and possibly select a floor plan that you like.

If you plan to come up with a unique design, unquestionably you will need the services of a good architect. As we discussed in the last chapter, that is the only person truly capable of transforming your own ideas into a satisfactory finished product.

A word should be said here about blueprints. For many people this word has magical overtones suggesting some mysterious procedure in the building process. Blueprints are nothing more than duplicates of the original plans. Since house plans often are very large (2- by 3-foot sheets are not uncommon), they cannot easily be duplicated in standard copying machines. Instead a large, special machine is used and it turns out blue prints.

You may not need a set of blueprints. You do need a set of plans. These plans, if accurately drawn, can be made on 8½ × 14 inch legal-size paper and then run off on the local copying machine. Several can be taped together to show large areas. Most building departments and construction workers can use these just as easily as blueprints.

When you have a set of plans that you are happy with and that you feel will meet with building code requirements, you'll need to submit them to the local building department for approval. Depending on the department and how busy they are, this could take anywhere from a few minutes to a few months. You'll have to pay for building permits (you will need a general permit plus special permits for electrical, mechanical, plumbing, and whatever other work your house may require) and this fee could run into several hundred dollars.

Once your plans are approved, or perhaps before depending on how your local government works, you'll also have to get the approval of a local planning department. This department determines if the house you propose to build will meet local zoning restrictions and any "covenants, conditions and restrictions" (CC&R's in the trade language) that may be attached to your deed. These are exactly what they say they are (covenant is a promise not to do something) and are very frequently added to deeds by developers or owners of large plots of land to ensure that the homes built will be uniform. They often require houses to be a minimum number of square feet, not more than two or three stories tall, have a certain type of roof or exterior, and they may even specify the color that may be painted on the exterior!

Now you're ready to build. While it's beyond the scope of this book to outline exactly how to build a house, information is included to help you make your own decision on what you are able to do yourself and what you will want to have skilled workers do. If you plan to do none of the work yourself, simply find a good general contractor. But if you're like most of us and plan to save some money, you'll probably find these clues helpful.

The reader should take careful notice that the following information is intended solely as a general guide to the difficulty involved in various construction jobs. Since construction techniques and materials vary dramatically from one area to another, the information should only be considered approximate. And since people differ in abilities, skills, and knowledge, no guarantee or assurance is given that any job can be performed successfully by any reader regardless of the degree of difficulty.

Grading

If your lot has a grade of more than 3 percent, chances are you're going to need some leveling work done. You'll also need to have the actual building site laid out. Unless you're handy with a bulldozer or pick and shovel, this is a job for an expert. Nonetheless, the tendency by some, myself included, is to save money here. Why pay $1,000, $5,000, or more to hire someone to come in with a tractor and truck and move around some dirt when for a few hundred dollars you can rent your own skip loader and do it yourself?

I've done it both ways and each has its advantages. Where there's a lot of earth to be moved, a bulldozer (identified by having tracks instead of wheels) is usually the only answer. A bulldozer requires a skilled operator who can handle almost any normal job in a day or two.

For smaller jobs, a small tractor (identified by having rubber tires) will do, particularly if you only need to move dirt from one area to another. If you plan to do this work yourself, be sure you allow a full day for wasted time while you learn how to operate the machinery properly.

Any grading that involves holding back hillsides, erecting supporting walls, or terracing should probably be done by an experienced operator. For small jobs, just "eyeing" the job may be sufficient to get it done right. For slopes, it probably will be necessary to get a survey and stakes put into the ground to show how much earth to move and where.

For these bigger jobs your best bet probably is an engineering firm. They can arrange for a skilled surveyor or engineer to do all the leg work on your job. You'd better count on spending extra money here as any type of engineering is expensive. Look under civil engineers in your phone book unless a contractor or someone you know can suggest a reputable firm.

Cement

Your next step will probably be pouring the foundation. If you will have a basement or wooden floors, this will consist of pouring a concrete footing around the edge of the house and at support joints in the center. (In some cases premade concrete supports can be used.) If you're going to have a slab floor, as is commonly the case in the Southwest, you'll still need the footings, but you'll probably also be required to put down about a foot of sand, a plastic membrane to prevent moisture from coming through, and then about 4 inches of concrete in a slab under the entire house. In the Northeast when creating a basement, you may be required (or want) to make special provisions for installing insulation. You may be required to install heavy steel rods or wire mesh in the concrete to give it added strength.

The major requisite for pouring concrete is a strong back. There are only two areas where special skill is involved. The first is in making the forms that will hold the concrete in place until it dries. These must be the right shape and of sufficient strength or they won't work. Any novice, however, can construct them with only a slight amount of direction. (But if they're not done correctly and collapse under the weight of the concrete, you'll have an enormous cleanup problem.)

The other special skill involves finishing the surface. A finisher gives cement that smooth surface that we've all come to expect. This is not a skill that can be learned in a day. If you're going to do the concrete work yourself, it will be worth your time and money to hire a finisher to do the final surface work.

One final word about concrete foundations. Cement sets up quickly, usually within a few hours. That means you don't have time to learn while you work. Typically a cement truck (don't ever mix the cement you need for a big job on the site yourself) will arrive from a cement yard and you'll be given only a few minutes to unload it and get it where you want it. The driver doesn't help you do this. Typically you may be allowed five minutes a "yard" to unload. (A yard is short for a cubic yard—an awful lot of cement.) Since you may only need 30 yards for a whole house, you may have only three hours or so to get all the cement off the truck and where you want it. (You can't just dump it on the ground and move it later or it will harden where it falls.) Two methods are used to get the cement from the truck to where you want it: the age-old wheelbarrow and the pumper. The pumper is a device that pumps cement through a large hose from the truck to the building site. It can often be rented for a few hundred dollars. Either way, plan to have a lot of friends and relatives helping pour the concrete if you plan to do it yourself.

Plumbing

The plumbing will have to be done at various stages in the building process. Some will undoubtedly need to be done before the foundation is poured, some during the framing, and the last after all the other work is finished.

Plumbing used to be a difficult task requiring heavy work and skill. (Try getting a perfect seal on a cast-iron sewer pipe using caulking and hot lead sometime if you don't believe this.) But today with the advent of plastic pipe and copper plumbing, almost anyone who can solder and glue can do the job. (Although it's not really quite that easy.) Building code regulations for plumbing tend to vary considerably, so you should be sure you're familiar with the code in your area. Safety requires the exercise of great care to see that no pollutants enter the fresh water through the plumbing. Pipes that will be laid either under or in concrete should be pressure-tested before the concrete is poured, since the only way to fix them should a leak develop afterward is to break up the concrete. An individual I know, Jay, hired a retired plumber as an advisor when he built his house. The older man did no actual physical work, but showed Jay how to handle all the plumbing.

Electrical

Electrical work, like plumbing, requires no great skill, but it does require that the work be done properly. With plumbing if you make a mistake the worst that's likely to happen is that you'll get a leak. With electricity, a mistake could result in someone getting electrocuted. Most people simply leave electricity to an expert. It's safer that way. If you're determined to do it yourself, however, and you are careful, handy, and know what you're doing through expert advice, you should be able to do as good a job as anyone. (It goes without saying that no electrical work should be done unless the power is off.)

The electrical work is usually done after the framing is up (unless a few circuits need to be buried in the concrete). Usually your city will have very specific requirements for electrical work—the type of wire that can be used, the type of boxes, how the wire is to be attached to the outlets, use of ground wires, etc. If you're going to do the work yourself either spend a lot of time at the city finding out what they require, get a code book, or find an advisor.

In recent years a big controversy has arisen over the use of copper wire versus aluminum wire. Aluminum costs about two-thirds the price of copper and so naturally anyone building with an eye toward saving money tends to opt for the aluminum wire. But aluminum has drawbacks. Usually you must use a thicker wire for the same service as compared to copper. And any kinks or crimps in the wire can cause overheating when electricity finally flows through it, which can eventually result in a fire. If aluminum is not properly attached at the terminals it can eventually work its way loose and cause shock or fires.

If properly installed, good aluminum wiring probably will serve as well as copper. If you're a beginner, however, stick to copper wire. It's easier to work with and will tolerate mistakes better.

Gas

If your home is going to be heated by natural gas, you'll need to make the proper pipe connections. These are usually done at the same time as the plumbing.

One special word about electricity and gas. You can save an enormous amount of money by doing the work yourself since in most areas the cost of labor is far higher than the cost of materials. If, however, you're careless or make a mistake, you could endanger both the property and someone's life (in some areas only licensed specialists may do this work—check your local regulations first). If you're not competent, or can't secure competent advice and guidance, you should not attempt either of these tasks yourself. Some homeowner-builders rely on their local building department to determine whether or not they've done a good job. They know that gas and electrical work will be inspected and so they assume that if it passes inspection, the job was done correctly.

Not necessarily so. Inspectors often have heavy loads and may only give the quickest and most superficial examination. If it looks all right they may pass it without really checking it thoroughly. In addition, the quality of inspectors varies from area to area—sometimes the person doing the inspection may not know much more than you! The important thing is that the job be done right, regardless of whether or not it passes inspection.

Masonry

If you can mix concrete and work with a plumb line, you can probably lay bricks. But don't expect your rows to be even the first time out. And you'd better hire an expert if you plan to go more than one story tall.

Lath and Plaster

Exteriors and interiors are frequently plastered. A lather simply sticks up the wire or wood that holds the plaster. Lathers work fast and they provide an inexpensive service. You might be able to save a few dollars by doing the work yourself, but the headache and hammer-smashed fingers are probably not worth it.

Plastering, whether interior or exterior, requires a skilled hand, more so because the results of the work will show in the completed house. Unless you absolutely can't afford it or unless you happen to have some experience yourself, it is probably best to hire an experienced worker here.

Insulation

In new construction insulation is usually very easy to apply. All that's required is a staple gun (or in the case of rigid insulation, hammer and nails). Insulation is sold on the basis of its "R" rating. R-14 gives better insulation than R-11, R-21 is better than R-14. The insulation rating you should use will depend entirely on the heat of the summers and cold of the winters in your area of the country. A quick call to the local building department will give you the answer. Be careful to ask where the rating applies, since ratings may differ for walls, floors, or ceilings.

Drywall

Drywall or sheetrock is plaster already prepared that comes pressed between two pieces of paper. It comes in a variety of lengths (usually multiples of 4 feet) by 4 feet wide. It is simply nailed to the framing.

Anyone who can lift sheetrock (it is quite heavy) can install it. The critical thing is to have as few joints as possible. Each joint must be taped and the more there are, the more it costs. Also the boards must all be flat and properly nailed. Usually there is a city inspection to determine if the nailing was done properly (commonly a nail every 4 to 6 inches along every stud is required).

Taping

After the sheetrock is installed, plaster and then a paper tape is applied to every joint. This gives the sheetrock an appearance of being solid wall and not a series of cut-up pieces. The paper is applied only once, but usually the plaster must be applied three separate times in order to get it smooth. Finally it is sanded to remove any rough spots. Nails are also plastered over.

Anyone can tape—only an expert can get it smooth. If you have a lot of time to spend and are adventurous, you can try taping yourself. But if you want a good job, hire an expert here.

Texturing

A final coat of plaster, often in the form of a texture, is usually applied to the drywall. I have seen individuals totally inexperienced simply put this on with a rough paint roller and have it come out looking terrific. For special effects, however, a professional is required.

Heating and Air Conditioning

Heating systems vary dramatically from sun to natural gas to coal to oil to wood. Whatever kind of system you have, there is usually a central heating unit and then duct work leading the heat to the different parts of the house. In California you might have a gas blower furnace installed in a closet in a central hallway; in Minnesota there would be an oil furnace in a basement.

There is no special skill required in installing the furnace. It's much like installing a dishwasher. You get it where you want it and connect it. (Although, unlike a dishwasher, you will want to take special care to see the connections are done properly.) Installing the ductwork is another matter.

Ductwork comes in a variety of types from sheetmetal to pipes made entirely out of compressed fiberglass. Again your local code will determine the cheapest type you may use. Installing it usually involves hanging it from floors or roofs, cutting openings in walls, installing a plenum or central box from which the ducts originate, and so forth. No special skill is normally involved and often the store where you buy the materials can instruct you on how they are to be installed.

Air conditioning can also vary in type. There can be the evaporative coolers typically found in the Southwest, and the refrigerated units of the South. Or they can be simply attic fans. Evaporative units and attic fans are easily installed and usually instructions come with the units explaining how to install them. Refrigerated air conditioning requires expert installation (although the ducting for it is almost the same as for furnace work).

TABLE 9-4
Beginner's Work Comparison Chart

Job	Skill or craftsmanship required	Technical knowledge required	Money saved by doing it yourself (labor vs. cost of materials)*
Grading	modest	little	modest
Cement foundation	modest	little	modest
Framing	modest	little	modest
Roof—shingles	little	little	modest
Roof—joists	little	very great	little
Electricity	little	great	great
Plumbing	little	great	great
Heating	little**	modest	great
Air conditioning	little**	very great	great
Insulation	little	little	modest
Stucco and plaster (texturing)	very great	little	great
Drywall—hanging	modest	little	little
Drywall—taping	great	little	little
Bricklaying (masonry)	great	modest	great
Doors and windows (prefab)	little	little	modest
Cabinets (prefab)	little	little	modest
Appliances	little	little	modest
Painting	little	little	modest

*See cautions on pages 182–184, top of 199, and 202–203.
**If premanufactured parts are purchased.

Buying Materials

When you begin your project and start buying materials you will notice a curious thing. Some materials such as lumber, nails, pipe, sheetrock, cement, and steel are readily available from a large number of sources and you can get almost as good a price on them as would a contractor. Some building materials, however, particularly certain electrical parts and nearly all sheetmetal or heating and air conditioning parts, are not readily available. There may be no retail source in your area. The reason is that almost all the individuals who use these materials are contractors, and to get what you want you'll probably have to buy from a contractor (who bought it wholesale) and pay a markup. You may even discover that the cost of the materials you have to buy from a contractor in order to do a project yourself is not much less than to have the contractor do the entire job. It may be worth your while to save a few aches and pains and pay the contractor to do it.

It is interesting to note from Table 9-4 that the most money can be saved in jobs requiring not much skill but a lot of technical knowledge, such as plumbing, heating, and electricity. For those prospective home builders who can learn quickly, the knowledge is readily available in books.

On the other hand, it will do little good to gain the knowledge of plastering, even though a great amount of money can be saved by doing it yourself, since it takes years of experience to be able to do a professional job. And though certain jobs like hanging and taping sheetrock require little skill or knowledge, the small amount to be saved by doing the work yourself indicates you could better spend your time doing something else and hire someone to do these. Finally, some jobs like assembling roofs require such great knowledge (though little skill) that to save headaches and ensure a good job it might be best to either buy a prefabricated roof or hire someone knowledgeable to do the work.

TEN
Domes, Log Cabins, Barns, Kits, and Prefabs

Jason, my youngest son, recently received a present which I found more interesting than he did. It was a large box containing the parts necessary to construct a toy house. It had several doors, a good many windows, walls, a roof, and a floor. I urged him to try it out and although he is only three, within a few minutes he was able to put together something that looked very much like the model of a real house.

Jason did not think much of his accomplishment and within the hour had returned his house to its original form. But I found the toy of continuing interest because it closely resembled one portion of the real house building market that today accounts for about 30 percent of all residential construction in the United States.

Panelized Housing

The panelized housing industry is closely related to the manufactured housing industry we discussed back in Chapter 5, although there are important differences. Panelized housing consists of two-dimensional parts such as wall panels, roof panels, floors, room partitions, plumbing walls, and so forth. Unlike mobile and modular homes which are three-dimensional and are finished at the factory, panelized housing only offers plant-finished components which then must be assembled at the building site.

If you have ever seen a truck going down the road carrying already-assembled beams and trusses used on roofs, you've seen panelized housing. Although most residential tract builders and developers like to refer to their homes as "custom" or built stick by stick, a large proportion use the prefabricated parts at the very least for their roofs.

Panelized parts are built in much the same way that assembly line production puts together mobile and modular homes (see a factory walk-through in Chapter 5). A panel may be as short as 2 feet or as long as 40 feet. It may have pipes and drains and other plumbing already installed in it. It may have electrical wiring and insulation. In essence, like the parts of Jason's little house, it may be a complete component of a home finished on both sides at the plant and then delivered to the building site ready to be connected to another component in the final assembly.

There are many panelized home manufacturers in the country today and their catalogs often run into the hundreds of pages with a different home design for each page. It's easy to see how moving the interchangeable parts around can give an almost infinite variety. They can come up with a design just for you or help you blend your ideas into the products they offer. (A list of panelized home manufacturers is given in the appendix.) Prices usually begin at about $18 a square foot and can go up from there.

Panelized construction has some disadvantages. The cost of freighting materials to the building site is high, so manufacturers will be regional. Frequently they operate within a 300- to 400-mile radius of their plant. If they go further out, freight charges may eat up the savings offered by this type of assembly line construction.

There could be a "matching" problem if you tried to get a wall from one manufacturer and a roof or floor from another. If you've ever tried to put a Chrysler transmission into a Ford you'll understand the problem. If you stick with a single manufacturer this potential problem shouldn't exist.

Finally, as with all other types of construction, there is still the need to get building permits, prepare the lot, and pour a foundation. Unlike building one stick at a time, the construction itself goes very quickly. It usually consists simply of connecting the panelized parts to each other.

Panelized housing is for either the do-it-yourselfer or the builder,

Figure 10–1. Panelized housing. *(Courtesy of Northern Homes, Hudson Falls, New York.)*

Figure 10–2. Panelized housing. *(Courtesy of Lincoln Homes Company, Elizabeth, Pennsylvania.)*

Figure 10–3. Panelized housing. *(Courtesy of Scholz Homes, Toledo, Ohio.)*

Figure 10-4. Panelized housing. *(Courtesy of Pease Company, Hamilton, Ohio, Lon H. Purcell, A.I.A.)*

Figure 10-5. Panelized housing. *(Manufactured by and photo courtesy of Guildway Ltd., Surrey, England.)*

Figure 10-6. Panelized housing. *(Manufactured by Pease Company, Hamilton, Ohio, Lon H. Purcell, A.I.A.)*

although several manufacturers will sell their products only through their local representatives or only to builders. (These same manufacturers, when contacted directly, can frequently suggest builders in your area who have already used their products and can show you actual examples of completed homes. These builders usually will be happy to work for you on a single house basis.)

Panelized housing can save money and time and still result in an outstanding-looking home. If you are considering building, you should definitely not overlook this alternative. (See figures 10-1 through 10-6.)

Precut Homes

One of the most exciting fields in housing for the do-it-yourselfer is the precut home. Precut homes differ from panelized construction in that you, the owner-builder, do much of the assembly yourself. The manufacturer usually offers a combination of "sticks" and panels, all presawed, drilled, and prepared for quick assembly.

Precut manufacturers usually say that almost anyone who can read a set of plans and put board "A" into notch "B" can successfully build a precut home. It's not quite that simple, but it's not hard. And it tends to take the guesswork out of building. Precut homes are often sold as complete kits.

Geodesic Domes

The most unusual homes occur in the precut area. Geodesic domes modeled after Buckminster Fuller's famous design are a notable example. These are based on a six-sided figure, not separate walls or ceilings, but rather multiples of the same figure which when put together give the structure impressive strength. It's similar to the eggshell, which for its thinness is incredibly strong.

Many people familiar with the beginnings of geodesic domes feel that they are always small. This is no longer true. Although manufacturers frequently build kits of just a few hundred square feet in size, some manufacturers build two-story domes that connect for much larger sizes. Monterey Domes of Riverside, California, has a unit which it states is over 3,000 square feet in size!

Figure 10–7. Geodesic dome. *(Courtesy of Monterey Domes, Riverside, California.)*

Figure 10–8. Geodesic dome. *(Courtesy of The Big Outdoors People, Inc., Minneapolis, Minnesota.)*

Since the geodesic dome manufacturer often panelizes the geo-desics, the assembly of the basic structure (once the foundation has been prepared) can be accomplished with bolts and a wrench. Covering the frame can be a bit more difficult. Since the home is circular, the conventional building material which presupposes vertical studs (framing boards) every 16 inches apart on center does not fit. An easy answer to this offered by some manufacturers is to cover the outside with a coating of stucco or wood shingles or even a heavy plastic film. The inside walls can be handled more easily by the use of wood paneling attached after insulation has been installed.

Geodesic domes vary enormously in price, but it usually isn't the cost factor which prompts owners to build them. It's their unique-ness. In recreational areas, out in the woods, and sometimes even in traditional neighborhoods, a geodesic dome is always outstanding and draws attention to its owner. (See Figures 10-7 and 10-8.)

Log Cabins

There are more than three dozen manufacturers of log cabins now delivering close to 20,000 units a year. Log cabins are unusual in most areas and yet have a tradition dating back to the foundings of this country.

Figure 10-9. Log cabin. *(Courtesy of Alta Industries, Ltd., Halcottsville, New York.)*

Figure 10–10 Log cabin. *(Courtesy of Alta Industries, Ltd., Halcottsville, New York.)*

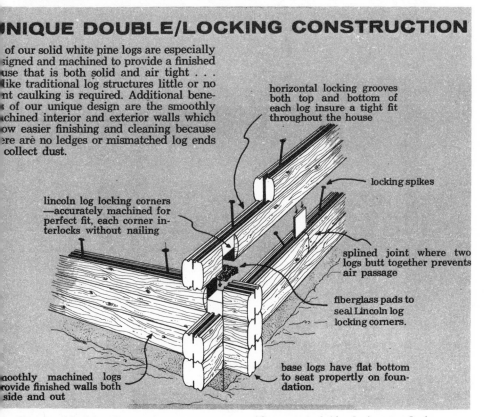

▌NIQUE DOUBLE/LOCKING CONSTRUCTION

of our solid white pine logs are especially ≥igned and machined to provide a finished ꭒse that is both solid and air tight . . . ▐ike traditional log structures little or no ꭒnt caulking is required. Additional bene- ꭤ of our unique design are the smoothly ꭤchined interior and exterior walls which ꭤow easier finishing and cleaning because ꭢre are no ledges or mismatched log ends ꭢ collect dust.

horizontal locking grooves both top and bottom of each log insure a tight fit throughout the house

locking spikes

lincoln log locking corners —accurately machined for perfect fit, each corner interlocks without nailing

splined joint where two logs butt together prevents air passage

fiberglass pads to seal Lincoln log locking corners.

ꭟoothly machined logs ꭢovide finished walls both side and out

base logs have flat bottom to seat properly on foundation.

Figure 10–11. Log cabin construction. *(Courtesy of Alta Industries Ltd., Halcottsville, New York.)*

Figure 10–12. *(Courtesy of Yankee Barn, Grantham, New Hampshire.)*

Manufacturers of log cabins tend to aim their products toward young do-it-yourselfers. They point out that the log house is rapidly constructed and easy to maintain, inexpensive to heat and very durable. If you've ever worked with the small toy log houses that are widely distributed for children, you have some idea of how a log cabin goes together. Even weekend carpenters who are mostly thumbs shouldn't have too much trouble with the assembly process, provided they can lift the heavy timbers.

Log cabins are primarily sold on the basis of their unique construction material. In an age when we have become saturated with synthetic products, the back-to-nature feeling of these homes has an appeal for many home seekers. If you're looking for rustic flavor in a house, a log kit is a definite possibility. (See Figures 10-9 through 10-11.)

Barns

At one time, particularly in New England, the countryside was dotted with big barns. They were highly utilitarian, providing shelter

Figure 10–13. *(Courtesy of Yankee Barn, Grantham, New Hampshire.)*

for farm animals. As the centuries passed many people began to notice that these barns had a striking architectural flavor all their own. It has been several decades since converting old barns into homes became fashionable in several areas of the country.

There are big problems with converting old barns into houses. First you have to find a usable old barn (a real impossibility in most urban areas), and then it costs a considerable amount of money to have it rehabilitated (100 or more years of wear can do fatal damage to almost any structure). One answer to this problem is to buy a brand new old barn.

Manufacturers of barns offer a basic design that is becoming increasingly popular. It offers great utility: There tends to be little wasted space in a barn.

Barn prices vary greatly. One manufacturer, Yankee Barn Homes, Inc., of Grantham, New Hampshire, will deliver anywhere in the United States. Prices for a Yankee Barn package as of this writing vary from a little over $8,000 to a little over $30,000 and include frame, wall components, windows, roof components, doors, building instructions, and even old-time nails. The company esti-

[217]

mates that by the time the structure is erected, costs including labor, flooring, heating, plumbing, and interior partitions (the whole barn) should run about $15,000 to $60,000 depending on the model chosen. And there are a wide variety of options including fireplace and decking.

If you finally get tired of considering all the alternatives open to you when building a house and decide that even a barn will do, there's one available today. (See Figures 10-12 and 10-13.)

Conclusion

Whether it's called panelized, prefabricated, modular, or mobile, housing that is manufactured in a plant on an assembly line offers the greatest variety and lowest cost in housing today. While this is just being discovered in America, it is something that has been known for a long time in other parts of the world. In the Soviet Union, for example, it has been estimated that nearly $1^{1}/_{2}$ million manufactured residential units are built each year—more than the total number of residential units built in the United States during several of the leaner years of this decade.

That doesn't mean that a manufactured home is for you. As we've seen, other alternatives may be superior for your needs. Perhaps the lifestyle of a condominium suits you best. Or the challenge of rehabilitating an older home. Or even adding on or stick building your own home.

Whatever your choice, these are the alternatives. I sincerely hope that you'll be able to move into one of them soon.

APPENDIX

A List of Producers of Modular Homes, Log Cabins, Domes, Barns, Panelized Houses, and Other Manufactured Homes and Home Products.

There are many hundreds of producers of manufactured homes across the United States. This is a listing of those belonging to the National Association of Home Manufacturers—a professional organization.

This listing is intended as a guide. The reader who is interested in a particular product should contact the manufacturer directly. Most will respond immediately with brochures, photos, and other information about their products. In those cases where manufacturers work only through builders or dealers, many may suggest builders or dealers in your area who can offer you direct assistance.

While every effort has been made to give correct addresses, phone numbers, contacts, and descriptions of products, changes in a company's service, personnel, and even location may occur over a period of time. The reader, therefore, would be wise to contact several companies that manufacture a particular product to be sure of getting a good response.

[219]

Active Homes Corporation, Department TN, 7938 S. Van Dyke, P.O. Box 127, Marlette, Mich. 48453, (517)635-9771

Contacts: Henry A. Drettman, vice president; Jack C. Ramsay, general manager; Edgar F. Connery, sales manager

Products: Closed panel, mechanical cores, stack modular homes.

Market area: 4

Acorn Structures, Inc., Department TN, P.O. Box 250, Concord, Mass. 01742, (617)369-4111

Contacts: John R. Bemis, president; Arthur N. Milliken, general sales manager

Marketing Area Key

Refer to this map shown as Figure A-1 when checking which area of the country is served by a home manufacturer.

1—Northeast	5—North Central
2—Mid-Atlantic	6—Southwest
3—Southeast	7—West
4—Midwest	8—Northwest
	9—International

Figure A–1. Marketing area key. Refer to this map when checking which area of the country is served by a home manufacturer.

Products: Panelized, architect-designed, contemporary homes. Year-round, vacation, single and multifamily, light commercial, and special purpose buildings. Solar heating system components can be supplied with panelized packages.

Market areas: 1, 2, 3

Adrian Housing Corporation, Department TN, Box 246, Adrian, Ga. 31002, (912)668-3231

Contacts: Carl L. Gillis, Jr., president; Billy Flanders, vice president; J. H. Wheeler, vice president

Products: Modular homes.

Market area: 3

Air-lock Log Co., Inc., Department TN, P.O. Box 2506, Las Vegas, N.Mex. 87701, (505)425-8888

Contacts: Frederic B. Oster, manager (president)

Products: Log homes.

Market areas: 3, 4, 6, 7

All American Homes, Inc., Department TN, 309 S. 13th Street, P.O. Box 451, Decatur, Ind. 46733, (219)724-9171

Contacts: Larry Bultemeier, president

Products: Sectional homes.

Market area: 4

Alta Industries, Ltd. Department TN, P.O. Box 88, Halcottsville, N.Y. 12438, (914)586-4490

Contacts: Edward Perazone, general manager; Frank Mann, vice president; Vincent Giacci, president

Products: Log homes.

Market areas: 1, 2, 3, 4

Authentic Homes Corp., Department TN, 310 Grand Avenue, Box 1288, Laramie, Wyo. 82070, (307)742-3786

Contacts: E. P. Fillion, president

Products: Log homes.

Market areas: 3, 4, 5, 6, 7, 8

Beaver Log Homes, Division of Chisum Industries, Inc., Department TN, Box 1966, Grand Island, Neb. 68801, (308)381-0421

Contacts: Harold Green, Jr., president; Gary Duncan, executive vice president; Russ Gertsch, controller

Products: Log homes.

Market areas: 3, 6

Bell Housing Components, Division of Del E. Webb Development Co., Department TN, P.O. Box 1705, Sun City, Ariz. 85351, (602)974-7610

Contacts: T. L. Rittenhouse, general manager

Products: Mechanical cores and components including bathrooms, utility walls, wall panels, and trusses.

Market area: 7

Bendix Home Systems, Inc., Department TN, Building #9, 12155 Magnolia Avenue, Riverside, Calif. 92503, (714)687-3634

Contacts: Robert E. Miller, executive vice president; Joe Sheehan, vice president, marketing and sales; Richard Mahnken, vice president, operating services; Dave McKenzie, director of modular marketing, United States Division

Products: Sectional homes for residential builder-developers in its twelve plants; single and multifamily units.

Market areas: 1, 2, 3, 4, 5, 6, 7, 8, 9

The Big Outdoors People, Inc., Department TN, 2201 N. E. Kennedy Street, Minneapolis, Minn. 55413, (612)331-5430

Contacts: Dennis H. Kelly, president

Products: Architectural designers, manufacturers, and marketers of precut, component dome homes, dome cabins, commercial domes and systems for wood heating, waste handling, water saving, solar energy, wind generators, methane digestors.

Market areas: 3, 4, 5, 6, 9

Boise Cascade Corporation, Manufactured Housing Division, Department TN, 61 Perimeter Park, Atlanta, Ga. 30341, (404)455-6161

Contacts: Rudy A. Brown, general manager, Eastern Operations; Kenneth R.

Ramsey, general manager, Western Operations, P.O. Box 50, Boise, Idaho 83728, (208)384-7272

Products: Eastern Operations markets panelized models in forty states and sectionals in eight southeastern states; Western Operations' modulars are distributed to builders in ten Pacific Northwest states.

Market areas: 1, 2, 3, 4, 5, 6, 7, 8

Boozer Lumber Company, Department TN, P.O. Box 9244, Columbia, S.C. 29209, (803)776-1326

Contacts: William L. Boozer, board chairman; L. Dale Boozer, president

Products: Open wall panels and roof trusses.

Market area: 3

Boyne Falls Log Homes, Inc., Department TN, Boyne Falls, Mich. 49713, (616)549-2421; Department TN, 32900 Log Bow, Birmingham, Mich. 48010, (313)642-2957

Contacts: Robert Mock, president (Birmingham); Floyd Hausler, vice president and general manager (Boyne Falls); Stephen Biggs, vice president, sales

Products: Log homes.

Market areas: 1, 2, 3, 4, 5, 6, 7, 8

Cardinal Industries, Department TN, 2040 S. Hamilton Road, Columbus, Ohio 43227, (614)861-3211

Contacts: Austin Guirlinger, president; David Baker, vice president; Jim McLaughlin, vice president

Products: Modular apartment and motel units.

Market areas: 3, 4

Cary-Way Building Company, Department TN, 50 Almeda-Genoa Road, P.O. Box 26937, Houston, Tex. 77207, (713)991-5111

Contacts: David Hampton, general manager; George Woods, plant manager

Products: Sectional homes.

Market areas: 3, 6

Castle Homes, Inc., Division of Reed Supply Co., Department TN, 1100 National Highway, Thomasville, N.C. 27360, (919)475-2171

Contacts: R. D. Reed, president

Products: Single as well as multifamily units, primarily custom-built from customer's plans; floors, precut; panels, open frame; trusses; millwork.

Market areas: 2, 3

CBS Homes, Inc., Department TN, 184 Main Street, LaCrescent, Minn. 55947, (507)895-4770

Contacts: John W. Welch, president; Donald H. Schumacher, general manager

Products: Single and multifamily panelized units, glued-deck system with exposed lower, up to 42-foot panels, with siding, doors, and windows installed. Sold through builders and brokers.

Market area: 4

Cedar Homes, Inc., Department TN, 555 116th Avenue Northeast, Suite #150, Bellevue, Wash. 98004, (206)454-3966

Contacts: Michael O. Hool, vice president; Jon R. Hook, vice president; C. L. Hook, president

Products: Panelized "packaged" homes.

Market areas: 7, 8

Component Homes, Inc., Department TN, 817 S. Capitol Street, P.O. Box 2146, Iowa City, Iowa 52240, (319)338-5448

Contacts: Robert D. Strub, president; Donald E. Strub, vice president; Norm Fanning, director of marketing

Products: A panelized package marketed through a dealership network in five states. Single-family, apartment, leisure home, and light commercial units.

Market areas: 4, 5

Components, Inc., Department TN, 4400 Homerlee Avenue, P.O. Box 2266, East Chicago, Ind. 46312, (219)397-3950

Contacts: Richard J. Dye, president; Arthur L. Clemens, executive vice president; Richard P. Metzger, vice president, marketing

Products: Custom fabrications of all building components for the builder's plans to the builder's specifications, including bath and kitchen modules, walls, floors, roofs, complete millwork packages. Single-family, multifamily, and commercial structures.

Market areas: 4, 5

Continental Homes, Division of Wylain, Inc., Department TN, P.O. Box 13106, Roanoke, Va. 24031, (703)334-5000

Contacts: J. Dillard Powell, president; James M. Mason, vice president, marketing and sales

Products: Panelized and sectional buildings and an innovative two-story sectional with fold-down upper level; single and multifamily units and vacation homes.

Market areas: 1, 2, 3, 4

Continental Homes of New England, Division of Wylain, Inc., Department TN, Daniel Webster Highway South, Nashua, N.H. 03060, (603)888-2191

Contacts: T. W. Cahow, president; Robert P. Killkelly, vice president, sales and marketing

Products: Vacation homes, single-family sectionals, single and multifamily panelized, and stacked modulars.

Market areas: 1, 2

Davidson Louisiana, Inc., Department TN, P.O. Box 1162, Jennings, La. 70546, (318)824-4865

Contacts: Richard Boisture, vice president, manufacturing; Karl Conrad, sales manager

Products: Wood-framed components to customer plans; single-family, multifamily, commercial styles; one-, two-, and three-story work; gang-nail roof and floor trusses; Truswal "Space Joist" floor and roof trusses.

Market areas: 3, 6

Dynamic Homes, Department TN, Box 875, Detroit Lakes, Minn. 56401, (218)847-9225

Contacts: L. Clark Tollefson, president, Wayne Baumgart, production director; Jack Lillis, transportation director; Richard J. Price, advertising and marketing manager

Products: Sectional homes.

Market areas: 4, 5

Empire Homes Inc., Division of Janssen/Dakota Corp., Department TN, 206 So. Frontage Road, Beresford, S. Dak. 57004, (605)763-5043

Contacts: T. E. Janssen, president; Jim Hansen, executive vice president

Products: Panelized packaged homes; lumber-treating and wood foundation fabricator.

Market areas: 4, 5

Fabricon Corporation, Department TN, 1780 Rohrerstown Road, P.O. Box 1701, Lancaster, Pa. 17601, (717)569-6471

Contacts: James Phillips, president; F. Lance Neuman, sales manager

Products: Panelized house packages sold through builders within a 200-mile radius. Complete pre-engineered product line plus capability to customize to builder's individual requirements. Optional factory-applied siding and crane erection. Engineering, marketing, and financial assistance.

Market areas: 1, 2

Fleetwood Enterprises, Inc., Department TN, 3125 Myers Street, P.O. Box 7638, Riverside, Calif. 92503, (714)785-3500

Contacts: Gerald G. Biddulph, vice president, housing group; Glenn Kummer, executive vice president, operations; William Weide, president; Don Wichman, marketing director

Products: Mobile homes, 24-foot-wide modular units: recreational vehicles.

Market areas: 1, 2, 3, 4, 5, 6, 7, 8

Fleetwood Homes, Inc., Department TN, Highway 60 North, Box 308, Worthington, Minn. 56187, (507)376-3128

Contacts: Richard D. Stout, president; Gerald F. Jansen, sales manager, Worthington; Dennis E. Rydell, sales manager, Minneapolis

Products: Custom-designed, crane-erected, panelized package homes, apartments, townhouses, motels, wood foundations, certified wood truss roof systems, and other light commercial structures, manufactured to the builder's plans and specifications.

Market areas: 4, 5

Fuqua Homes, Inc., Department TN, 7100 S. Cooper, Arlington, Tex. 76015, (817)275-3211

Contacts: Dooley E. Culbertson, president; William C. Noble, executive vice president; William Gambrell, marketing manager

Products: Mobile homes, entering into the modular unit line.

Market areas: 2, 3, 4, 5, 6, 7, 8

GBH-Way Homes, Inc., Department TN, 101 N. Main Street, P.O. Box 488, Walnut, Ill. 61376, (815)379-2166

Contacts: Charles D. Hill, president

Products: High quality packages for small commercial, single and multifamily, and vacation homes with extensive design flexibility. Complete line of optional refinements at combined home center. Distribution through franchised builder-dealers.

Market area: 4

General Electric Company, Department TN, 3198 Chestnut Street, Philadelphia, Pa. 19101, (215)823-4822

Contacts: Alexander Lengyel, general manager, Industrialized Housing and International Programs Department; William Dwyer, program general manager, Housing Technology; Robert Bell, international marketing manager

Products: Develops basic new technology including steel and cast-plaster surface structure as applied to modular housing systems. Will sell technology and industrialized housing factory for overseas application.

Market area: 9

Great Plains Homes, Department TN, P.O. Box 157, Kensett, Iowa 50448, (515)845-2201

Contacts: Otto Lehmann, general manager; Duane DeLonias, assistant manager; Dean Thompson, sales manager

Products: Modular housing units 24, 26, and 28 feet wide. Construction components for open wall sections and trusses for customer erection. Sells through dealers and direct plant sales.

Market areas: 4, 5

Green Brothers Lumber Corporation, Department TN, Ashville, N.Y. 14710, (716)763-8518

Contacts: C. Craig Rustay, vice president; Errol E. Green, chairman of the board; George C. Gribbroek, president

Products: Single and multifamily package homes; panels; roof trusses; commercial and vacation homes; all marketed as C. R. Homes.

Market areas: 1, 2

Guerdon Industries, Inc., Department TN, P.O. Box 4132, North Little Rock, Ark. 72116, (510)758-5757

Contact: John Monaweck, vice president

Products: Primarily mobile homes with some modular housing.

Market areas: 1, 2, 3, 4, 5, 6, 7, 8

Guildway Limited, Department TN, Portsmouth Road, Guildford, Surrey, England, Guildford 69201

Contacts: J. R. More-Molyneux, president

Products: Packaged homes.

Market areas: England

Harvest Homes, Department TN, 1 Cole Road, Delanson, N.Y. 12053, (518)895-2341

Contacts: William H. Bartlett, general manager; Lester Taylor, production foreman

Products: Panelized residential, commercial, and vacation structures. Fabricated custom houses as well as standard product line. Also trusses, windows, and door assemblies, wholesale lumber.

Market areas: 1, 2

Havelock Homes Corporation, Department TN, U.S. 70 West, P.O. Box 249, Havelock, N.C. 28532, (919)447-7122

Contacts: Gene A. Jackson, general manager

Products: Sectional homes and mobile homes.

Market area: 2

Haven Homes, Inc., Department TN, Box 178, Beech Creek, Pa. 16822, (717)962-2111

Contacts: Charles M. Ballard, president and treasurer; Charles Mogish, executive vice president; David C. Ballard, director

Products: Sectional homes (one story).

Market areas: 1, 2

Haven Homes of Ilion, Inc., Department TN, 139 Central Avenue, P.O. Box 390, Ilion, N.Y. 13357, (315)895-7708

Contacts: John J. Bauer, general manager; Charles Ballard, president; Charles Mogish, vice president

Products: Modular single-family housing, tri-level, bi-level, and ranches; offices and medical buildings on request.

Market area: 1

Heartland Homes Corporation, Department TN, One Heartland Drive, P.O. Box 217, Etna Green, Ind. 46524, (219)858-2514

Contacts: Donald L. Corl, president

Products: Stack modular homes and sectional homes.

Market areas: 2, 4

Hendrich Building Systems, Inc., Department TN, 111 W. Second Street, Jamestown, N.Y. 14701, (716)664-6014

Contacts: William Craddock, vice president in charge of marketing, Hendrich Building Systems Inc., 1350 Avenue of the Americas, New York, N.Y. 10019

Products: Stack modular homes and panelized homes.

Market areas: 3, 6, 7

Heritage Building Products, Division of Heritage Corporation, Department TN, 4850 Boxelder Street, Murray, Utah 84107, (801)262-4601

Contacts: LaMar Bradshaw, president; Larry Bradshaw, secretary-treasurer

Products: Panelized, packaged homes and commercial units.

Market area: 7

Heritage Homes of New England, Inc., Department TN, 456 Southampton Road, Westfield, Mass. 01085, (413)568-8614

Contacts: Robert T. Goyette, president

Products: Custom-designed and engineered wood structures. Panelized single and multifamily, vacation homes, light commercial, and agricultural buildings. Components are customized to builder specifications.

Market area: 1

Homecraft Corporation, Department TN, P.O. Box 359, South Hill, Va. 23970, (804)447-3186

Contacts: William B. Pepera, vice president; H. R. Legg, president

Products: Panelized homes.

Market areas: 1, 2, 3, 4

Home Manufacturing and Supply Company, Inc., Department TN, 4401 East 6th Street, Sioux Falls, S. Dak. 57103, (605)336-0730

Contacts: D. Wayne Ronning, president; Richard Skancke, vice president, sales

Products: Custom homes (each individually designed) sold as Holiday Homes. Component packages sold at wholesale to builders and realtors. Single and multifamily homes, commercial and vacation structures.

Market areas: 4, 5

Intermountain Precision-Bilt Homes, Inc., Department TN, 2525 North Highway 91, Ogden, Utah 84404, (801)782-8090

Contacts: Ross Olsen, marketing manager; Blaine Wade, president; Robert Wade, vice president

Products: Standard and customized component and modular single and multifamily homes, vacation homes, and commercial structures.

Market area: 7

Key-Loc Modular Homes, P.O. Box 226, Suncook, N.H. 03275, (603)485-7131

Contacts: Lawrence E. Haiman, general manager and vice president; William R. Zolla, operations manager and vice president

Products: Single detached, two and four box modulars. Specializes in colonial-designed ranches, splits, and two-story homes. Sells through developers, builders, and dealers.

Market area: 1

Lodge Logs by Mac Gregor, Division of Pressure Treated Timber, Department TN, 3200 Gowen Road, Boise, Idaho 83705, (208)336-2450

Contacts: Robert Lewandowski, manager; Robert Darrow, president

Products: Log home kits.

Market areas: 1, 2, 3, 4, 5, 6, 7, 8

Lumber Enterprises, Inc., Department TN, Star Route, Box 203, Bozeman, Mont. 59715, (406)763-4411

Contacts: David Johnson, president; Glen Hargrove, superintendent; Phillip Auble, office manager

Products: Precut custom-designed log homes.

Market areas: 3, 4, 5, 6, 7, 8

Manufactured Homes, Inc., Department TN, 29089 Lexington Park Drive, Elkhart, Ind. 46514, (219)294-5463

Contacts: Robert Willard, president; Richard Oliver, director of engineering; Arthur Willard, general manager

Products: Sectional homes.

Market area: 4

Midland Industries, Inc., Department TN, First National Bank Building, 111 E. Fourth Street, Cincinnati, Ohio 45202, (513)721-3777

Contacts: C. M. Fellows, executive vice president

Products: Mobile homes in widths of 12, 14, and 24 feet and lengths ranging from 36 to 70 feet; Modular homes 24 feet wide and ranging from 40 to 60 feet in length.

Market areas: 3, 4

Mill-Craft Housing Corporation, Department TN, Tower Road, P.O. Box 327, Waupaca, Wis. 54981, (715)258-8531

Contacts: Erwin G. Rehbein, president; I. Lee Kabat, vice president, Waupaca Plant; Gerald W. Schultz, vice president, Iowa Plant, Box 505, Clear Lake, Iowa 50428

Products: Modular homes and apartments.

Market area: 4

Modern Homes & Equipment Company, Department TN, 2467 N. Dog River Drive, P.O. Box 5068, Mobile, Ala. 36605, (205)478-6339

Contacts: James D. McPhillips, president; Frank J. Lott, Jr., plant manager; Earl F. Aubrey, vice president

Products: Panelized packaged homes.

Market area: 3

Mod-U-Kraf Homes, Inc., Route 40 East, P.O. Box 573, Rocky Mount, Va. 24151, (703)483-0291

Contacts: O. Z. Oliver, board chairman and chief executive: Robert K. Fitts, president; Robert L. Cooper, executive vice president

Products: Modular homes through builder-dealer organization throughout mid-Atlantic states.

Market areas: 2, 3

Monterey Domes, P.O. Box 5621-J, Riverside, Calif. 92517

Contact: Bob Gunther, president. (The company, not an NAHB member, has a nationwide dealer network where models may be seen. A 52-page full-color catalogue of domes is available for $3, and a dome assembly book for $5.)

Products: Geodesic domes from 300 to 4,500 square feet in size.

Market areas: 1, 2, 3, 4, 5, 6, 7, 8 and in Australia and other foreign countries

Morton Systems, Inc., Department TN, Morton, Minn. 56270, (507)697-6158

Contacts: Dean Limoges, president; Harry Wahldick, senior vice president; Dan Nielsen, junior vice president

Products: Panelized, packaged homes; mid- to high-rise systems buildings.

Market areas: 4, 5

Namretaw Manufacturing, Inc., Department TN, Domingo Rt. 60-A, Algodones, N. Mex. 87001, (505)867-2382

Contacts: Robert K. Waterman, president

Products: Stack modular homes. Truss and panel fabricator.

Market area: 6

Nanticoke Homes, Inc., Department TN, P.O. Box F, Greenwood, Del. 19950, (302)349-4561

Contacts: John Mervine, president; Merle Embleton, vice president

Products: Custom-built sectional homes.

Market area: 2

National Homes Corporation, Department TN, Earl Avenue at Wallace Street, P.O. Box 680, Lafayette, Ind. 47902, (317)448-2000

Contacts: David R. Price, president; Larry C. Geyer, president, National Homes Manufacturing Company; William G. Ikins, director of product development, National Homes Manufacturing Company

Products: Panelized packaged homes and mobile homes.

Market areas: 1, 2, 3, 4, 5, 6

Nationwide Homes, Inc., Department TN, 1100 Rives Road, P.O. Box 5511, Martinsville, Va. 24112, (703)632-7101

Contacts: James W. Severt, president and chief executive officer; George W. Coleman, senior vice president; Thomas G. Harris, vice president, Dealer Division

Products: Sectional modular and panelized single and multifamily homes and commercial buildings; distributed in mid-Atlantic and southeastern United States by company-owned vehicles and installed on dealers' foundations by Nationwide Homes personnel.

Market areas: 2, 3

New England Homes, Inc., Department TN, Freemans Point, P.O. Box 1138, Portsmouth, N.H. 03801, (603)436-8831

Contacts: Daniel J. Donahue, president; Tony Curtiss, vice president operations

Products: Sectional homes and panelized homes.

Market area: 1

New England Log Homes, Inc., Division of Plasticrete Corporation, Department TN, P.O. Box 5056, Hamden, Conn. 06518, (203)562-9981

Contacts: Vito M. Vizziello, president; Mitch Watson, engineer; Edward Sink, sales manager

Products: Log home packages.

Market areas: 1, 2, 3, 4, 5, 6, 7

Northeastern Log Homes, Inc., Department TN, Route 302, P.O. Box 126, Groton, Vt. 05046, (802)584-3200

Contacts: Peter K. Chaples, president

Products: Log homes.

Market areas: 1, 2, 3, 4, 5, 6

Northern Homes, Inc., Department TN, 10 LaCrosse Street, Hudson Falls, N.Y. 12839, (518)747-4128

Contacts: L. Michael Carusone, president; Sherril Cronin, executive vice president; Robert Lynch, vice president and treasurer; Joseph Carusone, vice president marketing

Products: Single and multifamily housing, vacation homes, commercial buildings, farm buildings, pole structures—all of wooden construction.

Market areas: 1, 2

Northern Homes of Pennsylvania, Inc., Department TN, Route 2, P.O. Box 515, Chambersburg, Pa. 17201, (717)264-5132

Contacts: Lewis R. Bowers, president; Samuel H. Oliver, vice president

Products: Single and multifamily housing, vacation homes, commercial buildings—all of wooden construction.

Market areas: 1, 2, 3

Northern Products, Inc., Department TN, Bomarc Road, Bangor, Maine 04401, (207)945-6414

Contacts: Brian E. Carlisle, sales manager; Ernest A. Caliendo, Jr., president

Products: Panelized packaged homes.

Market areas: 1, 2, 3, 4, 5

[234]

Ohio Valley Homes, Inc., Department TN, 1326 N. Harlan Avenue, P.O. Box 4347, Station A, Evansville, Ind. 47711, (812)425-3137

Contacts: C. A. Frank, president; L. G. Whipple, general manager

Products: Manufactured homes.

Market area: 2

Pacific Buildings, Inc., Department TN, P.O. Drawer C, Marks, Miss. 38646, (601)326-8104

Contacts: S. A. Walters, executive vice president; Henry C. Self, president; Eric L. Williams, engineer

Products: Open and closed wall sections, roof trusses, and kitchen cabinets. Uses a combination of components and precut, supplying total house packages for single and multifamily units from standard or custom plans.

Market area: 3

Parco Building Corporation, Department TN, 120 Parker Lane, Virginia Beach, Va. 23454, (804)340-5600

Contacts: Warren E. Parkhurst, president; Frank F. Lusby, vice president and general manager; Milton R. Smith, general sales agent

Products: Modular homes, steel-framed and featuring new energy saver design; offices; classrooms; banks.

Market areas: 2, 9

Pease Company, Department TN, 900 Forest Avenue, Hamilton, Ohio 45023, (513)867-3333

Contacts: C. William Stricker, vice president and general manager, Builder Division; Lon H. Purcell, A.I.A., chief architect, Pease Co.

Products: Precut homes, single and multifamily, vacation homes, packaged homes, components for builders.

Market areas: 2, 4

Progress Homes, Inc., Department TN, P.O. Box 220, Charlottesville, Va. 22902, (804)296-5111

Contacts: Richard L. Nunley, president; Ronald McCormick, housing general manager

Products: Sectional homes.

Market area: 2

R-Anell Homes, Inc., Department TN, Highway 16, P.O. Box 236, Denver, N.C. 28037, (704)483-5511

Contacts: Rollan L. Jones, president; Robert Stout, general manager; Wilbur Boltz, engineering manager

Products: Modular housing built for 24-foot-wide finished homes, up to 60 feet long. Varied elevations and sidings with split foyer homes included.

Market area: 3

Raphael Development Corporation, Department TN, 606 S. Euclid Street, Anaheim, Calif. 92802, (714)635-5664

Contact: Raphael Weiner, president

Products: Closed panel, mechanical core single-family homes.

Market area: 7

Redman Homes, Department TN, 2550 Walnut Hill Lane, Dallas, Tex. 75229, (214)350-3761

Contacts: Jim Redman, president; Jim Miller, vice president, sales; Bill Rowe, vice president, research and development

Products: Sectional homes and mobile homes.

Market areas: 1, 2, 3, 4, 5, 6, 7, 8, 9

Rycenga Homes, Inc., Department TN, 1053 Jackson Street, Grand Haven, Mich. 49417, (616)842-8040

Contacts: Charles Rycenga, president; Louis Rycenga, vice president

Products: Panelized single and multifamily homes, vacation homes, and commercial structures.

Market area: 4

Scholz Homes, Inc., Department TN, 3103 Executive Parkway, Toledo, Ohio, 43606, (419)531-1601

Contacts: Walter E. Ekblaw, president; Jack L. Piper, general sales manager;

James A. Jones, vice president, manufacturing; James M. Sattler, marketing services manager

Products: "Scholz Design" single and multifamily homes and apartments, component packages for multifamily or commercial construction; specializes in custom construction also.

Market areas: 1, 2, 3, 4, 5, 6

Skyline Corporation, Department TN, 2520 By-Pass Road, Elkhart, Ind. 46514

The country's largest manufacturer of mobile homes. Products are sold nationwide primarily through dealers. There is probably a Skyline dealer in your area. If not, contact the national headquarters listed above and they will direct you to the nearest dealer. (Not listed as active member of NAHM.)

Standard Homes Company, Department TN, U.S. Highway 169 & I-35, P.O. Box 1900, Olathe, Kans. 66061, (913)782-4220

Contacts: Eugene D. Smith, vice president and manager; Frank H. Woodbury, assistant manager

Products: Panelized material packages for single and multifamily units sold from a catalog to owner-builders and franchised builder-dealers.

Market areas: 4, 5, 6

Steele & Haurberg Company, Department TN, RR #2, Walnut, Ill. 61376, (815)379-2161

Contacts: Volmer B. Haurberg, vice president; Volmer H. Haurberg, president

Products: Trusses, panels, and packaged homes.

Market area: 4

Sterling Custom Homes Corporation, Department TN, 225 W. McWilliams Street, P.O. Box 830, Fond du Lac, Wis. 54935, (414)923-2000

Contacts: Donald E. Ahonen, board chairman and chief executive officer; Earl T. Hunt, president and general manager; Donald T. Ahonen, secretary and vice chairman

Products: Custom manufacturers, panelized single-family, multifamily, and vacation homes, apartments, and light commercial buildings, manufactured to the builder's plans and specifications.

Market areas: 4, 5

[237]

Stylex Homes, Inc., Department TN, 1863 Scottsville-Mumford Road, P.O. Box 9, Scottsville, N.Y. 14546, (716)889-4450

Contacts: William Fleming, president

Products: Manufactured sectional homes.

Market areas: 1, 2

Suburban Homes Corp., Department TN, 816 N. County Road 360W, Valparaiso, Ind. 46383, (219)762-2118

Contacts: L. Paul Saylor, president; Robert A. Miller, vice president; Donald V. Hanson, plant manager and purchasing agent

Products: Single and multifamily homes, mechanical cores and closed panels, precut and nonassembled.

Market area: 4

Swift Industries, Inc., Department TN, 1 Chicago Avenue, Elizabeth, Pa. 15037, (412)892-0700

Contacts: Ira H. Gordon, president; Francis X. Bannon, vice president, purchasing; Michael Dzura, vice president housing

Products: Manufactures and distributes prefabricated (Lincoln Homes) and precut (Swift Homes) homes in eastern half of the United States through company-owned and dealer-franchised sales offices.

Market areas: 1, 2, 4

Trademark Homes, Inc., Department TN, 214 N. 2nd Street, P.O. Box 549, Guttenberg, Iowa 52052, (319)252-1740

Contacts: Elmer Rome, Executive officer; Floyd Farmer, president; Robert Ernster, vice president of sales

Products: Sectional homes.

Market area: 4

Traditional Living, Inc., Department TN, Box 202, Hartland, Vt., 05048, (802)436-2121

Contacts: Tod Schweizer, executive vice president; Lance Collister, director of Technical services

Products: Precut log building kits.

Market areas: 1, 2

Tri-Co Builder's Supply Co., Department TN, 9 South 104 Frontenac Road, Naperville, Ill. 60540, (312)420-3300

Contacts: H. R. (Herb) Tison, president; Carl Bryant, director of sales

Products: Component fabricators of roof trusses, floor trusses, wall panels, interior balustrades, and stairs.

Market area: 4

Unibilt Industries, Inc., Department TN, 4671 Poplar Creek Road, P.O. Box 373, Vandalia, Ohio 45377, (513)890-7578

Contacts: Douglas Scholz, president; Curt Bowling, vice president; Ken Gift, sales

Products: Single-family sectional homes. Ranches and bi-levels 960 to 1400 square feet. Wood-framed with finished drywall interiors. Full service package includes freight, erection, and carpentry finish work.

Market areas: 4, 5

Unibuilt Structures, A Division of the Reasor Corporation, Department TN, 905 West Lincoln Avenue, P.O. Box 460, Charleston, Ill. 61920, (217)345-3921

Contacts: William Reasor, president; Donald W. Hutton, executive vice president

Products: Produces single and multifamily modular housing constructed in plant as a three-dimensional cube produced to 90 percent completion, including framing, electrical heating, plumbing, drywall finish, trim carpentry, and decorating.

Market areas: 4, 5

Union Manufacturing and Supply Company, Inc., Department TN, 725 E. Vine Drive, P.O. Box 1696, Fort Collins, Colo. 80522, (303)484-4015

Contacts: Robert H. Morton, vice president and general manager; John C. Campbell, assistant general manager; Robert S. Everitt, president; Kenneth Nelson, vice president

Products: Thirteen models of manufactured homes delivered and set on foundation provided by dealer; component division panelizes custom homes to builder's specifications.

Market areas: 5, 6

Vacation Land Homes, Inc., Department TN, 733 Cayuga Street, P.O. Box 292, Bellaire, Mich. 49615, (616)533-8611

Contacts: Ordon D. Hierlihy, Jr., president; Robert Larson, sales manager; Dennis Robinson, chief engineer

Products: Panelized packaged homes.

Market areas: 2, 3, 4

Van-Ler, Inc., Department TN, 505 S. Second Street, Tipp City, Ohio 45371, (513)667-2414

Contacts: Nelson C. Borchers, president; James Collins, sales manager

Products: Components, roof trusses, panelized homes.

Market areas: 2, 4

Vindale Corporation, Department TN, 630 Hay Avenue, Brookville, Ohio 45309, (513)833-4091

Contacts: Daniel P. Riedel, president

Products: Sectional modular and mobile home products which meet the conventional building codes and are designed for permanent foundation placement.

Market area: 1, 2, 3, 4, 9

Wakefield Homes, Inc., Department TN, P.O. Box 729, Spring Hope, N.C. 27882, (919)478-3682

Contacts: R. A. McGilvary, president; W. R. McGilvary, general manager

Products: Sectional homes and stack modulars.

Market area: 2

Ward Cabin Company, Department TN, Houlton Airport, P.O. Box 72, Houlton, Maine 04730, (207)532-6531

Contacts: Michael A. McLaughlin, assistant manager; Aubrey A. McLaughlin, president; Norman Hubert, director, research and development

Products: Log homes.

Market areas: 1, 2, 3, 4

Appendix

Wausau Homes, Inc., Department TN, P.O. Box 1204, Wausau, Wis. 54401, (715)359-7272

Contacts: Earl Schuette, president; Marvin C. Schuette, executive vice president

Products: Single and multifamily homes, commercial buildings, vacation homes, panelized, closed construction, mechanical core system; complete assistance through manufacture and product erection.

Market areas: 4, 5

Western Development Company, Department TN, 9821 Loan Lane, N. E., Albuquerque, N. Mex. 87111, (505)821-6800

Contacts: Gerhard Muller, president; Bo K. Johnson, vice president, engineering; Carl Conroy, senior vice president

Products: Panelized packaged homes.

Market area: 6

Western Valley Log Homes, Department TN, Box 254, Victor, Mont. 59875, (406)961-4421

Contacts: Rex J. Clothier, director, sales and marketing; Kirk Parmenter, general manager

Products: Log homes.

Market areas: 5, 6, 7, 8

Weston Homes, Inc., Department TN, P.O. Box 126, Rothschild, Wis. 54474, (715)359-4281

Contacts: Robert T. Wagner, general manager, Earl Schuette, president; Marvin Schuette, executive vice president; Paul Ott, sales manager

Products: Closed panel with mechanical core, single and multifamily homes, apartments, townhouses, motels, and light commercial structures.

Market areas: 4, 5, 6, 9

Wick Homes, Division of Wick Building Systems, Inc., Department TN, 2415 Parview Road, P.O. Box 217, Middleton, Wis. 53562, (608)836-7401

Contacts: Kenneth R. Welton, executive vice president and division manager; James G. Muench, division operating manager; John G. Pollis, division marketing manager

Products: Wet core, closed panel, single-family homes. Fifty-three basic plans with many structural options available.

Market areas: 4, 5

Wickes Shelter Systems, Department TN, 515 N. Washington Avenue, Saginaw, Mich. 48607, (517)754-9121

Contacts: Robert Welsh, vice president, shelter systems; Charles T. Sparks, operations manager; Tom Kesling, marketing manager

Products: Roof and floor trusses, complete line of panelized packaged single-family and vacation homes, complete line of prefabricated garages and wood storage buildings.

Market areas: 1, 2, 3, 4, 5, 6, 7

Yankee Barn Homes, Inc., Department TN, P.O. Drawer A, Grantham, N.H. 03753, (603)863-4545

Contacts: Emil Hanslin, board chairman; Tony Hanslin, president

Products: Post and beam houses with stressed skin panels.

Market areas: 1, 2, 3

Index

Index

Federal National Mortgage Administration
(FNMA), 7
Financing:
collateral, 131, 162–163, 189–192
costs of, 165–168
government, 39–44
(*See also* Federal Housing Administration; Veteran's Administration)
land advance, 193
lenders, 26–27
100 percent, 193–196
Private Mortgage Insurance (PMI), 37
red-lining, 129–132
(*See also* Mortgages)
Footings, 172–173

Geodesic domes, 212–214

Hammurabi, Code of, 92–93
Harris, Patricia, 3
Home Builders, National Association of,
126, 138
Home Manufacturers, National Association
of, 219
Homes:
additions to (*see* Additions to homes)
alternative comparison chart, 23
"cheapies," 8
comparison of housing in Los Angeles,
Minneapolis, and Atlanta, 15–16
dream, 2–18
1890, 4–5
1930, 5
1950–1970, 9
manufactured (*see* Manufactured homes)
market for, 57–58
market value, 144–150
median sales price of, 8, 16
tables, 13, 14, 17
mobile (*see* Mobile homes)
modular, 88–92
presenting offers on, 53–58
sales price of, 5, 9–10, 13–17, 185
second, 9
single-family suburban, 19, 25
starts, number of, 5, 8, 16
Housing and Urban Development, Department of (HUD), 3, 61, 89, 94
Community Development Block Grant
Program, 132, 135
condominium study, 61
Mobile Home Standards code, 93

Income, median, in United States, 8, 16–18
Inflation, 2
rate of, in United States, 12
International Conference of Building Officials (ICBO), 93

Land, 2–3, 185–186
Leverage, 26–27
Loans (*see* Financing)
Log cabins, 214–216
Lot, preparation of, 10, 184–186

Manufactured homes, 84–117, 208–242
benefits vs. disadvantages of, 20–23
defined, 84–85
list of manufacturers, 219–242
Mechanic's liens, 160–161
Minimum property standards (MPS), FHA,
93
Mobile homes, 84–117
attitudes against, 85–88, 109–111
"Blue Book" listing value of used, 113
building codes, 91–94
chattel mortgages, 92
construction of, 96–108
Covered Wagon Company, 86
dealer's profit, 116
double-wide, 87
"empty nesters" in, 111–112
financing, 112–117
Ford Motor Company, 86
foundation for: peripheral, 105–106
pier, 105–106
General Motors, 86
"gypsy wagons," 86
insulation for, 101
lifestyle, 111
luxury units, 112
pad for, buying, 116
parks for, 87–88, 111
as real estate, 94–96
rent for, monthly, 116
roof pitch of, 109
taxation of, 94–96
Modular homes, 88–92
(*See also* Mobile homes)
Mortgages:
amortization table, 168
construction, 162–163, 190, 194
compared to permanent loan, 194
debt ratio, 114
down payment chart, 36
foreclosure of, 190–191

[245]